General Editor
ARNOLD GOLDMAN

AMERICAN LITERATURE
IN CONTEXT, I
1620–1830

AMERICAN LITERATURE IN CONTEXT, I

1620–1830

STEPHEN FENDER

METHUEN
LONDON AND NEW YORK

First published in 1983 by
Methuen & Co. Ltd
11 New Fetter Lane, London EC4P 4EE
Published in the USA by
Methuen & Co.
in association with Methuen, Inc.
733 Third Avenue, New York, NY 10017

Typeset in Great Britain by
Scarborough Typesetting Services
and printed by
Richard Clay (The Chaucer Press) Ltd
Bungay, Suffolk

British Library Cataloguing in Publication Data

Fender, Stephen
American literature in context.
1 : 1620–1830
1. American literature – History and criticism
I. Title
810.9   PS88

ISBN 0–416–74590–3

Library of Congress Cataloging in Publication Data

(Revised for vol. 1)
Main entry under title:
American literature in context.
Includes bibliographies and indexes.
Contents: 1. 1620–1830 / Stephen Fender –
2. 1830–1865 / Brian Harding –   – 4. 1900–
1930 / Ann Massa.
1. American literature – History and criticism –
Addresses, essays, lectures. I. Goldman, Arnold.
PS92.A425 1983   810′.9   81–22302

ISBN 0–416–74590–3 (v. 1)

Contents

General Editor's Preface

The object of the *American Literature in Context* series is to offer students of the literature and culture of the United States a coherent, consecutive and comprehensive sequence of interpretations of major American texts – fiction and non-fiction, poetry and drama.

Each chapter is prefaced by an extract from the chosen text which serves as a springboard for wider discussion and analysis. The intention of each analysis is to demonstrate how students can move into and then from the pages of literature in front of them to a consideration of the whole text from which the extract is taken, and thence to an understanding of the author's *oeuvre* and of the cultural moment in which he or she lived and wrote. The extract and its interpretation *ground* the wider interpretation: students need not just take the critic's overall view on trust, but can test it against the extract from the primary text.

The selection of texts is intended to represent the critic's choice from the variety, quality and interest of important American writing in the period. In these essays students can see how a literary and cultural critic responds to the page of writing before him or her, and how sustained critical response to particular passages can be linked to broader analyses of texts, authors, culture and society. With this integrated format, students can better see how background material relates to the text and *vice versa*. While the chapters are not precisely intended as models for students to imitate, those who are learning to write about literature are encouraged to treat extracts of their own choosing in a comparable manner, relating the particular response to wider matters.

Arnold Goldman

Note on the extracts

The extracts in each chapter, further citations and page references are from the texts cited in the further reading lists. Copy has been corrected against first editions and orthography modernized where relevant.

PART ONE

America as Type and Thing

Introduction

First America was imagined — only then was it discovered, and then 'invented'. European mythology associated sleep, death, rest and eternity with one or another unknown land in the west, where the sun set in diurnal imitation of these ideas. To die was to 'go west'; Hesiod's Garden of the Hesperides and Homer's Elysian Fields lay west of the Pillars of Hercules. Avalon, the mythical island to which King Arthur was carried when he died, was supposedly situated in the west of the British Isles.

Another persistent idea was that of a continent, or country, once great but since sunk somewhere in the western ocean. The sometime existence of Atlantis, which gave the Atlantic ocean its name, was a widely held belief in classical times (it is mentioned in Plato's *Timaeus* and *Critias*, for example), and Celtic legend placed the birth of Tristram in Lyonesse, a large island west of Cornwall, since overwhelmed by the sea (see Jones, 1964, 1–5).

Magical lands were postulated in European fiction too, and sometimes they were put to quite specific use. The landscape of the pastoral, whether in Theocritus's *Daphnis and Chloe*, Virgil's *Eclogues*, or the great romances of the English renaissance by Sidney, Spenser, Shakespeare and Thomas Lodge, was an artificial, idealized country setting, away from the distracting influence of the court or city, in which meditations could flourish on the relative influences of nature and culture. What all these heavens, havens, lost islands and pastoral retreats had in common was an agrarian economy and a perfection of climate, natural process and human government. The place was sunny without being desert (a spring or river kept it watered), the season was spring-like without stasis, and there was no war or commercial competition, no harsh laws or private property — in fact none of the usual impositions of fallen man when he forms a government in cold climates.

The similarity between visions of past and future, of the lost land and the place of bliss 'proposed for the deserver', is no more surprising than that between the Christian paradise from which man was banished and that to which he would go if he was good. Paradise was both lost in the past and to be regained in the last days. Even classical myth, for all its concern with overwhelmed Atlantis, had its apocalyptic visions of worlds still to be discovered:

> Venient annis, saecula seris,
> Quibus Oceanus vincula rerum
> Laxet et ingens pateat tellus
> Tiphysque novos detegat orbes
> Nec sit terris ultima Thule.

(In the last days there will come an age in which Ocean shall loosen the bonds of things; the vast globe will lie open; another Tiphus [the first was Jason's pilot in the Argo] shall make known new worlds, and Thule [the frozen North] shall no longer be the extremity of the world.)

Nor were these lines from Seneca's *Medea* (ll. 375–9) unknown to the renaissance chroniclers of American exploration. In his biography of his illustrious father, Don Fernando Columbus cites them, sharpening their prophetic aspect by mistranslating 'et ingens pateat tellus' as 'a great country will be discovered', then adding that 'This prediction may assuredly be considered as accomplished in the person of the Admiral'.

The English renaissance synthesized all this classical and medieval myth from oral tradition, from a renewed interest in Arthurian materials stemming from the pseudo-Celtic content of the Tudor myth of the succession, from the general recuperation of the classics in renaissance education, and above all from the intensified millennial fervour of the Reformation. But the English of the sixteenth century had something else that Columbus did not have: the idea of progress, of knowledge advanced through the discovery of new data. When Francis Bacon needed a metaphor for the 'Advancement of Learning' for which he argued so passionately, he turned to the enterprise of discovering and developing new-found lands then progressing as he wrote: 'Thus I have made as it were a small globe of the intellectual world, as truly and faithfully as I could discover; with a note and description of those parts which seem to me not constantly occupate, or not well converted by the labour of man.'

Bacon's last work was an unfinished utopia set in the framework of an imaginary voyage to the *New Atlantis*, where he discovers an idealized research institute, untainted by Plato, Aristotle and the medieval schoolmen, practising experimental science of the kind he wished to advance. Columbus escaped the schoolmen less easily. Edmundo O'Gorman (1961) has shown how hard he struggled to reconcile the facts of his discoveries over the course of four voyages with his assumption that he had landed on the outlying islands of the Chinese mainland. He simply could not escape the *a priori* belief of medieval theologians that the world consisted of a single, huge island. It was only when European intellectual development had reached the stage at which it was possible to conceive of a land not part of the *Orbis Terrarum* prepared by God for man, inhabited by human beings not descended from Adam and as yet beyond the influence of Christ's redeeming sacrifice, that America could truly be said to have been 'invented' as well as imagined and discovered.

*

Since all descriptions of the unfamiliar are a mixture of the perceiver's preconceptions and what is 'really' there, it comes as no surprise to find the early explorers of America encountering both good and ill in terms of European images of gardens or wastelands, noble savages or devils. Columbus's famous letter of 1493 to the Comptroller of the Spanish Treasury, translated and widely published throughout Europe, described the landscape of Española (now Haiti) in terms which a student of English literature might think more appropriate to Spenser's Garden of Adonis. The trees were 'as green and lovely [in December] as they are in Spain in May, and some of them were flowering, some bearing fruit, and some in another stage, according to their nature. And the nightingale was singing, and other birds of a thousand kinds . . .' (cited in Jones, 15). Giovanni da Verrazzano, who explored the American coast from Newfoundland to the Carolinas and who is credited with having discovered the mouth of the Hudson River, found the coast of North Carolina 'replenished with divers sorts of trees, as pleasant and delectable to behold as is possible to imagine', in the words of Richard Hakluyt's translation of 1582. At latitude 34 degrees north (Cape Fear, near where North and South Carolina meet) Verrazzano saw 'palm trees, bay trees, and high cypress trees', and he gave the resonant name of Arcadia to the coast of Maryland (Quinn, 1971, 61, 63). Sir Walter Raleigh described the interior of Venezuela, from the Orinoco River, as a sort of gentleman's park, with 'plains of twenty miles in length, the grass short and green, and in divers parts groves of trees by themselves, as if they had been by all the art and labour in the world so made of purpose. And . . . the deer came down feeding by the water's side, as if they had been used to a keeper's call' (cited in Emerson, 1971, 21).

On the other hand, the country could appear poisonous. Columbus, according to a letter to Pope Leo x published in the collection of travel accounts collected by Peter Martyr of Anghiera as *De Orbe Novo* (1511, 'Englished' by Richard Eden in 1555 as *The Decades of the New World or West India*), found 'plenty of sweet apples, but hurtful, for they turn into worms when they are eaten', and a tree whose shadow 'is contagious, for such as sleep under it any time, have their heads swollen and lose their sight' (ed. Arber, 1885, 106–7).

Yet for all the influence of European prototypes, these accounts seldom lack an element of factual description, sometimes rivalling the best writing produced by geographers and natural historians two centuries later. Thus though the Indians could be described alternately as promiscuous, cannibalistic devils, or inhabitants of 'that golden world of the which old writers speak so much: wherein men lived simply and innocently without enforcement of laws, without quarrelling judges and libels, content only to satisfy nature' (171), they could also be described as they actually looked, behaved and spoke. Gonzalo Fernandez de Oviedo y Valdes wrote a natural history of the West Indies (1526, translation included in Eden's edition of the *Decades*) which includes descriptions of plants, animals and native inhabitants: 'All the Indians are commonly without beards: In so much that it is in manner a marvel to see any of them either men or women to have any down or hair on their faces or other parts of their bodies. . . .' He tells how they fish for pearls, how they go into battle with 'certain shells of great whelks of the sea which they blow and make therewith great sound much like the noise of horns' (237). Thus the *First Decade* describes the eating and clothing of the natives: 'Their bread is made of roots. . . . They have sundry kinds of water pots, jugs, and drinking cups made of earth. . . . The men of this country, enclose their privy members in a gourd, cut after the fashion of a codpiece: or else, cover the same with the shell of a tortoise, tied about their loins with laces of gossampine cotton' (95). The variety of languages is represented ('In some places they call a king *Cacicus*: in other places they call him *Quebi*, and somewhere *Tiba*' [151]), and occasionally brief glossaries are included, beginning with a list of fourteen words rather grandly titled 'The Indian Language' at the foot of the table of contents. Finally, though there are giants and chimaeras enough in the *Decades*, there are other animals less fabulous than they seem at first, like the 'monstrous beast with a snout like a fox, a tail like a marmoset, ears like a bat, hands like a man, and feet like an ape, bearing her whelps about with her in an outward belly much like unto a great bag or purse' (98), which is plainly a possum.

America could not be experienced, then, without the inextricable interaction of concept and fact, 'type' and thing. The type might change; as explorers moved west over the continental landscape, so might the thing. The balance between them might be altered too. As the project for imperial expansion became more urgent, so the traveller's discourse was taken up more and more with the physical opportunities awaiting the colonist. In time, even the 'thinginess' of the optimist's projection might become a convention, a rhetorical recourse for a peculiarly American argument about America, and so the thing might become a type in its turn.

I

Captain John Smith
(1580–1631)

The surprising emergence of fact from apparent fiction is nowhere so well illustrated as in the career of Captain John Smith as represented in his own writings. His astonishing adventures in war and exploration, his claim to pre-eminence in the Virginia Company's settlement of Jamestown in 1607, his strenuous attempts, in which he failed, to get further employment as a leader of colonial projects in America, and above all the fact that his encounter with the Indian maiden Pocahontas has become part of American folklore – all these and other factors have caused modern American historians, from Henry Adams onwards, to treat the story of his life with a degree of scepticism.

The events of his life as set out in his autobiography of 1630, will demonstrate the causes for doubt. Born in 1580 in Lincolnshire, the son of a yeoman farmer, Smith was educated at free schools in Alford and Louth, where the curriculum would have called for study in Latin, grammar and composition. From an early age he wanted to seek his fortune abroad, an ambition which his father hoped to modify by apprenticing him to a merchant in King's Lynn. Only a year after he began work, however, his father died, and Smith took this chance to get away, serving with English forces against the Spanish in the Netherlands for three years. In 1600, during the temporary lull in the fighting after the Battle of Nieuport, he made his way through northern France to Brittany, thence to the French Mediterranean, where he took ship for Italy. In a spell of bad weather he was thrown overboard like Jonah (his Protestantism and Englishness rendering him suspect to a band of pilgrims bound for Rome), fetched up on a small island, and was rescued by a Captain La Roche, a Frenchman engaged in trade with the Levant. Travels with La Roche took Smith around the Italian peninsula to Cyrenaica and Alexandria, to Kalamata in Greece, and the islands of

---

* The extract for this chapter is to be found on pp. 16–18.

Cephalonia and Corfu. Off the coast of Sicily they fought, defeated and took as prize a rich 'argosy' from Venice. When they returned to France, Smith went ashore at Antibes with five hundred gold pieces in his pockets, enough to keep him for five years.

For a while he toured Italy, but soon he was soldiering again, this time against the Turks in the Balkans, where he was made captain of 250 horse troops in the Imperial Army of Rudolph II. During the siege of Alba Iulia, in Transylvania, one of the Turkish commanders holding the city challenged the attackers to single combat, the loser to part with his head. Smith accepted on behalf of the Christians, and on the first pass, ran his lance through his opponent's beaver. The next day another challenge followed, and on the third yet another. Smith won these too, and was granted both an annual pension of three hundred ducats, and the right to sport the impress of three Turks' heads on his shield ever after. But in a later engagement he was wounded, captured and sold as a slave by the Tartars to a pasha called Bogall, who sent him to Istanbul as a gift to his mistress, Charatza Trabigzanda (not her name, as Smith thought, but Greek for 'girl from Trebizond'). When she discovered he was a plain Englishman who had fallen on hard times, 'Charatza' sent Smith to her brother near Azak (Azov in what is now the Soviet Union). Here, treated abominably, Smith lost his temper and killed the brother, dressed himself in the clothes of the dead man, and took off across the steppes into Muscovy. There he was found by a Russian border official, who took pity on him, found him a place in a convoy heading north to Moscow, and gave him a certificate to explain his presence and assist his passage. From Russia Smith headed west across Lithuania into Poland and back to the Holy Roman Empire, where he finally collected, not his pension but a once-for-all honor-arium of 1500 ducats and a document attesting his service in the Imperial cause.

And all this – plus more travel and a bit more pirating – before 1605, his twenty-fifth year of life, and before embarking on the career for which he has gone down in history! And yet, his biographer, Philip Barbour, has managed to match most of the descriptions, dates and names in Smith's autobiography to historical events. As for the gentry and petty nobility of Slovenia whom Smith mentions as having served in the Imperial Army, says Barbour, 'he could hardly have *read* about them anywhere!' (1964, 27). Even the duels, which with their suspicious arrangement into three tournaments on three successive days seem to leap out of Sidney's *Arcadia*, were apparently 'in accordance with the contemporary conventions of single combat – however crude these were on the Turkish frontier' (49).

A man of such spirit would not rest long by the fireside, and now there was talk of an explicitly national, British venture overseas. Since the voyage of John Cabot to Nova Scotia in 1497 the English had taken a rather desultory interest in North America. At first, they used it for fishing (on one recent hypothesis deep-sea fishermen from Bristol had actually visited the Grand Banks before Cabot), but Spanish and Portuguese settlements in South America, the Caribbean and Florida began to concentrate British minds on forming an American colony of their own. Sir Humphrey Gilbert took possession of a part of New-foundland in 1583, but was drowned in a wreck on his return journey. The next year Sir Walter Raleigh financed an expedition, headed by Sir Richard Grenville, to claim Virginia for the English Crown. They landed on Roanoke Island, off the coast of present-day North Carolina. Despite twice being reinforced, the small settlement melted mysteri-ously away into the wilderness. A contemporary theory, advanced by William Strachey in his *History of Travel in Virginia Britannia* (1612) was that the Roanoke colonists had been wiped out by hostile Indians. A legend still supported by the major historian of the European discovery of America has it that the colonists amalgamated with the Croatan Indians and migrated to Robeson County in the southern part of the state: 'the existence of blue-eyed and fair-haired types among [the Indians], as well as the incorporation of Elizabethan English words in their language and their using surnames from [the] lost colonists bears this out' (Morison, 1971, 677).

By the end of the sixteenth century, not one British settlement remained in the New World. Yet the subject of colonization was far from dead in the public prints. Edward Haie, a surviving captain of one of Gil-bert's ships, had written a 'Report of the voyage and successes thereof' of the Newfoundland venture. Thomas Hariot's *A Brief and True Report of the New Found Land of Virginia* (1588) attempted a scientific geography of climate, typography, raw materials, foodstuffs and Indians. Sir Walter Raleigh's *The Discovery of the large and beautiful Empire of Guiana*, though it reported nothing discovered by an Englishman, was such a popular and optimistic account of new-world opportunities that it went into four editions in 1596. The first voyage by an Englishman to New England was described by the Anglican clergyman John Brereton. His *A Brief and True Relation of the Discovery of the North Part of Virginia* (1602) was an account of the expedition, led by Captain Bartholomew Gosnold, to survey the coast of Maine and Massachusetts. It made various landings, traded with the Indians and got on well with them, admired the climate and the possibilities for future planting. It also gave the region many of its place names, such as Cape Cod and the nearby island, Martha's Vineyard, named after Gosnold's daughter.

These descriptions were also collected and reprinted for wider circulation. The greatest propagandist for English colonies in America, Richard Hakluyt, included the reports of Haie, Hariot and Raleigh in his extremely influential *The Principal Navigations, Voyages and Discoveries of the English Nation* (1589; revised and enlarged, 1598–1600), which runs to eleven volumes in the modern reprint. The infectious enthusiasm for the western planting found a ready echo in contemporary literature. Michael Drayton's ode 'To the Virginian Voyage', written on the eve of the departure for Jamestown, praises 'Industrious Hakluyt, / Whose reading shall enflame / Men to seek fame', and promises 'Virginia, / Earth's only paradise, / Where nature hath in store / Fowl, venison, and fish. . . . Three harvests more, / All greater than your wish' – not to mention another 'golden age'. So popular was the topic that Shakespeare based a play on it, though it should be added that *The Tempest* was first performed at court, not before the general public. The storm in the first scene takes many of its details from an account by William Strachey of a wreck in the Bermudas of a ship sent to reinforce the Roanoke colony. (The accident was providential, Strachey argues, not only because crew and passengers were saved, but also because they discovered that islands previously shunned as inhabited by devils were really an earthly paradise.) Other borrowings show how much Shakespeare had read of contemporary travel literature. 'Setebos', the name of his island, comes from Richard Eden's *History of Travel* (1577), and the refrain of Ariel's first song ('Bow-wow' in I.ii) from a description of an Indian ceremonial dance, or 'pow-wow' in modern westerns, in James Rosier's *A True Relation of . . . the Discovery of the Land of Virginia* (1605). Other possible sources of the play, according to the Arden editor, Frank Kermode, include Hariot, Raleigh and Eden's translation of Peter Martyr (1954, xxxii–iii).

It was to such a ferment of curiosity and anticipation that the adventurous Captain Smith returned in 1604 or 1605. If the expectations for an American colony were to be met, this time the settlement would have to find a way of sustaining itself and not depend, as Smith himself was later to write, on 'privy men's purses'. 'The expansive flourishes of such individuals as Sir Humphrey Gilbert and Sir Walter Raleigh . . . were ended,' writes Barbour. 'Careful businessmen took over, disposed to invest (or gamble) the vast sums needed, in the hope – the certainty, as they saw it – of reaping commensurate rewards . . .' (82). It was exactly the right moment for the self-made man of action. Smith had some capital and a lot of experience of seamanship and warfare. Through a mutual acquaintance he met Bartholomew Gosnold, who was now connected with a new venture bound for Virginia. The result was that Smith joined a company of gentlemen, merchants and explorers to seek a charter from King James I for the founding of colonies in Virginia. Gosnold and Hakluyt were involved, so were the Lord Chief Justice, Sir John Popham, Sir Thomas Gates, Sir Fernando Gorges and the explorer Edward Maria Wingfield. Of these, Smith, Gosnold and Wingfield were to go on the voyage. They left with about 120 settlers in three ships early in 1607.

Almost from the start there was dissension among the leaders of the venture. The 'London Council' of the company had deposited sealed orders with the leading captain of the flotilla, Christopher Newport, which dictated, among other things, the membership of the Council of the new colony, and which were not to be opened until landing. During the inevitably trying voyage, therefore, no one knew who would eventually be in charge. Smith's very qualifications for participation in the venture – his practical sense, his decisiveness, his experience – were irksome to his social betters. The strong-minded Wingfield, particularly, opposed most of his ideas, and at one point, while the ships were provisioning in the Canaries, actually brought a charge of mutiny against Smith and insisted that he be confined below decks for the rest of the voyage. When they finally dropped anchor in Chesapeake Bay, Captain Newport opened the orders, only to find that Smith had been named to the Virginia Council. Almost three months were to pass, during which Smith more than proved himself as a useful member of the colony, before he was allowed to serve on it.

Prove himself Smith certainly did, and that through his practical modifications of theoretical diktat. For example, the London Council had issued ludicrously specific directions about where they were to establish the colony. It was to be on a river, and furthermore on whatever river ran furthest into the land in a north-westerly direction, and arose from a large lake, rather than from springs or smaller tributaries. The purpose behind this nonsense (which would, of course, necessitate a major survey before the colonists could settle and plant) was the evergreen search for a north-west passage to the Pacific. Then again,

Wingfield, the first president of the colony, had the notion that the Indians would be best pleased if the planters did not fortify the settlement. The instructions from the London backers said not to 'offend the naturals'. Later directions from home were to advise offering a crown to Powhatan, the local Algonquin chief. The coronation took place 'but did not have the desired effect', as another of Smith's biographers (Emerson, 1977, 30) adds laconically.

In the event the colony was settled just south of what is now Williamsburg, Virgina, on the north bank of the James River. It was a fair approximation of the London Company's wishes (the river does indeed run north-west, though it originates in the Blue Ridge Mountains and most assuredly not the Pacific Ocean), but it was not a particularly salubrious or convenient site for deep-sea trading and remains to this day only the small town of Jamestown. They did fortify their camp with a log palisade (even Wingfield's allies insisted on this), and they did begin the search for a north-west passage. It was in this business of subsidiary exploration that Smith's abilities began to show themselves. With Newport he went up river to prospect for wood and minerals, and to make contact with the Indians. Smith himself led later excursions, to explore the shores of Chesapeake Bay, and to trace the route of the Chickahominy River (parallel to the James). It was on this voyage, apparently, that he was captured and condemned to death by Powhatan, then rescued by the intervention of the chief's daughter, Pocahontas.

On the other hand, the colonists seem to have been lamentably slow in preparing for their immediate needs. Two months after unloading their supplies at Jamestown, they had still to plant much of anything, or to complete even one house. The summer heat brought typhoid to add to the general debility. Many died. Smith was made supply officer, and succeeded in trading with the Indians for food. He prodded the colonists into building stronger fortifications and proper houses, dividing up the labour into specialized units. At length Wingfield's arbitrariness eroded everyone's patience, and he was removed from the presidency of the Colony. Within a year John Smith succeeded him.

Thus the son of a small farmer promoted himself to the presidency of England's first successful colony in North America. His elevation was not the end of his troubles (he was to quarrel again with both local colonists and the London backers), but at least it showed what experience and natural ability could achieve in the new world. He was never again to be active in the enterprise of colonial settlement. Wounded by an explosion in 1609, he had to return to England, where he was refused a further role in the Virginia Company. In 1614 he accepted a commission from some London merchants to explore New England (Smith himself gave the region its name) for gold and copper. With two ships he sailed to Maine and Massachusetts, bringing back fur and salt fish, but no minerals. The disappointed merchants bestowed upon him the grand title 'Admiral of New England', but nothing further was heard of their venture. Next Sir Fernando Gorges, one of the original Virginia Company, suggested a colony in New England; he would raise the money if Smith would head the settlement. Two voyages were attempted; one returned after the lead ship sprung a leak and the other was diverted by adverse winds. Despite numerous subsequent attempts to get backing, Smith would never again set out on a colonial expedition.

This left writing. No doubt Smith thought it a dreary second best, but his career as an author turned out to be at least the equal of his more active pursuits, however exciting and historically portentous they had been. In fact, the two phases of his life overlapped somewhat. In Virginia he had written a forty-four-page pamphlet giving *A True Relation of such occurrences and accidents of note as hath happened in Virginia since the first planting of that Colony* (1608). It was the first book about America actually to have been written there. A vivid, first-person account in the form of a letter home, the *True Relation* is informative, concrete and has a lively narrative organization.

Back in London, Smith undertook a more formal account of the Virginia Colony in *A Map of Virginia. With a Description of that Country, the Commodities, People, Government and Religion* (1612). This was three times the length of the *True Relation* and included not only the map referred to in the title but also a description of the climate, the lay of the land, catalogues of plants and other materials suitable for export (an account borrowed partly from Hariot's *A Brief and True Report*) and a close, uncondescending examination of the Indians' way of life, which praises their practical ingenuity and harmony with their environment, while remaining unsentimental about their savage state and their occasional nuisance to the colonists.

Smith's exploration of the Maine and Massachusetts coasts resulted in his *A Description of New England* (1616). The 'description' of the title is in the vein of his second book on Virginia, but personal narrative of his experiences on the voyage and powerfully phrased arguments for English colonization add colour and urgency to the narrative. His most ambitious production was *The General History of Virginia, New England,*

and the Summer Isles (1624), a folio of 241 pages with maps, portraits and commendatory verses by, among other notables, his friend John Donne. Two stanzas (out of Donne's four) will give an idea of how Smith's career was assessed by an intelligent contemporary:

> This gentleman whose volume here is stored
> > With strange discovery of God's strangest creatures,
> Gives us full view, how he hath sail'd, and oared,
> > And marched, fully many miles, whose rough
> > > defeatures,
> > > Hath been as bold, as puissant, up to bind
> > Their barbarous strengths, to follow him dog-lind.
>
> But wit, nor valour, now adays pays scores
> > For estimation; all goes now by wealth,
> Or friends; tush! thrust the beggar out of doors
> > That is not purse-lined; those which live by stealth
> > > Shall have their haunts; no matter what's the guest
> > In many places; monies will come best.

The General History was really a compilation of Smith's earlier writings (somewhat expanded) and other accounts of new-world exploration, such as Brereton's *Brief and True Relation*, Rosier's *True Relation* of voyages to New England, Ralph Hamor's *True Discourse of the Present Estate of Virginia* (1615), Nathaniel Butler's *The History of the Bermudas*, which Smith saw in manuscript (it was not published until 1882), and the so-called *Mourt's Relation* (1622) of the Puritan colony at Plymouth.

His other works include *New England's Trials* (1620), a pamphlet in which he again describes New England, projects a plan for colonizing it, and complains frankly of his frustrated attempts to get backing for a voyage of his own. Even the Pilgrim Fathers, he reveals in a later edition of the work, were happy enough to use his maps and books, but too cheap to employ their author in person. *An Accidence, or the Pathway to Experience. Necessary for all Young Seamen* (1626) was recast a year later as *A Sea Grammar*, after Smith had seen a manuscript of Sir Henry Mainwaring's *Nomenclator Navalis*. Energetically told and packed with both terminology and material details, the *Grammar* is a fascinating source of information about how ships of those days were built and sailed. Smith's last major book was his autobiography, *The True Travels, Adventures, and Observations of Captain John Smith, In Europe, Asia, Africa, and America . . .*, published in 1630, the year before his death. Once considered 'pseudo-romance' by a nineteenth-century historian (see Emerson, 94) it is now thought to be nearly as true as the title claims.

* * *

The chief mountains, them of Pennobscot, the twinkling mountain of Acocisco, the great mountain of Sasanow, and the high mountain of Massachuset, each of which you shall find in the map: their places, forms, and altitude. The waters are most pure, proceding from the entrails of rocky mountains; the herbs and fruits are of many sorts and kinds, as alkermes, currants, or a fruit like currants, mulberries, vines, raspberries, gooseberries, plums, walnuts, chestnuts, small nuts, &c, pumpkins, gourds, strawberries, beans, peas, and maize; a kind or two of flax, wherewith they make nets, lines, and ropes, both small and great, very strong for their quantities.

Oak is the chief wood, of which there is great difference in regard of the soil where it groweth; fir, pine, walnut, chestnut, birch, ash, elm, cyprus, cedar, mulberry, plum tree, hazel, sassefras, and many other sorts.

Eagles, gripes [vultures], divers sorts of hawks, cranes, geese, brants, cormorants, ducks, sheldrakes, teal, mews, gulls, turkeys, dive-dappers, and many other sorts whose names I know not.

Whales, grampus, porpoises, turbot, sturgeon, cod, hake, haddock, coal[-fish], cusk or small ling, shark, mackerel, herring, mullet, bass, pinnas, cunners, perch, eels, lobsters, mussels, whelks, oysters, and divers others, &c.

Moose, a beast bigger than a stag, deer, red and fallow; beavers wolves, foxes both black and other; racoons, wildcats, bears, otters, martens, fitch[ews], musquashes, & divers sorts of vermin whose names I know not. All these and divers other good things do here, for want of use, still increase & decrease with little diminution, whereby they grow to that abundance. You shall scarce find any bay, shallow shore, or cove of sand, where you may not take many clams or lobsters, or both at your pleasure, and in many places load your boat if you please; nor isles where you find not fruits, birds, crabs and mussels, or all of them, for taking at a low water. And in the harbors we frequented, a little boy might take of cunners and pinnas, and such delicate fish, at the ship's stern, more than six or ten can eat in a day; but with a casting net, thousands when we pleased; and scarce any place but cod, cusk, hallibut, mackerel, skate or such like, a man may take, with a hook or line what he will. And in divers sandy bays, a man may draw with a net great store of mullets, basses, and divers other sorts of such excellent fish as many as his net can draw on shore: no river where there is not plenty of sturgeon, or salmon, or both, all which are to be had in abundance observing but their seasons. But if a man will go at Christmas to gather cherries in Kent, he may be deceived, though there be plenty in summer; so here these plenties have each their seasons, as I have expressed. We for the most part had little but bread and vinegar, and though the most part of July when the fishing decayed, they wrought all day, lay abroad in the Isles all night, and lived on what they found, yet were not sick. But I would wish none put himself long to such plunges, except necessity constrain it; yet worthy is that person to starve that here cannot live, if he have sense, strength and health, for there is no such penury of these blessings in any place but that one hundred men may, in one hour or two, make their provisions for a day; and he that hath experience to manage well these affairs, with forty or thirty honest industrious men, might well undertake (if they dwell in these parts) to subject the savages, and feed daily two or three hundred men, with as good corn, fish and flesh as the earth hath of those kinds, and yet make that labour but their pleasure, provided that they have engines that be proper for their purposes.

Who can desire more content that hath small means, or but only his merit to advance his fortunes, than to tread and plant that ground he hath purchased by the hazard of his life? If he have but the taste of virtue and magnanimity, what to such a mind can be more pleasant than planting and building a foundation for his posterity, got from the rude earth by God's blessing & his own industry, without prejudice to any? If he have any grain of faith or zeal in religion, what can he do less hurtful to any, or more agreeable to God, than to seek to convert those poor savages to know Christ and humanity, whose labours with discretion will triple requite thy charge and pains? What so truly suits with honour and honesty as the discovering things unknown, erecting towns, peopling countries, informing the ignorant, reforming things unjust, teaching virtue & gain to our native mother country a kingdom to attend her, find employment for those that are idle, because they know not what to do: so far from wronging any as to cause posterity to remember thee, and remembering thee, ever honour that remembrance with praise? Consider what were the beginnings and endings of the monarchies of the Chaldeans, the Syrians, the Grecians and Romans, but this one rule: what was it they would not do for the good of the commonwealth or their mother city? For example: Rome, what made her such a monarchesse, but only the adventures of her youth, not in riots at home, but in dangers abroad, and the justice and judgement out of their experience when they grew aged? What was their ruin and hurt but this: the excess of idleness, the fondness of parents, the want of experience in magistrates, the admiration of their undeserved honours, the contempt of true merit, their unjust jealousies, their politic incredulities, their hypocritical seeming goodness and their deeds of secret lewdness? Finally in fine, growing only formal temporists, all that their predecessors got in many years they lost in a few days. Those by their pains & virtues became lords of the world; they by their ease and vices became slaves to their servants. This is the difference betwixt the use of arms in the field, & on the monuments of stones, the golden age and the leaden age, prosperity and misery, justice and corruption, substance and shadows, words and deeds, experience and imagination, making commonwealths and marring commonwealths, the fruits of virtue, and the conclusions of vice.

Then who would live at home idly (or think in himself any worth to live) only to eat, drink, and sleep, and so die? Or by consuming that carelessly his friends got worthily? Or by using that miserably that maintained virtue honestly? Or for being descended nobly, pine with the vain vaunt of great kindred in penury? Or (to maintain a silly show of bravery) toil out thy heart, soul and time basely, by shifts, tricks, cards & dice? Or by relating news of others' actions, shark here and there for a dinner or supper, deceive thy friends by fair promises and dissimulation, in borrowing where thou never intendest to pay, offend the laws, surfeit with excess, burthen thy country, abuse thy self, despair in want, and then cozen thy kindred, yea even thy own brother, and wish thy parents death (I will not say damnation) to have their estates, though thou seest what honours and rewards the world yet hath for them that will seek them and worthily deserve them.

A Description of New England (1616)

*   *   *

In fact there is hardly a contemporary account of American exploration and settlement without the adjective 'true' in the title. The authors of these myriad books and pamphlets must have seen their purpose as countering, if not medieval and renaissance notions of golden ages and earthly paradises, then at least the wilder rumours that had found their way back to London about the exploits, quarrels and desperate straits of the colonists' ventures abroad, not to mention their backers' more fanciful expectations of instant wealth. Smith's *Description of New England* strives hard to achieve a sense of the actual. It begins and ends (except for a short peroration) with an informal account of how he happened to go to New England, how he returned, and the anticlimactic results of the voyage. They went to catch whales and to 'make trials of a mine of gold and copper', but in the event they came away with furs and dried fish. The facts defeated the expectations. The whales were not worth the time and effort. 'We saw many, and spent much time in chasing them, but could not kill any, they being a kind of jubartes [jupiter fish, or rorqual], and not the whale that yields fins and oil as we expected.' As for the gold, 'it was rather the master's device to get a voyage that projected it, than any knowledge he had at all of any such matter.'

But Smith had something to say in favour of fish. The English backers may think it an unexciting commodity, he writes, but look what the Dutch have done with it. They 'labour in all weathers in the open sea' and so become 'hardy and industrious'. Then they sell 'this poor commodity' for 'wood, flax, pitch, tar, rosin, cordage, and such like' for their ships. What is left over they trade again to the French, Spanish, Portuguese and English, and thus:

> are made so mighty, strong and rich, as no state but Venice, of twice their magnitude, is so well furnished with so many fair cities, goodly towns, strong fortresses, . . . as well of gold, silver, pearls, diamonds, precious stones, silks, velvets, and cloth of gold. . . . What voyages and discoveries, East and West, North and South, yea about the world make they? What an army by sea and land, have they long maintained in despite of one of the greatest princes of the world? And never could the Spaniard with all his mines of gold and silver pay his debts, his friends, & army, half so truly, as the Hollanders still have done by this contemptible trade of fish.

This passage, which comes some eighteen pages before the excerpt in the first edition, is nothing short of a paean to mercantilism. Its surprising discovery of excitement in the ordinary (the bourgeois sensibility is supposed to be incapable of imaginative conceits) is like Defoe's revelation of the astonishingly complex commercial relationships within the organism of the modern city in *A Journal of the Plague Year* (1722). Only the rich could escape London during the plague, and one would think everyone else would still need the necessities of life. But 'the real condition of the people' suffered when even this relatively minor proportion of the capital's population was removed. Master workmen in manufactures relating even to 'ornament, and the less necessary parts of the people's dress, cloths, and furniture for houses' stopped work and dismissed 'their journeymen and workmen, and all their dependants'. Soon 'merchandizing was at a full stop', and traffic up and down the river ceased; so ferrymen, boatmen, carmen and porters were out of a job. With people leaving their houses, demand for building came to an end, and so did the employment of 'bricklayers, masons, carpenters, joiners, plasterers, painters, glaziers, smiths, plumbers, and all the labourers depending on such'. And so on.

The catalogue, much of it redundant from the strict point of view of the information it transmits is an astonishing rhetorical display, reinforcing through a surplus of material evidence the idea of the moral interdependence of a great social unit.

Smith's *New England* is full of such delectable riches discovered in plain things. The language of the extract is certainly plain. It comes from the common stock of the English vernacular, from the same source as the English Bible (the Geneva Version primarily), Donne's sonnets (both holy and secular) and Shakespeare's great middle plays. Whatever the rhetorical tactics, there is little that is 'literary' about the diction. Metaphors too are almost totally absent. Even the excellent verb in 'shark here or there for a dinner', the seventeenth-century equivalent of the modern 'to sponge', is more likely to be related etymologically to 'shirk' than to an image of the ravenous fish. 'Plunge' too, as in 'But I would wish none put himself long to such plunges', is not Smith's original figure but contemporary vernacular for 'crisis' or 'dilemma'.

The place in the discourse where 'reality' really seems to break through, however, is in the lists of 'herbs', fruits, trees and the various kinds of animals. Here even normal syntax all but falls away, as though to suggest that faced with such material plenty, European formulae, even to the most radical rules of conventional sentence structure, must be broken down. Only after contact with material fact can they be reconstituted – except that now, of course, they are no longer European. The more elaborate syntax of the later paragraphs (more complex, in fact, than most of what Smith had written up to this time) is in a sense grounded on these bare catalogues. They authenticate it.

The insistence on the native American *thing*, and on its power over the European *type*, is what makes this passage, despite its date, such a characteristic piece of American writing. As for its explicit, paraphrasable argument, it is clearly an early version of what has since come, rather loosely, to be called 'the American dream'. America is not a pleasant never-never land, but it affords a chance for the hard-working immigrant, without the old-world advantages of inherited wealth or social rank, to get a fair return on his investment of courage and labour. This vision of individual worth triumphing over the accidents of fortune in a fallen world owes a lot to Smith's own hopes and disappointments, but it was to become a recurrent theme in later American literature.

The plainness, both argued and exemplified, is achieved with great art, of course. The passage begins with a survey of headlands, mountains, waters, plants and animals. The bare summary is soon fleshed out; the catalogues consisting almost entirely of substantives are worked into a more complex structure in paragraph five. Now the sense of plenty is enhanced by subordination. Each bay, shore or cove teems with lobsters or clams; each 'isle' with fruits, birds, crabs and mussels, each harbour and river with all manner of fish. As the cells of the categories divide, each spawns a new sub-set, as though to mime in syntax the very idea of perpetual 'increase'. This is how the bare lists of things in paragraphs one to five serve to rebuild the dismantled 'European' formulae and re-invent them as American; they infiltrate the new structures based on the local landscape, then harden into supporting members.

But rather than allow the series to extend further, perhaps because he wants to preserve his major force for the paragraphs arguing the motives for colonization, Smith interrupts with the homely apothegm about how one should not expect to find cherries in Kent at Christmas. This qualification serves to authenticate his claims for New England, for in addition to warning inexperienced stay-at-homes against premature disappointment, it reinforces the idea of his own common sense (he was not carried away by paradisal visions, only reporting what he saw). 'These plenties have each their seasons', with its almost liturgical sound, is by way of saying that although the various species of New England move to their own, and not a European, natural rhythm, they at least obey the general rules of nature, and are not, therefore, the figments of a visionary projection. The vivid detail of their 'bread and vinegar' further supports the hope invested in the geography of New England with a personal reference reinforcing the idea of their hard experience in the adventure.

By the time it moves on to more abstract subject matter, Smith's writing remains plain only in the sense that it still derives from speech. The rhetoric now begins to accumulate repetitions. In paragraph six the word 'what' begins six questions (and the questions themselves are 'rhetorical' in the popular modern sense). In the following paragraph no fewer than five begin with 'or', with the effect (especially since the sense units in paragraph seven are by now much shorter) of accelerating the pace of his urgent interrogation. Abstract analysis need not necessitate words drawn from Latin origins (Smith does well enough with 'idleness', 'fondness', 'lewdness' and other equivalents of German words ending in '-heit'), but in English there is no doubt that Latin-derived words are a richer source of abstract terms than are those coming from the Anglo-Saxon. Even so, there is some hint here that Smith is using latinate words in a rather special way. For example, 'building a foundation for his posterity, got from the rude earth' is almost a metaphysical conceit epitomizing the theme of the whole book, suggesting the unlikely yoking together of the monosyllabic, concrete material and the polysyllabic, abstract promise for a whole network of hypothetical dependencies. The word 'foundation' is a perfect mediating term – either abstract or concrete, depending on how you read it. Then again, the concatenation of words derived from Latin (and Greek) in 'the want of experience in magistrates, the admiration of their undeserved honours, the contempt of true merit, their unjust jealousies, their politic incredulities, their hypocritical seeming goodness', though on one level precisely denoting the shortcomings of old-world society, also suggests (because it is hard to construe the polysyllabic abstraction) a world of preposterous, empty values, a suspension that is brought down to reality with the English balance between 'seeming goodness' and 'secret lewdness'.

Indeed, even the plainest parts of the passage recall a verbal model. The English Bible not only stems from the same vernacular roots as Smith's *New England*, but is also a direct source for it. The kinship of the two texts can be seen not only in their common diction, but in their fondness for redundant double constructions like 'sorts and kinds', 'ropes both great and small' and 'All these and diverse other'. Sometimes the biblical echoes in Smith's words and phrases amount to allusions conveying information. 'Yet worthy is that person to starve that here cannot live, if he have sense, strength and health, for there is no such penury of these blessings in any place . . .' borrows the 'Blessed are . . . for . . .' formula of the Beatitudes, as in, 'Blessed are they which suffer persecution for righteousness' sake: for theirs is the kingdom of heaven' (Geneva Bible, Matt. 5: 3). The apparently neutral – indeed, reportorial – cataloguing of the New England landscape which begins 'The herbs and fruits are of many sorts and kinds' suggests the account of the Creation in the Geneva Bible: 'Then God said, Let the earth bud forth the bud of the herb, that seedeth seed, the fruitful tree, which beareth fruit according to his kind . . . and it was so' (Gen. 1:11). Smith's categories (herbs, woods, birds, fishes, beasts) are very like the headings for creation in Genesis, in almost the same order (the Bible has herbs, trees, heavenly bodies, fish, fowl and cattle). Most striking of all, perhaps, is the echo of the exhortation to the Apostles in Acts 20: 28 'to feed the Church of God, which he hath purchased with his own blood' in 'Who can desire more content . . . than to tread, and plant that ground he hath purchased by the hazard of his life?'

So for all his claim to present things as they are, Smith buries a providential plot beneath the hard material reality of his surface argument: New England is also a new Eden in which the planter, having redeemed his individual worth from the false values of a fallen social and economic system, is blessed to live, to tend as a new church and for which to hazard (but this time not sacrifice) his life – as a more fortunate Jesus might have done. For all his experience of the real world he finds, Smith is also quite close here to Andrew Marvell's paradisal garden, where the Fall is reinvented as a harmless stumble onto soft grass ('The Garden', l. 40).

But surely the catalogues themselves – so slight of syntax, so stripped down to bare lists of things actually there – belong to no old-world formula? Actually catalogues are plentiful in early European accounts of the new world, appearing in the work of Edward Haie, Hariot, Raleigh, Brereton, and many others. William Wood's *New England's Prospect* (1634) even sets them out in verse, in the context of an otherwise prosy, informal and accurate account of the physical landscape, the Indians and their language – or what Wood himself, in his subtitle, calls a 'true, lively, and experimental description of that part of *America*, commonly called New England'. Chapters 5 to 9 describe the vegetable, mineral and animal world of New England (the animals being classified by habitat), and each kind has its verse catalogue:

> Trees both in hills and plains in plenty be,
> The long-lived oak and mournful cypress tree,
> Sky-towering pines, and chestnuts coated rough,
> The lasting cedar, with the walnut tough;

> The rosin-dropping fir for masts in use,
> The boatmen seek for oars light, neat-grown spruce. . . .
> Within this Indian orchard fruits be some,
> The ruddy cherry and the jetty plum,
> Snake-murthering hazel, with sweet saxifrage,
> Whose spurns in beer allays hot fever's rage.
> The dyer's sumac, with more trees there be,
> That are both good to use, and rare to see.

Thus set out, Wood's catalogues declare their family likeness, not only to other descriptions of America, but also to the much older European convention of what Ernst Curtius (trans. Trask, 1953) calls the 'idealized mixed forest' of classical literature. Chaucer's 'Parlement of Foules' provides a medieval instance of the trope:

> The byldere ok and eek the hardy asshe;
> The piler elm, the cofre unto carayne; . . .
> The saylynge fyr; the cipresse, deth to playne; . . .
> The olyve of pes, and eke the dronke vyne;
> The victor palm, the laurer to deveyne.
>
> (ll. 176–82)

And Spenser chimes in with an almost identical list in Book One of *The Faerie Queene*: 'The builder Oake, sole king of forrests all, / The Aspine good for staves, the Cypresse funerall. / The Laurell, meede of mightie conquerours . . .' and so on down to ash, maple and olive. The catalogue, as Curtius (194) reminds his readers, 'is a fundamental poetic form that goes back to Homer and Hesiod'.

Yet Wood's verse lists do mark a departure from the rhetorical convention. In the first place, they are not mixed: Chaucer and Spenser cite species that could not all live in the same place, whereas Wood, Smith and the other new-world travellers record only what might be seen in that part of America they describe. Secondly, the traditional catalogue was a closed set in which the circle of species representing all that was pleasant or fruitful was brought right round, while Wood leaves his series open-ended: 'more trees there be, / That are both good to use, and rare to see.' Smith too ends his lists of birds, fish, and so forth, with 'and many other sorts, whose names I know not', 'and diverse others, etc.' and 'diverse sorts of vermin, whose names I know not'. Even Columbus's letter to Luis de Santangel, the first 'real' description of the new world, tails off with 'And the nightingale was singing, and other birds of a thousand kinds. . . .'

Obviously one reason for the refusal to close the series is the traveller's genuine uncertainty what to call some of the unfamiliar species he saw (the doubt was certainly justified, as witnessed by Columbus's nightingale, which is not native to the new world, and the infamous case, which has reverberated down the years in language textbooks, of the American thrush with a red front which English settlers dubbed a robin). But as Wayne Franklin suggests, in his *Discoverers, Explorers, Settlers* (1979, 3–5), the open ending, in miming breakdown, dramatizes the struggle of language to domesticate the wilderness of America, and also expresses its limitless creation. America goes beyond Europe in fruitfulness, manifestly by outrunning its linguistic energy.

These narratives of discovery were to be a rich source for later Americans whenever they needed a text to authenticate their country or their culture. For instance, Thomas Jefferson's *Notes on the State of Virginia* (1784), written to answer the scepticism of French scientists and philosophers who thought that species in the new world must decline in both size and variety, takes a rigorously scientific line in its defence of its author's native state. Like Strachey's *History of Travel into Virginia Britannia*, Smith's *A Map of Virginia* and the formal part of his *Description of New England*, Jefferson's *Notes* begins by placing the territory on the map – literally – by lines of latitude and longitude. By the time Jefferson wrote, this act must have been something less than necessary. Like earlier descriptions of American travel, Jefferson divides creation into categories of catalogues, and through them he also expresses more than the data he records. In tables opposing American and European species, Jefferson demonstrates that the former exceed the latter in both weight and variety. Tell-tale blanks appear in the European column, opposite species aboriginal to America. Wayne Franklin's comment on this juxtaposition is illuminating:

> Jefferson's argument with [the French naturalist] Buffon uses reason in the cause of truth. There is a touch of American audacity in the whole performance, even a sense of frontier humor: simple Jefferson with his concrete beasts outsmarts the French dandy with his grand speculations, his civilized scheme of reality. (35)

The catalogue, particularly, became naturalized as an American trope. American writers struggling to establish a national identity used the bare list of things to be found in American nature as a weapon against another kind of list frequently uttered by Europeans – or more often by Americans living in, or newly returned from Europe – the long rehearsal of traditional titles, institutions, prerogatives and customs missing from the American social and political scene. The most famous example is the one in Henry James's monograph on Nathaniel Hawthorne, published in the 'English Men of Letters' series in 1879, in which America is said to be a nearly impossible setting for the novel because it lacks a sovereign, an aristocracy, an established church, army, country gentlemen, castles, manors, thatched cottages – even an Eton and Ascot. Similar negative catalogues had already been published in James Fenimore Cooper's two-volume study of American society, *Notions of the Americans* (1828) and the preface to his novel *Home as Found* (1838), in which he claimed that an interesting *roman de société* was impossible in a country lacking a 'standard for opinion, manners, social maxims, or even language', and in Hawthorne's own preface to *The Marble Faun* (1860), in which he complained how difficult it was to write 'a romance about a country where there is no shadow, no antiquity, no mystery, no picturesque and gloomy wrong, no anything but a commonplace prosperity'.

But the supposed deficiency of 'quality' could be answered with an assertion of the immense quantity of nature in America. 'The English, when they sneer at our country,' wrote the Cincinnati editor Timothy Flint, 'speak of it as sterile in moral interest. . . . It has, they say, no monuments, no ruins, none of the massive remains of former ages; no castles, no [etc., etc.] . . . nothing to connect the imagination and the heart with the past, no recollections of former ages to associate the past with the future.' But if the Europeans had proportion, the Americans had size and variety; what the old world husbanded and distributed by inherited prerogatives, the new world poured forth profuse for all to take. The Mississippi Valley alone, wrote Flint, is larger than half of Europe, and compared to its great waterway, 'all but two or three of the rivers of Europe are but rivulets'. America has lakes 'which could find a place for the Cumberland lakes in the hollow of one of their islands' (ed. Brooks, 1966, 124). Noticing Flint's book, the *North American Review* praised the variety of novel types to be discerned in it: 'The scene is changed, and we are introduced to the rough, but frank and hospitable *backwoodsman*. . . . The preachers, the lawyers, the Indian, the negro, the fanatic, the venerable chronicler of "the olden time," the fresh and lovely "rose of the prairies," successively pass in review before us' (XXIII, 362).

These were types, not in the sense of 'kinds' or conventional signifiers, but in the meaning more commonly found in the term as used in biblical exegesis – prototypes or precursors of fulfilments to come. They were the human equivalent of the teeming nature encountered by the early explorers: unranked by hierarchical systems, not fitting any European tradition, and – above all – native. In time (as the hope was expressed, anyway) they would find their place in American fiction; meanwhile they had 'colour', interest and particularity of their own. In the early stages of the project for a truly native literature, 'bare lists of words are found suggestive to an imaginative and excited mind', as Ralph Waldo Emerson was to write in 'The Poet' (1844), before going on to utter a catalogue of 'types' strikingly similar to those the *North American Review* drew from Flint, except that this time novel institutions were included as well as individuals: 'Our log-rolling, our stumps and their politics, our fisheries, our Negroes and Indians . . . are yet unsung. Yet America is a poem in our eyes; its ample geography dazzles the imagination. . . .'

To pose material abundance against abstract qualities supposedly missing is to make the latter appear not only insubstantial but unimportant. And the bravado of the catalogue is that it mimes the very freedom from convention which it celebrates on another level; its extremely simple (almost non-existent) syntax eschews all subordination while the series, because it appears infinitely extendable, expresses the idea of fruitful increase. Nature flouts culture, just as in the fruitful exploration accounts of Captain John Smith.

By the middle of the nineteenth century the catalogue had become so firmly associated with excited 'boosters' of western development and with others projecting the great literature to come, that Herman Melville could parody the form as part of his satire on American optimism in *The Confidence Man* (1857):

As among Chaucer's Canterbury pilgrims, or those oriental ones crossing the Red Sea towards Mecca in the festival month, there was no lack of variety. Natives of all sorts and foreigners; men of business and men of pleasure; parlor men and backwoodsmen; farm-hunters and fame-hunters; heiress-hunters, gold-hunters, buffalo-hunters, bee-hunters, happiness-hunters, truth-hunters, and still keener hunters after all these hunters. Fine ladies in slippers and moccasined squaws; Northern speculators and Eastern philosophers . . . Kentucky boatmen, and Japanese-looking Mississippi cotton planters . . . hard-shell Baptists and clay-eaters; grinning negroes, and Sioux chiefs solemn as high-priests. . . .

As pine, birch, ash, hachmatack, hemlock, spruce, basswood, maple, interweave their foliage in the natural wood, so these varieties of mortals blended their varieties of visage and garb . . . in one cosmopolitan and confident tide.

This comic series – too full and self-interfering to be taken entirely seriously – is really a condensed history of the trope. The reference to Chaucer is a reminder that, for all its insistence on actuality, the catalogue has often been set in a literary context (to take just the examples we have examined, Wood's catalogues are – at least in form – the most 'literary' thing about his book on New England, and Emerson's was expressly set out as the foundation of a new American literature). The biblical double constructions ('Natives . . . and foreigners', 'men of business and men of pleasure', and so on) recall a similar introduction to Smith's categories of 'many sorts and kinds'. Finally, the mock-epic simile at the end of his series – quite anti-climactic, if not downright meaningless, unless it is read as an allusion, reasserts the literariness of the convention, and shows where it began – with the original arboreal catalogue.

Yet, as Emerson hoped, the trope did provide a rhetoric for later American writers. Walt Whitman, in particular, seems to have been given voice by it; without the relatively uncomplicated syntax of the endless list of particulars it is hard to imagine him having written at all. Finally the argument from profusion, as a counter to 'tradition', has become part of the apology for modernist poetics. 'We seek profusion, the Mass – heterogeneous – ill assorted – quite breathless – grasping at all kinds of things,' as William Carlos Williams said in 1948. 'We should be profuse, we Americans; we need to build up a mass, a conglomerate maybe, containing few gems but bits of them . . . that shine of themselves, uncut as they are.' In going over to the (European) enemy, T. S. Eliot had elected 'to go where there was already a mass of more ready distinction . . . already an established literature in what to him was the same language (?) an already established place in world literature – a short cut, in short.' The American poet's task was to 'make anew . . . not at *this* time an analysis so much as an accumulation' (1954, 284–5). The echo of Ezra Pound's dictum 'make it new' should be sufficient reminder that he, Williams and other exponents of the American long poem had been doing just this: accumulating catalogues of 'found objects' in an (apparently) unplotted, open-ended series. Williams's 'field' was the city of Paterson, New Jersey – its geography, what its people said, the documents relating to its history that lay in the library. Into the poem they went, uncut and unpolished as they were. For Pound the field was wider in both time and space: everything from Sienese banking through early American history and a commentary on Magna Carta down to the ephemera of contemporary life. Again, in it went – in small fragments or large slabs, apparently as found, though not without a purpose. Like the early explorers of America, the modernist American poets found the most appropriate celebration of their rich world to be a simple, paratactic collection of the material that lay around them. The most fitting style, then as now, would be one celebrating the happy accident, the fortunate fall into a redeemed Eden where everything encountered would be good. Which is why it is so pleasing that Charles Olson, another theorist and practitioner of the long, open-field poem, should have 'found', among other things, the writing of Captain John Smith. His *Maximus* includes excerpts from the Sixth Book of *The General History*, from the *Sea Grammar*, from the title page, dedication and epigraph of *Advertisements for the Unexperienced Planters of New England* (Smith's last book, published in 1630) and this tribute, in Olson's own words, to the verbal accuracy of the explorer who gave New England her name:

> the Admiral of New England Smith proudly
> took himself to be, rightly, who sounded
> her bays, ran her coast, and wrote down
> Algonquin so scrupulously Massachusetts
> And I know who lived where I lived
> before the small-pox took them all away
> and the Pilgrims
> had such an easy time of it
> to land
> What further wowed us was
> he had a swooning Turkish Princess
> in his arms:
>   Historie
> come bang into the midst of
> our game! Actors,
> where I have learned another sort of
> play
> 2
> Smith also got shoved aside.
>   ('Maximus, to Gloucester, Letter 11', 1–2)

References

Barbour, Philip (1964), *The Three Worlds of Captain John Smith*, London: Macmillan.

Curtius, Ernst (1953), *European Literature and the Latin Middle Ages*, trans. Willard Trask, New York: Pantheon Books.

Emerson, Everett (1971), *Captain John Smith*, New York: Twayne (United States Authors Series, 177).

Flint, Timothy (1966), *Recollections of the Last Ten Years in the Valley of the Mississippi*, ed. George Brooks, Carbondale and Edwardsville, Ill.: Southern Illinois University Press.

Franklin, Wayne (1979), *Discoverers, Explorers, Settlers; the Diligent Writers of Early America*, Chicago, Ill.: University of Chicago Press.

Jones, Howard Mumford (1964), *O Strange New World; American Culture, the Formative Years*, New York: Viking Press.

Kermode, Frank (1954) (ed.), *The Tempest*, London: Methuen (Arden Shakespeare).

Martyr, Peter (1885), (*The Decades of the Newe Worlde or West India . . .*, in Edward Arber (ed.), *The First Three English Books on America*, Birmingham.

Morison, Samuel Eliot (1971), *The European Discovery of America; the Northern Voyages, AD 500–1600*, New York: Oxford University Press.

O'Gorman, Edmundo (1961), *The Invention of America*, Bloomington, Ind.: Indiana University Press.

Quinn, David (1971) (ed.), *North American Discovery*, New York: Harper & Row.

Williams, William Carlos (1954), 'The poem as a field of action', in *Selected Essays*, New York: New Directions.

Further reading

TEXTS

Peter Martyr of Anghiera, *The Decades of the Newe Worlde, or West India . . .*, trans. Richard Eden, London, 1555; in Edward Arber (ed.), *The First Three Books on America . . .*; Birmingham: 1885.

David and Alison Quinn (eds), *Virginia Voyages from Hakluyt*, London: Oxford University Press, 1973.

John Smith, *Travels and Works*, ed. Edward Arber, 2 vols, Edinburgh: J. Grant, 1910.

Louis B. Wright (ed.), *The Elizabethan's America; a Collection of Early Reports by Englishmen on the New World*, Cambridge, Mass.: Harvard University Press, 1966.

CONTEXTS

Wayne Franklin, *Discoverers, Explorers, Settlers; the Diligent Writers of Early America*, Chicago, Ill.: University of Chicago Press, 1979.

Howard Mumford Jones, *O Strange New World; American Culture, The Formative Years*, New York: Viking, 1952.

Samuel Eliot Morison, *The European Discovery of America; the Northern Voyages, AD 500–1600*, New York: Oxford University Press, 1971.

Edmundo O'Gorman, *The Invention of America*, Bloomington, Ind.: Indiana University Press, 1961.

William Spengemann, *The Adventurous Muse; the Poetics of American Fiction, 1789–1900*, New Haven, Conn.: Yale University Press, 1977.

CRITICAL AND BIOGRAPHICAL

Philip Barbour, *The Three Worlds of Captain John Smith*, London: Macmillan, 1964.

Everett Emerson, *Captain John Smith*, New York: Twayne (United States Authors Series, 177), 1971.

2

Robert Cushman
(c. 1599–1625)

Forasmuch as many exceptions are daily made against the going into, and inhabiting of foreign desert places, to the hindrances of plantations abroad, and the increase of distractions at home, it is not amiss that some which have been ear witnesses of the exceptions made, and are either agents or abettors of such removals and plantations, do seek to give content to the world, in all things that possibly they can.

And although the most of the opposites are such as either dream of raising their fortunes here, to that than which there is nothing more unlike, or such as affecting their home-born country so vehemently, as that they had rather with all their friends beg, yea starve in it, than undergo a little difficulty in seeking abroad; yet are there some who out of doubt in tenderness of conscience, and fear to offend God by running before they be called, are straitened and do straiten others, from going to foreign plantations.

For whose cause especially, I have been drawn out of my good affection to them, to publish some reasons that might give them content and satisfaction, and also stay and stop the wilful and witty caviller; and herein I trust I shall not be blamed of any godly wife, though through my slender judgement I should miss the mark, and not strike the nail on the head, considering it is the first attempt that hath been made (that I know of) to defend those enterprises. Reason would therefore, that if any man of deeper reach and better judgement see further or otherwise, that he rather instruct me, than deride me.

And being studious for brevity, we must first consider, that whereas God of old did call and summon our fathers by predictions, dreams, visions, and certain illuminations to go from their countries, places and habitations, to reside and dwell here or there, and to wander up and down from city to city, and land to land, according to his will and pleasure. Now there is no such calling to be expected for any matter whatsoever, neither must any so much as imagine that there will now be any such thing. God did once so train up his people, but now he doth not, but speaks in another manner, and so we must apply ourselves to God's present dealing, and not to his wonted dealing: and as the miracle of giving manna ceased, when the fruits of the land became plenty, so God having such a plentiful storehouse of directions in his holy word, there must not now any extraordinary revelations be expected.

But now the ordinary examples and precepts of the Scriptures reasonably and rightly understood and applied, must be the voice and word, that must call us, press us, and direct us in every action.

Neither is there any land or possession now, like unto the possession which the Jews had in Canaan, being legally holy and appropriated unto a holy people the seed of Abraham, in which they dwelt securely, and had their days prolonged, it being by an immediate voice said, that he (the Lord) gave it them as a land of rest after their weary travels, and a type of eternal rest in heaven; but now there is no land of that sanctimony, no land so appropriated, none typical; much less any that can be said to be given of God to any nation as was Canaan, which they and their seed must dwell in, till God sendeth upon them sword or captivity; but now we are in all places strangers and pilgrims, travellers and sojourners, most properly, having no dwelling but in this earthly tabernacle; our dwelling is but a wandering, and our abiding but as a fleeting, and in a word our home is nowhere, but in the heavens: in that house not made with hands, whose maker and builder is God, and to which all ascend that love the coming of our Lord Jesus.

'Reasons & Considerations touching the lawfulness of removing out of *England* into the parts of *America*' (1622)

* * *

The long history of the Reformation can be summarized as an attempt to re-establish the direct contact between God and the individual worshipper thought to have existed in the early days of the Christian Church. The most fervent reformers wanted no mediator, apart from Jesus Christ, between the Word and the dictates of their own consciences – no parish priest licensed by the hierarchy and supported by a local landowner, no ritual, no vestments, no music or idolatrous decorations, no soteriological machinery of confession, penance, absolution and varying degrees of time spent in Purgatory. A man was either saved or damned – predestined to one or the other state since the time of the

Creation – and nothing he did in his lifetime would affect the case. The Word of God was to be made readily available through vernacular translations in every parish, and its plain exposition was to be the chief business of whomever presided at the weekly or monthly service. The pulpit was to supplant the altar of pagan sacrifice – as indeed it did in the design of non-conformist chapels. If these arrangements seemed somewhat makeshift, that was no accident. Early Protestantism had a strong millennial flavour; the purifying, the stripping away of centuries-old accretions of habit, tradition and unwarranted authority, was to be a preparation for the rigours of the Last Days. The only argument was over how quickly the Apocalypse was coming. Luther taught that it was imminent, and that there was time only for each individual worshipper to make a reformation in his own heart, while Calvin supposed there was time for a body of the elect to work out their salvation as a reformed community.

This, at least, was the vision at its purest. In fact, the inevitable compromises with state authority halted the movement a long way from its fullest expression. The Elizabethan Settlement consolidated the separation from Rome and authorized the Bible and liturgy in English, but the Prayer Book of 1559 was actually more conservative than one produced in 1552 under Edward VI. Vestments and ritual were allowed to continue, only slightly altered from Roman usage. Bishops still maintained control over the parishes. Projects for improving the education of the clergy were discouraged, and the hierarchy did not require the parish priest to preach more than four times a year. The reason for this caution was the established nature of the English Church. Independent parishes, the individual reading the Bible, hearing the Word and working out his own salvation, all tended to 'disputaciousness' and might lead even to sedition.

The rise of English Puritanism was a response to Anglican conservatism. The *OED* defines 'Puritan' as 'A member of that party of English Protestants who regarded the reformation of the church under Elizabeth as incomplete, and called for its further "purification" from what they considered to be unscriptural and corrupt forms and ceremonies retained from the unreformed church'. There was more than one sect of Puritans, and occasionally they seemed to spend most of their energy in disputes among themselves, but in a famous sermon at Paul's Cross in 1589, Archbishop Richard Bancroft argued that they were all a threat to the state. Richard Hooker's *Of the Laws of Ecclesiastical Polity* (Books I–IV, 1593) defended Anglicanism against the Puritans, not by pleading the need for a middle way between Roman Catholicism and antinomian enthusiasm (a common claim for the thirty-nine Articles of Anglican belief), but by posing a positive project for a faith based on reason, which would reveal the common cause of peace in the outer worlds of nature and the state, and the inner one of the individual spirit. *Of the Laws of Ecclesiastical Polity* did in prose what Archbishop Laud, according to a well-known history of Puritanism, was later to do in the Church itself: 'to impose decency, decorum, order and cleanliness, good manners and respect for law and authority, learning, beauty and good taste, all the things that England most needed short of the one thing that half of England most passionately desired, namely freedom for the individual to work out his own salvation in his own way' (Haller, 1957, 229).

For a while the Puritans had hopes in the accession of the Calvinist James I. Even before he had arrived in London, he had received a deputation of several hundred Puritan ministers asking that the reformation of the Protestant Church be resumed without further delay. He promised to meet them in more formal circumstances, but meanwhile seems to have been persuaded of the old maxim that no bishop means no king. At the Hampton Court Conference of 1604 he came down in favour of the episcopacy; any Puritans who did not conform to the Church of England he 'would harry . . . out of the land, or else do worse'.

The Puritans could still meet and hear sermons in private houses waiting for a congregational polity eventually to become acceptable – or more hopefully, for the whole of the English Church to be reorganized on a presbyterian model. But those who wished to form open confederations electing their own ministers now had to separate from the body of the Church, and separatism was schism, and schism was punishable by death. Overt separatists were indeed harried from the land, and they could only survive in foreign countries sympathetic to their condition, such as Holland. One such congregation went to the Netherlands from Scrooby, Nottinghamshire, in 1608.

The Scrooby separatists settled in Leyden, a cloth-making town, where they had a hard time. Powerful craft guilds kept them out of all except unskilled trades. If they wanted to learn how to weave or be tailors, they needed time and money for a long apprenticeship. Only the minister of the group, John Robinson, got a job commensurate with his abilities, teaching English in the University of Leyden. After more than ten years of barely making a living, with the truce between Spain and

the Netherlands about to end, and with some of their children beginning to be tempted by the more worldly youth of Holland, the Scrooby
Puritans began to think of moving on. They wanted somewhere where
they could be on their own, but still make a living. America was the
only possibility. Virginia was too Anglican, but New England, according to Captain John Smith's 1616 account, would support anyone
willing to work, and that they certainly were. Eventually, after much
discussion among themselves and negotiations with prospective London
backers, Robinson's congregation chartered two ships and, together
with a larger number of 'strangers', or non-Puritans enlisted by the
backers from London and other parts of England, the 'saints' set out for
Massachusetts, promising to work for seven years for a common stock
to be divided among the London adventurers.

This, then, was the origin of the Plymouth Colony, the original
Pilgrim Fathers of later American legend. At first, it seemed an inaus-
picious venture. John Robinson could not accompany them (the
Plymouth Colony was not to have the services of a professional minister
for some eight years); the king would not grant them a charter, though
he would not refuse them permission for unmolested passage either; one
of the two ships sprung a leak, and after two attempts they had to put
back for Plymouth, where they discharged some of their cargo and
those colonists who were least confident of the venture or least able-
bodied, and took the rest on board the one remaining ship, the *Mayflower*. Finally, in the middle of September 1620, they got away to a fair
wind and crossed with little further trouble, landing just inside the
hook of Cape Cod, at what is now Provincetown, Massachusetts, at the
end of November. After four or five weeks of exploring the Bay coast of
the Cape, they sailed across to Plymouth, where they settled.

A brief account of these events was given in *A Relation or Journal of . . .
the English Plantation at Plimouth*, known as *Mourt's Relation*. It was
published in London less than two years after the Plymouth Colony had
set out from England, in order to inform the backers of their success, and
to encourage new recruits. 'Mourt' was probably George Morton, who
was associated with the Plymouth colonists but remained in England as
their agent until he came to America in 1623. Although he probably
edited the pamphlet and saw it through the press, only a brief
introduction 'To the Reader' is signed by him. Other authors probably
included William Bradford, governor of the colony from 1621, Robert
Cushman, and Edward Winslow, who continued the history of the
colony in his *Good News from New England* (1624). John Robinson

sent a 'Letter written by a discreet friend unto the planters in New England', which appears as a preface to the book. The *Relation* itself comprises five chapters. The first and longest covers the journey to Massachusetts, the explorations of the coast and the process of settling and building at Plymouth. The other four are short narratives of minor explorations and trade missions to the Indians. The book is concluded by two brief arguments for further support and numbers.

The main body of the *Relation*, an informal narrative arranged more or less in the form of a journal, is lightly plotted. Occasionally something is said to have happened 'by God's providence' or 'after [they] had given God thanks for [their] deliverance', but for the most part things are told in the order in which they happened, without especial heightening or selection, except that 'the starving time' of the first winter, when almost half of the planters died of scurvy, exhaustion and malnutrition, is not emphasized. The first sentence gives an idea of how undramatic the narrative is: 'Wednesday, the sixth of September, the wind coming east-north-east, a fine small gale, we loosed from Plymouth, having been kindly entertained and courteously used by divers friends there dwelling, and after many difficulties in boisterous storms, at length, by God's providence, upon the ninth of November following [i.e. 19 November by the modern calendar], by break of the day we espied land which we deemed to be Cape Cod, and so afterwards it proved.'

So much for the perils of crossing the Atlantic. Except that it lacks notes of latitude, directions sailed and miles covered, the account might have come from the log of the *Mayflower*. And the narrative continues unadorned. In the Bay they saw whales, which they could have caught if they had 'had instruments and means to take them'. The master of the *Mayflower* 'professed we might have made three or four thousand pounds' worth of oil'. They saw no cod, but guessed there would be plenty 'in their season'. After they had assembled their shallop (a long-boat that had been knocked down for storage between decks) they began to explore the shallow waters of the Cape. Their first encounter with the Indians was unexciting; they 'espied five or six people with a dog, coming towards them, who were savages, who when they saw them, ran into the wood and whistled the dog after them, etc.'. For a while their only contact was through Indian artefacts abandoned, either in fright or on purpose, like the 'certain heaps of sand, one whereof was covered with old mats, and had a wooden thing like a mortar whelmed on the top of it, and an earthen pot laid in a little hole at the end thereof'.

The explorers, 'musing what it might be', dug down a bit, and found a bow; then, realizing it might be a grave, delicately left off their researches, because 'it would be odious unto [the Indians] to ransack their sepulchres'. Later they did help themselves to a store of 'two or three baskets full of Indian wheat [i.e. maize], and a bag of beans' but that was because they were starving and needed seed native to the country; besides, so far no Indian had stayed to trade with them.

Mourt's Relation gives a very different idea of the early American Puritans from the personal traits with which they are commonly invested. It is a childlike account – or what one feels children would write if only they could write well – innocent and full of respectful, yet unfeigned delight in the unfamiliar. There is no wisdom after the event, little sense of a solemn mission prosecuted against the grain of natural occurrence, not even an attempt to save face. When they came across an Indian deer trap (a noose sprung by a young sapling 'bowed down over a bow, and some acorns strewed underneath') they puzzled over it, until 'William Bradford being in the rear, when he came looked also upon it, and as he went about, it gave a sudden jerk up, and he was immediately caught by the leg'. The story admits even this comic posture of the soon-to-be governor of the colony. Nor does the narrative dwell on the great man's loss of dignity; what is of interest is the trap itself: 'It was a very pretty device, made with a rope of their own making and having a noose as artificially made as any roper in England can make, and as like ours as can be, which we brought away with us.'

Yet the voyage was not just a lark, or a tour, and even the *Relation* was more than a chronicle of what the colonists first encountered on Cape Cod. An early index of a more serious purpose is the first description of the woods around Provincetown. The country looked 'like the downs in Holland, but much better; the crust of the earth a spit's depth excellent black earth; all wooded with oaks, pines, sassafras, juniper, birch, holly, vines, some ash, walnut; the wood for the most part open and without underwood, fit either to go or ride in.' When they finally sailed across the Bay to the site of Plymouth, on which they were to settle, they again found soil that was deep, friable and rich, 'two or three great oaks but not very thick, pines, walnuts, beech, ash, birch, hazel, holly, asp [aspen], sassafras in abundance, and vines everywhere, cherry trees, plum trees, and many others we know not'. The catalogue continues through vegetables, building materials, a clay that 'will wash like soap' and brooks that 'now begin to be full of fish'.

Here was the profuse world poured out, and in utilitarian terms the

London investors could understand (the stress on sassafras, here and twice elsewhere in the *Relation*, relates to its value as a drug). Yet the catalogue also works, as the convention does in other exploration narratives, to give the idea of natural bounty outrunning European words for its variety, a fruitfulness still within the confines of nature yet richer and more plentiful than anything encountered in the old world.

At the end of the Pilgrims' journal of their first explorations, building and planting, two brief essays attempt to persuade other emigrants to join the colony. Now the purpose is not narration but argument, yet the two addenda appeal to very different motives in the would-be planter. The first, in the form of a letter from Edward Winslow to a 'loving and old friend' (probably Morton himself who received the manuscript of *Mourt's Relation* by the same ship), summarizes their achievement during the first year. 'We have built seven dwelling-houses, and four for the uses of the plantation, and have made preparation for divers others. We set last spring some twenty acres of Indian corn, and sowed some six acres of barley and peas, and according to the manner of the Indians, we manured our ground with herrings, or rather with shads, which we have in great abundance.' The Indians, he reports, have kept the peace 'very faithfully'. The climate 'agreeth well with that in England, and if there be any difference at all, this is somewhat hotter in summer'. Fish and fowl they have in 'great abundance' and variety. Then follows a brief catalogue. The plenty of nature, the Indians, 'very loving and ready to pleasure us', form the background for his story of the first Thanksgiving:

> Our harvest being gotten in, our governor sent four men on fowling, that so we might after a special manner rejoice together after we had gathered the fruit of our labours. . . . At which time, amongst other recreations, we exercised our arms, many of the Indians coming amongst us, and among the rest their greatest king Massasoit, with some ninety men, whom for three days we entertained and feasted, and they went out and killed five deer, which they brought to the plantation and bestowed upon our governor. . . . And though it be not always so plentiful as it was at this time with us, yet by the goodness of God, we are so far from want that we often wish you partakers of our plenty.

The theme of bounty reciprocated, latent in the rest of the *Relation*, is made salient here. Yet Winslow ballasts the account with an accurate qualification – if indeed something of an understatement – that 'it has not always been so plentiful', and he ends his letter with an extremely detailed, practical list of things which the intending emigrant should bring, both for his own use and that of the colony. Winslow's letter brings *Mourt's Relation* to the classic mood of exploration narrative, because it is both rhapsodic and realistic, so as to catch the imagination and speed the actual progress of the hesitant colonist. For as he says, 'The country wanteth only industrious men to employ'.

Winslow's argument was a secular one; it might have been intended to attract more 'strangers', not to mention more finance, to allow the struggling colony to pursue its way in the world. The other addendum, however, was certainly addressed to the 'saints' still dawdling in the old country. Written by Robert Cushman in the form of a sermon, it offers 'Reasons and Considerations for removing out of England into the parts of America' that would move the Puritan imagination most urgently. The extract comes from the first three pages of Cushman's appeal. How does the argument work?

Having dispensed with those who fancy they may still grow rich here (i.e. in England) or who dote on their mother country so idolatrously that they would not leave it even if they were starving there, Cushman turns to the serious believers who may be still searching their consciences for evidence of God's call to remove. There will be no miraculous call, says Cushman; in biblical times God addressed his people through signs and miracles, but now He 'speaks in another manner', through the ordinary occurrences of nature. Nor is there any promised land, so there is no point in hanging about England expecting the Apocalypse to begin there. Our only 'proper' dwelling is our own bodies, our only permanent home 'nowhere, but in the heavens'. The material benefits of the new world are then offered, not to satisfy longings of self-interest (the usual plea of other exploration accounts) but as a means of doing good to others. Following the passage in the extract, Cushman goes on to argue that the new land is empty, except for the Indians who welcome the English and acknowledge the supremacy of the British monarchy ('neither has this been accomplished by threats and blows', he adds, but rather 'by friendly usage, love, peace, honest and just carriages, good counsel, etc.'); so they would not be stealing the land to settle in it. The Indians were a reminder, too, that the good work of converting heathen was still to be done. If only the English Puritans could divert the energy they now spend on 'writing, disputing, and inveighing earnestly one against another' into this work of conversion, if only their 'zeal . . . were turned against the rude barbarism of the heathens, it might do more good in a day than it hath done [in England] many years'. Finally (and here again Cushman departs sharply from the usual inducements), the prospective emigrant should not be deterred by thoughts of hardship, want of variety in food or comfort in housing. 'Nature is content with little, and health is much endangered by mixtures upon the stomach.' Anyway, such comforts are badly distributed in England. 'The rent-taker lives on sweet morsels, but the rent-payer eats a dry crust often with watery eyes.' In New England what there is will be shared by all.

It is a brilliant work of persuasion – superbly written in the cleanest and most balanced prose imaginable, and acutely aimed at the Puritans' appetite for self-abnegation, their wish to do good, and the tenets of their reformed faith. For example, it was a common notion among Puritans that the Apocalypse would begin in England, because the work of reform was furthest advanced in that country. 'Why else was this Nation chosen before any other, that out of her as out of Sion should be proclaimed and sounded forth the first tidings and trumpet of Reformation to all Europe?' asked Milton in *Aeropagitica* (1644). In 1655 Cromwell even invited the Jewish theologian Menasseh ben Israel and three rabbis to London to discuss the resettlement of the Jews in England, from which they had been officially banned since the rule of Edward III. The reason advanced was that the conversion of the Jews was one of the three signs of the Last Days, and the English Puritans were more likely to convert them than continental Catholics (though Cromwell may also have been interested in using the Jews, with their connections throughout Europe, for intelligence work).

To disabuse his readers of this notion that England was the only site of the millennium, Cushman appeals to an even deeper Puritan belief, that (as he says) 'God having such a plentiful storehouse of directions in his holy word, there must not now any extraordinary relevations be expected.' The belief that miracles had ceased after the time chronicled by Holy Scripture was fundamental, not only to Puritanism but to Protestantism generally and this was one of many points of the reformers' discontent with Roman Catholic doctrine.

Associated with this issue was the question of typology, the system by which an event or person in the Old Testament was interpreted as prefiguring a fulfilment, or 'antitype', in the New. The strictest opinion about biblical exegesis held that Old Testament types could refer only to the New Testament – or, to put it another way, that all the Old Testament prophets, priests and kings, and all the instances of

God's special favour to his Chosen People, were recapitulated in the person and mediating presence of Jesus Christ. Searching the Bible for types prophetic of anti-types in *contemporary* history (though clearly this was done regularly – and still is – by the more extreme millennial sects, at least as far as concerned signs of the Last Days) was, according to the 'purest' theory, unwarranted. Following the revelation of God's Word in Christ, as the great Cambridge Puritan theologian John Preston wrote in *The New Covenant, or the Saints' Portion* (1629), we have no need of the baby-talk by which He addressed the people of the Old Testament:

> the Old was expressed in types, and shadows, and figures. . . . These were elements, and rudiments that God used to them as children; that is, as children have their A, B, C, their first elements, so God did show to the Jews these spiritual mysteries, not in themselves, but in these types and shadows they were able to see them from day to day . . . whereas now in the time of the Gospel, these things are taught to us, these we comprehend in our minds, we serve the Lord in spirit and in truth, but there is not that visible sight, that was a help to their weakness.

Or as the Puritan divine Samuel Mather wrote in the introduction to his *The Figures and Types of the Old Testament* (1683), 'It is not safe to make any thing a type merely upon our own fancies and imaginations; it is God's prerogative to make types.' So God feeding the Jews in the wilderness with manna, and His promise of a land flowing with milk and honey in Canaan was not a type of a special country reserved for the saints today, but of the redeeming mission of Christ in the New Testament. Canaan prefigures Heaven, not England. Cushman is emphatic about this, reiterating the negative formulation in 'no land . . . none typical . . . much less any . . .'.

So what is left? Where is 'home'? At first the answer comes as an anti-climax. After the repeated negatives, the reader expects a more convincing positive formulation than Cushman's assertion that our earthly bodies must be seen as home enough for the pilgrim spirit bent on a more permanent and glorious resting place than the richest palace earth can afford. If at first this seems a meagre compensation, gradually it comes to chime with the deepest beliefs of the Puritans; for what, apart from this, can be the ultimate implication of their rejection of empire, episcopacy, ritual and church trappings? It is this delayed realization of coincidence between the disappointing offering of 'nowhere' as a settling place and the deepest logic of the faith that makes the long sentence beginning 'But now we are all in all places strangers . . .' so powerful. Of course the repetitions, on both a small and a large scale, strengthen it too. So does the clever use of 'tabernacle', the biblical word for 'tent', which is a miniature type within a larger denial of typology reminiscent of the Jews wandering in the desert. The pun on 'properly' adds another rib to the frame; the true pilgrim has 'no dwelling but in this earthen tabernacle' both 'correctly' (when he thinks about his faith) and 'in his own person'.

To make the force of paragraph five more acceptable, Cushman prepares his readers by a clever juxtaposition of values in paragraphs one to four. On the one side he places 'dream', 'affecting' (in the sense of 'taking a fancy to'), 'predictions', 'visions', 'illuminations', 'imagine', 'extraordinary' and 'type'; and on the other, 'ordinary', 'examples', 'precepts', 'reasonably', 'rightly', 'properly' and 'earthen tabernacle'. The opposition between fancy and the ordinary could not be clearer.

But how does he make the reality seem preferable? First, and most obviously, by making the first category insubstantial. Where once we had vague promises we now have less attractive but more concrete fulfilments. 'Manna' (whatever that is, he implies) has become 'fruits' – not the abstract 'fruit' but real and several 'fruits'. Secondly, and more daringly, he associates with dreams and illuminations, not freedom, as one might expect, but confinement. Dreams do not liberate, but 'straiten' and cause people to 'straiten' others from free action. The 'witty' cavillers are not joyous free spirits but 'wilful' constrainers of other people's freedom to do good.

So, by this devious rhetorical strategem, the 'ordinary' is made to seem exhilarating, the accidents of the contemporary, material world an occasion for their (perhaps first ever) free expression of the spirit. The effect of Cushman's argument is very like that of the end of *Paradise Lost* which can produce a sense of exhilaration more than compensating for sorrow over the loss of Paradise. Adam and Eve have been denied the comforts of Eden (the 'capital seat' of their *imperium*) and the easy observance of the Covenant of Works. Now they are 'on even ground . . . with [their] sons'. Yet God dwells too 'in valley and in plain', and 'The world was all before them, where to choose / There place of rest, and providence their guide'.

Robert Cushman's 'Reasons and Considerations' advances the subtlest reason for emigration to America of all the arguments in the various exploration narratives – and for Puritans surely the most powerful – that truly serious, mature people have no need of a metropolitan centre. The message was a hard one: to leave friends, perhaps the family, land, occupation or profession, and all the architectural and institutional props of a settled community. Yet the appeal to one's sense of being 'straitened' by routine (perhaps – who knows? – even felt by Adam and Eve in their flowery intensive-care unit), the invitation to strip oneself down to the only 'proper' habitation of one's body and the offer of a whole world for the play of their conscientious intent, must have been an extremely potent counterweight to the agoraphobia of departure for the wilderness. Once accepted, this difficult conviction was to speed the emigration, not only of younger sons awaiting an uncertain inheritance, of restless adventurers, vagabonds and even separatists who had nothing to lose but the near certainty of persecution, but also men and women, or whole families, of solid achievement, conscience, and possibly even of education – people, in other words, who would contribute from the beginning to the moral and material well-being of the struggling new settlements.

References

Haller, William (1957), *The Rise of Puritanism*, New York: Harper Torchbooks.

Further reading

(Texts and contexts relating to the New England Puritans follow the chapter on William Bradford's *Of Plymouth Plantation*, p. 60.

3

William Bradford
(1590-1657)

Being thus arrived in a good harbor, and brought safe to land, they fell upon their knees and blessed the God of Heaven who had brought them over the vast and furious ocean, and delivered them from all the perils and miseries thereof, again to set their feet on the firm and stable earth, their proper element. And no marvel if they were thus joyful, seeing wise Seneca was so affected with sailing a few miles on the coast of his own Italy, as he affirmed, that he had rather remain twenty years on his way by land than pass by sea to any place in a short time, so tedious and dreadful was the same unto him.

But here I cannot but stay and make a pause, and stand half amazed at this poor people's present condition; and so I think will the reader, too, when he well considers the same. Being thus passed the vast ocean, and a sea of troubles before in their preparation (as may be remembered by that which went before), they had now no friends to welcome them nor inns to entertain or refresh their weatherbeaten bodies; no houses or much less towns to repair to, to seek for succour. It is recorded in Scripture as a mercy to the Apostle and his shipwrecked company, that the barbarians showed them no small kindness in refreshing them, but these savage barbarians, when they met with them (as after will appear) were readier to fill their sides full of arrows than otherwise. And for the season it was winter, and they that know the winters of that country know them to be sharp and violent, and subject to cruel and fierce storms, dangerous to travel to known places, much more to search an unknown coast. Besides, what could they see but a hideous and desolate wilderness, full of wild beasts and wild men – and what multitudes there might be of them they knew not. Neither could they, as it were, go up to the top of Pisgah to view from this wilderness a more goodly country to feed their hopes; for which way soever they turned their eyes (save upward to the heavens) they could have little solace or content in respect of any outward objects. For summer being done, all things stand upon them with a weather-beaten face, and the whole country, full of woods and thickets, represented a wild and savage hue. If they looked behind them, there was the mighty ocean which they had passed and was now as a main bar and gulf to separate them from all the civil parts of the world. If it be said they had a ship to succour them, it is true; but what heard they daily from the master and company? But that with speed they should look out a place (with their shallop) where they would be, at some near distance; for the season was such as he would not stir from thence till a safe harbor was discovered by them, where they would be, and he might go without danger; and that victuals consumed apace but he must and would keep sufficient for themselves and their return. Yea, it was muttered by some that if they got not a place in time, they would turn them and their goods ashore and leave them. Let it also be considered what weak hopes of supply and succour they left behind them, that might bear up their minds in this sad condition and trials they were under; and they could not but be very small. It is true, indeed, the affections and love of their brethren at Leyden was cordial and entire towards them, but they had little power to help them or themselves; and how the case stood between them and the merchants at their coming away hath already been declared.

What could now sustain them but the Spirit of God and His grace? May not and ought not the children of these fathers rightly say: 'Our fathers were Englishmen which came over this great ocean, and were ready to perish in this wilderness; but they cried unto the Lord, and He heard their voice and looked on their adversity,' etc. 'Let them therefore praise the Lord, because He is good: and His mercies endure forever.' 'Yea, let them which have been redeemed of the Lord, shew how He hath delivered them from the hand of the oppressor. When they wandered in the desert wilderness out of the way, and found no city to dwell in, both hungry and thirsty, their soul was overwhelmed in them. Let them confess before the Lord His lovingkindness and His wonderful works before the sons of men.'

Of Plymouth Plantation (this part written *c.* 1630)

* * *

'Men must not indulge their own fancies, as the Popish writers used to do, with their allegorical senses as they call them,' wrote Samuel Mather, and even typological exegesis had to be confined to connections latent in the Bible.

As long as they remained *within* the system of Holy Writ, the American Puritan ministers had confidence in their right – indeed their duty – to explore the most elaborate connections between the Old and New Testaments for the purposes both of private meditation and of instructing their flocks. Within the mysteries of the faith, fully explored, there could be no plain style. Edward Taylor, the frontier minister of Westfield, Massachusetts, some 100 miles to the west of Boston, wrote 217 verse meditations over 43 years, each one preparatory to his celebration of the Lord's Supper with his congregation. Some of his sermons and many of these poems examine the exegetical possibilities of biblical typology. For example, Meditation 9 (Second Series), on the text Deuteronomy 17: 15, 'The Lord thy God will raise up unto thee a prophet . . . like unto me', poses a number of typological connections between Moses and Christ. Both were mediators between God and man; both came of poor parents while Israel lay 'in bondage state'; both escaped a decree that all male children were to be slain; Moses led his people through the Red Sea to freedom, and Christ led his to salvation 'through no less / Than [His] red blood', and so forth (*Poems*, ed. Donald Stanford, 1960, 96). A sermon on John 1: 14 ('And the Word became flesh, and dwelt among us . . . full of grace and truth') exhibits no great concern with distinctions between typology, prophecies and even promises, as long as the events referred to all lie within the confines of Scripture. Christ is:

> said to be full of Truth. . . . Objectively. As He is the object of all the Old Testament prophecies, and metaphorical descriptions of the Messiah. He was variously foretold in the Old Testament even from Adam to the latter end of Malachy. As in prophecies, promises and types, which differ one from another, only as to the manner in which he was shewn.
>
> (*Christographia*, ed. Norman Grabo, 1962, 269)

Within this system even metaphor conveys truth:

> And all languages admit of Metaphorical forms of speech, and the Spirit of God abounds in this manner of speech in the Scripture and did foreshew that Christ should abound in this sort of speech Ps. 78.2 Matt. 13.35, and this sort of speech never was expected to be literally true, nor charged to be a lying form of speech, but a neat rhetorical, and wise manner of speaking.
>
> (ibid., 273)

This represents one aspect of the frontier mentality. A well-educated man leaves England after refusing to take the oath demanded of the Act of Uniformity of 1662, completes his education at Harvard, and takes his faith on a mission into the wilderness. He also takes a large library (Taylor was extremely well read in matters of biblical exegesis, and the Meditation on 'Full of . . . truth' follows Henry Ainsworth's commentary on the five Books of Moses, the Psalms and the Song of Songs – published in 1627 – almost point by point on this text) and practises almost until his death in 1729 a form of devotional verse shaped in the days of Donne and Herbert. Separated from the country of his birth, and all but cut off from the colonial settlements on the coast, he pursues orthodoxies of art and faith long out of fashion in the metropolis. Even the sermon cited above is one of a set defending the integrity of the Lord's Supper against progressives like Solomon Stoddard of Northampton, Massachusetts, who wanted even the confessedly unregenerate to be allowed access to communion, on the grounds that the sacrament was a 'converting ordinance'.

Yet if Taylor buttressed his exposed condition with rigidified conventions, he at least felt free, within those strict confines, to allow varying conduits of truth, and alternative modes of interpretation. For American Puritans more concerned with the business of the emerging colonies, however, the strains and temptations were greater. People like William Bradford of Plymouth Plantation and the first governor of the Massachusetts Bay Company, John Winthrop – not to mention Samuel Mather's brother and nephew, Increase and Cotton – confronted problems beyond those faced by ordinary Puritans on the frontier. For in addition to the threats of starvation and attack by Indians, and the normal Puritan anxiety of trying to determine whether one was saved or damned in a system in which good behaviour made no contribution to the individual's salvation, they had to justify the investments of the merchant adventurers and other backers of their colonies and maintain the connections between the colonies and the Crown. The Plymouth colonists had no royal charter, were separatists as well as Puritans. The Massachusetts Bay Company, though chartered and better established than its predecessor at Plymouth, ran into trouble with London as the political climate changed there, and as Massachusetts Bay began to take its independence so far as to coin its own money. This crisis of its legal existence was only resolved after the Glorious Revolution of 1688, and even then the renewed charter established Massachusetts as a Royal Colony along the lines of other American colonists, without some of its former freedoms.

When it came to justifying to the sceptics of the old world their millennial mission in the new, therefore, the American Puritans could not allow themselves the luxury of Samuel Mather's proscription of typology adduced outside the framework of biblical narrative, or respond to Robert Cushman's bracing reminder that 'there is no land of that sanctimony, no land so appropriated, none typical, much less any that can be said to be given of God to any nation as was Canaan . . .'. The surest sign that Bradford, Winthrop and the Mathers were thinking and writing about an emergent *nation*, whereas Taylor was not, is their tendency to appropriate typology to the purpose of history, especially at times when that history did not seem to be working out quite as expected. It was in moments of disappointment and frustration, particularly, when justifications had to be found to satisfy metropolitan doubts, and the justifications were arrived at, more often than not, by incorporating the apparent reverses into a larger providential plan, in which the new world would become that 'home' for the spirit which England was not.

For example, the Plymouth colonists had hoped to plant their corn in common, because the ideal of common ownership best represented God's disposition of nature in Eden before the Fall, and because their enterprise in the new world would allow them to institute this pattern free of the entangling contracts of Europe. But after two years, during which there never seemed to be enough corn for everyone, they reverted to a system based on the economy of the family, allotting 'to every family a parcel of land according to the proportion of their number'. But, adds William Bradford, in his history *Of Plymouth Plantation*, 'only for present use' and making no concession to the old-world 'division for inheritance'. The new plan 'had good success'; now even 'the women . . . went willingly into the field, and took their little ones with them to set corn; which before would allege weakness and inability; whom to have compelled would have been thought great tyranny and oppression' (120).

A modern historian might have let this bare narrative tell its own story. Captain Smith might have drawn from it a lesson about practical reality prevailing over theory. Bradford, though, lays the blame on a pagan philosopher (however enlightened) who lived before the revelation of God's Word in Christ:

The experience that was had in this common course and condition, tried sundry years and that amongst godly and sober men, may well

evince the vanity of that conceit of Plato's and other ancients ap-
plauded by some of later times; that the taking away of property and
bringing in community into a commonwealth would make them
happy and flourishing; as if they were wiser than God.   (121)

They had been misled by Plato; but God had revealed His truth in time.
He also had His way with men sent to try them, like John Lyford, the
false preacher shipped out by the London company as their minister,
who fell out with the colonists and wrote critical letters home to
strengthen growing opposition to the Plymouth venture; and Thomas
Morton, who set up a more relaxed colonial regime near present-day
Quincy, Massachusetts, which the Plymouth Puritans thought little
short of pagan, and whose *New English Canaan* (1637) attacked the
solemnity and hypocrisy of the Pilgrim Fathers while expressing love
and respect for the country and the Indians. In trading spirits and gun-
powder to the Indians, Morton fell foul of Massachusetts Bay Company
law, and was transported to England in 1630. There 'he was vehemently suspected for the murder of a man that had adventured
moneys with him when he came first into New England' (Bradford,
216), but 'he got free again, and writ an infamous and scurrilous book
against many godly and chief men of the country'. Finding himself on
the wrong side of the English Civil War, Morton once again set off for
America, where 'he was imprisoned in Boston for this book, and other
things, being grown old in wickedness' (217).

Was it just to imprison Morton for writing an uncanonical 'history' of
the Puritan enterprise in Massachusetts? If any doubts remain, there are
'other things' to take into account, not to mention that he had been
steeped 'in wickedness' authenticated by the late revelation that he was
accused of murder by the English authorities. (That the vehement
suspicion was apparently unfounded is passed over in silence.) Similarly,
Lyford was banished from Plymouth, from where he went to Nantasket,
Salem and finally to Virginia, where he died. He was banished because he
was a danger – real enough, no doubt – to the colony, but in telling the
story, Bradford places a number of hitherto hidden 'facts' about his
character just before the account of his banishment. It is revealed, by
several sources including Lyford's own wife, that the 'minister' had
seduced a girl in Ireland before first coming over to America, and that his
wife 'could keep no maids but he would be meddling with them; and some
time she hath taken him in the manner, as they lay at their beds' feet, with
such other circumstances as I am ashamed to relate' (167).

These are minor, and unattractive, instances of the settlers' need to exclude the unorthodox from their precarious millennial project in the wilderness. And the means by which these injustices are justified are always the same: the recourse to an inherent pattern of behaviour corresponding to God's predestined distribution of all human beings into ranks of damned and saved. The surface nuisances of such as Morton and Lyford were merely incidental; the 'real' cause, revealed only after the immediate events had raised the local alarm, was the deep depravity of the transgressors.

But the same habit of justifying disappointment by late revelation of God's purpose was less conclusive when the pattern adduced was explicitly typological and the purpose to dramatize a communal, or even national, 'mission' in history. Here, perhaps because the project was larger and the method theologically more risky, the question was left at least partly open as to whether the interpretative method had settled the matter. William Bradford's account of the Plymouth Colony's landfall at Provincetown, from which the extract is taken, illustrates vividly this drama of interpretation.

Bradford probably never intended his manuscript history *Of Plymouth Plantation* to be printed. It was not published entire until 1856, but it certainly circulated freely in the Plymouth and Massachusetts Bay settlements, and was used in the preparation of other histories written in the seventeenth century. Bradford's nephew Nathaniel Morton made extensive use of it in his *New England's Memorial* (1669), the first published history of a New England colony. Increase Mather used it for his *A Brief History of the War with the Indians* (1676), and his son Cotton drew on it for his monumental *Magnalia Christi Americana*, written before the end of the century and published in 1702. The manuscript is divided into two 'books', the first narrating the separatists' departure for Holland, their life there and their voyage to New England, and the second comprising chapters for each year of the Plymouth Colony's existence from 1620 to 1646.

There was hardly a moment when Bradford was not busy with the affairs of Plymouth (he was governor of the colony from 1621 to 1656, except for five years when he served as assistant to the governor), so it is interesting to speculate on why he wrote his history when he did. None of it was written as the events happened. Book One, the narrative of the removals and voyages, was begun in 1630 and completed within a year or two; Book Two, the twenty-six annals, was written between 1644 and 1650. Jesper Rosenmeier (1974) has made the intriguing suggestion that both periods coincide with times at which Bradford might have felt particularly doubtful about the primacy of Plymouth's millennial mission. In 1630 the more prosperous, better educated, more numerous and above all unseparated body of Massachusetts Bay colonists arrived to settle in Boston. In 1644 and 1645 the Parliamentary forces defeated the Cavaliers at Marston Moor and Naseby. Each event seemed to augur a site for the Last Days other than Plymouth. 'In these two periods . . . Bradford's feelings of joy at the spreading light and his fear of God's judgement on Plymouth grew so acute that he felt compelled to picture the glorious past, so that the younger generation might see and emulate their ancestors' (88–9).

Certainly the arrival of the Massachusetts Bay settlers must have filled Bradford with powerfully mixed feelings. The one thousand colonists who arrived in the first wave in 1630 included distinguished Cambridge-educated theologians, like John Cotton and the lawyer and landed gentleman John Winthrop who had been selected as governor of the new colony. Although they had rejected episcopal polity in favour of the congregational model, the colonists of Massachusetts Bay remained in communion (however tenuous) with the Church of England and never denied the thirty-nine Articles of the Anglican faith. Because of this politic allegiance, their company, unlike Plymouth Plantation, had been awarded a royal charter.

Bradford must have been pleased to see the cause of reformed religion thus advanced in New England, but he must have been equally fearful that such a powerful colony and illustrious settlement would lure his more promising confederates away from Plymouth. In any case, it is not difficult to imagine him sitting down in 1630 to write a history of the earlier colony, in order both to remind the youth of Plymouth of the glorious work done there over the last ten years, and also to stake a claim specifically for Plymouth in the history of the Reformation in America. Certainly a comparison of the passages in *Mourt's Relation* and *Of Plymouth Plantation* dealing with the landing and exploration on Cape Cod seems to lend weight to this notion of Bradford's purpose in writing Book One of his history. *Mourt's Relation*, written soon following these events so as to attract more venturers to the colony, mentions the depth of good soil, and the initial shyness of the Indians. The first paragraph about their first steps ashore contains a catalogue of useful trees encountered there. The *Relation* is replete with details of the colonists' explorations as they happened, not omitting their perplexity and wonder at the Indian burial ground, their concern whether to take the votive corn, and accidents reflecting their inexperience, like Bradford's mishap with the deer trap, or the occasion when they shot off their muskets into the night at 'a great and hideous cry' which turned out to be 'a company of wolves or foxes'.

In Bradford's history, written by the same man who probably wrote at least a good part of the earlier account, everything is more purposeful, and the purpose is God's. There is nothing of the material wealth to be found in New England. The doubts and frailties of the explorers are elided; so is their delight in exploring the material world around them. Though the *Relation* refers to God's providence, in the fortunate discovery of Indian corn and in their success in a skirmish with the Indians, these allusions are brief and subordinated to the flow of the narrative: 'And sure it was God's good providence that we found this corn, for else . . .'; 'So after we had given God thanks for our deliverance, we took . . .'. In *Of Plymouth Plantation* these events are heightened to become major testimonies to the colonists prevailing, by God's grace, over a hostile environment. The skirmish occupies a climactic position, almost at the end of Book One. And the references to Providence are expanded into separate paragraphs interrupting the narrative.

The plot of God's Grace is manifest in the excerpt. Again, the environment is made hostile. The Indians become 'savage barbarians' and the episode of that first skirmish provides the sole index of their behaviour. The winter, which Winslow in the *Relation* calls no worse than that in England, is 'sharp and violent, and subject to cruel and fierce storms' in Bradford's history. (In fact, that winter was an unusually warm one for the coast of Massachusetts, which is, in any case, milder in winter than the interior.) Sandwiched between 'woods and thickets [of] a wild and savage hue' and 'the mighty ocean . . . as a main bar and gulf to separate them from all the civil parts of the world', the isolated colonists had no sustenance – certainly not the material riches offered by Captain Smith or *Mourt's Relation* – save the 'blessed God of heaven who had brought them over the vast and furious ocean'.

As the physical landscape disappears, so the references outwards, to other times and other dimensions of reality, expand. An allusion to Seneca provides a historical justification for their dislike of sea travel. A long excursion (explicitly announced as such: 'But here I cannot but stay and make a pause . . .') plots the occasion of their arrival on the chart of God's divine plan for his chosen people. As the narrative moves from the physical to the metaphysical world, so it shifts from chronological to millennial time – that is, from time passing to time as in 'an idea whose time has come'.

Yet here we too should make a pause, because in the two paragraphs concluding the excerpt (and also the chapter, as it happens) the discourse changes in more than just its area of reference. What happens is that the narrative ceases to be a transparency through which the events and their import are seen, and begins to thicken, to call attention to its own process of interpretation. Whereas the narrative voice might well have announced a certain meaning to be attached to the events as told, with all the authority that third-person narratives usually convey, here it begs an interpretation before it commands one ('May not and ought not the children of these fathers rightly say . . .?'), and even then – because the escalation from request to command is foregrounded within the discourse – leaves open the possibility that the children may do nothing of the sort.

Connected with this sense of uncertainty is the debate, all but announced in the preceding paragraph, about whether the Plymouth colonists may consider their 'errand into the wilderness' as properly antitypical to that of the Israelites. Against the proposition, but adding to the evidence for their heroism, was the fact that unlike Moses, they could not go up on to the top of Mount Pisgah to glimpse the promised land lying in the distance; wherever they looked, there was no 'goodly country to feed their hopes'. One is reminded of Cushman's, 'now there is no land of that sanctimony . . . none typical'. And if the chosen people of the Old Testament, carrying the Ark of the Covenant through the wilderness, offer no type of the colonists' venture, neither do the peregrinations of St Paul carrying the Gospel abroad, for when he was shipwrecked on Malta, 'the barbarians showed us no common kindness' (Acts 28: 2).

With nothing to sustain them – no food, no comfort, no shelter, not even the thought that they were fulfilling types in the Bible – what had they left but the 'Spirit of God'? But since that very spirit is what motivates the divine *logos*, what better pivot on which to swing the argument round in favour of their prophetic mission? For if they have nothing but God and wilderness, they have at least the kernel of the narrative of the Israelites wandering in the desert. From there the argument finds its way with relative ease: via God's Englishmen and 'ocean' to 'wilderness' (a word which entails so much of the earlier story), Bradford infiltrates the colonists' case into the very verbal structure of the Bible story of the desert wandering. Note that the account in

Deuteronomy, to which he refers his readers, is also phrased as reported speech handed down from father to son: 'And thou shalt answer and say before the Lord thy God, A Syrian ready to perish was my father, and he went down into Egypt, and sojourned there . . . and the Egyptians . . . afflicted us, and laid upon us hard bondage: and we cried unto the Lord, the God of our fathers, and the Lord heard our voice . . . and brought us forth out of Egypt . . . [to] a land flowing with milk and honey' (Deut. 26: 5–9). The even fuller citation of Psalm 107 ('Let them therefore praise the Lord . . .') completes the pattern.

Thus from their absolute zero, having stripped them of even the hope of comfort, Bradford recuperates the colonists' fortunes within the pre-existing text of God's word. It is a daring rhetorical manoeuvre, which he begins hesitantly and ends breathlessly, as though running away from his work and afraid to look behind him. His excitement has little to do with what happened to the colonists; now the narrative interest is centred on the process of interpretation, and the dramatic suspense on whether or not the events can be made to fit a typological plot.

But the important point is that the matter is never really settled in Bradford's history. The rest of *Of Plymouth Plantation* is a running dialogue between advances and disappointments in the colony's fortunes; between attacks by Indians in America and detractors in London, countered by Bradford's explanations, justifications and accounts of minor providences. The story proceeds in starts and reverses, and the drama is in the restless search for evidence, the overriding interest in how to interpret contemporary events in the light of God's plan. The narrative rhythm is that of spiritual autobiographies like Bunyan's *Grace Abounding to the Chief of Sinners*, in which the devout pilgrim can never be certain of his election and the story, whatever it offers in the way of fitful spiritual progress, comes to no very definite conclusion.

The arrangement of Bradford's Book Two into annals provides a convincing pretext for these oscillations, obviating the need for an overall narrative sweep. Indeed, the most characteristic form of American Puritan prose is the diary or journal, with dated entries each containing its own local spiritual crisis, and the common subject the spiritual struggle (of person or community) played out in reiterated dramas of interpretation. John Winthrop's *Journal* (kept from his journey to New England in 1630 to his death in 1649, first published 1790) and Samuel Sewall's *Diary* for 1674–7 and 1685–1729 (published 1878–82) provide many typical examples of the trivial local event, interpreted and moralized according to the larger plot of God's Providence. Winthrop's entry for 13 April 1641 mentions fire in the house of 'a godly woman of the church of Boston' which destroyed 'a parcel of very fine linen of great value, which she set her heart too much upon'. 'But it pleased God,' he adds helpfully, 'that the loss of this linen did her much good, both in taking off her heart from worldly comforts, and in preparing her for a far greater affliction by the untimely death of her husband, who was slain not long after at Isle of Providence.' On 1 October 1697, Samuel Sewall and some friends dined rather well on some 'very good roast lamb, turkey, fowls, apple pie', after which they sang Psalm 121. Then the diarist's attention was alerted by a minor accident. 'Note: a glass of spirits my wife sent stood upon a joint-stool which, Simon Willard jogging, it fell down and broke all to shivers; I said 'twas a lively emblem of our fragility and mortality.'

The restless interpretation of contemporary events can be exhibited most clearly in cases in which the chief narrative interest might be expected to lie in a more conventional story. The conflict between whites and Indians has been a staple of American literature almost from its beginnings, and the struggle between the codes and values of the two races has often been expressed as the story of a white man or (more usually) woman kidnapped by the Indians. In Cooper's Leather-Stocking romances, in the dime novels of the nineteenth century and myriad western films, the suspense has centred on whether the victim will escape, or how he or she will be rescued, and the thematic interest (if any) on how the experience will have changed the captive's moral outlook. Earlier instances of the captivity narrative, however, concentrated on how the victim, or the white community, could explain the event in the light of God's benign programme for his elect.

The first and deservedly the most popular of these captivity narratives was *The Sovereignty and Goodness of God ... a Narrative of the Captivity and Restauration of Mrs Mary Rowlandson* (1682, many reprints through the eighteenth century). In a first-person narrative Mary Rowlandson tells how during the course of the settlers' fights with the Wampanoag and other tribes known as 'King Philip's War', her house was attacked and fired, her sister and brother-in-law and one of their children killed, and her own little daughter shot 'through the bowells and hand'. The Indians then took her on a trek through north-western Massachusetts, during which her child died of her terrible wounds.

The attack on the house, the armed struggle and the various incidents of the long march make exciting reading, but only between the lines, as it were. The real energy of the narrative is expended on attempts to incorporate the major tragedy and many smaller inconveniences of her situation into the paradigm of Holy Scripture. 'One hill was so steep', she writes, 'that I was fain to creep up upon my knees, and to hold by the twigs and bushes to keep myself from falling backwards. . . . But I hope all those wearisome steps that I have taken, are but a forewarding of me to the heavenly rest. *I know, O Lord, that thy judgements are right, and that thou in faithfulness hast afflicted me*. Psalm 119: 75' (Galleon Press, 1974, 52). Though the Indians fed her as regularly as possible, the food was strange and she remained always hungry. Only then 'could I see that scripture verified, there being many scriptures that we do not take notice of, or understand till we are afflicted. Mic. 6: 14. *Thou shalt eat and not be satisfied*' (p. 74). Perhaps the greatest test of her faith (because the hardest event to square with the biblical plot) came when the Indians took her safely over a river which the pursuing English were unable to cross. 'I cannot but admire [that is, wonder] to see the wonderful providence of God, in preserving the Heathen for further affliction to our country. They could go in great numbers over, but the English must stop' (103). Similarly, far from starving in the wilderness, the Indians could eat anything and survive. 'Strangely did the Lord provide for them, that I did not see . . . one man, woman or child die with hunger. Though many times they would eat that, that a hog or dog would hardly touch' (104).

Here was a seemingly diabolical reversal of God's bounty to the Israelites wandering in the wilderness. Now it was the heathen's turn to be fed in the desert and God's elect who were stopped by the water. Mrs Rowlandson cannot bring herself to cite the relevant texts, which could relate only ironically to the present case, and the best she can muster of the divine plan is the rather lame 'God had an overruling hand in all those things' (103), and 'yet by that God strengthened them to be a scourge to his people' (104).

Not every captivity narrative, however, admitted this dialectic of interpretation. In some cases the technique of prophetic typology could be used ruthlessly to foreclose alternative readings. In the *Magnalia Christi Americana* (1702) Cotton Mather tells the story of Hannah Dustin, kidnapped with her infant daughter and the nurse attending her lying-in in 1697. On the forced march of over 150 miles, the Indians 'dash'd out the brains of the infant against a tree; and several of the other captives as they began to tire in their sad journey, were soon sent unto their long home'. Hannah and her nurse survived and were taken into an Indian family of 'two stout men, three women,

and seven children', which had already 'adopted' an English youth.
One night:

> when the whole crew was in a dead sleep, (reader, see if it prove not
> so!) one of [the captive] women took up a resolution to imitate the
> action of Jael upon Sisera; and being where she had not her own life
> secured by any law unto her, she thought she was not forbidden by
> any law to take away the life of the murderers by whom her child had
> been butchered. She heartened the nurse and the youth to assist her in
> this enterprise; and all furnishing themselves with hatchets for the
> purpose, they struck such home blows upon the heads of their sleep-
> ing oppressors, that e'er they could any of them struggle into any
> effectual resistance, 'at the Feet of those poor prisoners they bow'd,
> they fell, they lay down; at their feet they bowed, they fell; where
> they bowed, there they fell down dead.' Only one squaw escaped
> sorely wounded from them in the dark; and one boy.
>
> (Magnalia vii, Appendix, xxv)

It is not just the gallows humour of the parenthesis and the note of
triumph that makes this story so terrible, but the sense that for once, the
typology of the Old Testament (in this case Judges 5: 27) has been
adduced with absolute certitude to settle a moral question. No sooner
has the issue been canvassed, quite legitimately, of whether Hannah
Dustin is entitled to kill a whole Indian family, than it is clamped within
the words of the Holy Bible – the very words – celebrating Jael's
triumph as she drove a tent peg into the side of Sisera's head. This time
one feels that (except in its gruesome accidents) the analogy does not fit
the case, and that the moral question has been prematurely closed.

But Mrs Rowlandson, though no more forgiving of the Indians and
inclined to discount even their small kindnesses shown to her, at least
leaves some doubt about the status of her own faith. For her the references to Scripture are comforts, but uncertain and only temporary relief
– good only until the next thwart. This is partly the way in which she
tells her story (the narrative is divided into twenty 'Removes', each
with its local crises, rather like a journal or Bradford's annals), and
partly because of her quiet lesson drawn at the end of the book about the
'vanity of . . . outward things'. 'If trouble from smaller matter begin
to rise in me,' she writes in her last paragraph, 'I have something at
hand to check myself with, and say, Why am I troubled? It was but the
other day, that if I had had the world, I would have given it for my
freedom.' But above all her captivity narrative is more open to human

experience than Mather's account of Hannah Dustin's, because her story is teased apart with the unease of interpretation; the Bible is turned to the purpose of spiritual pilgrimage.

The comparison between these two narratives of Indian captivity demonstrates the moral and rhetorical neutrality of prophetic typology. The procedure could be used either to suppress doubt or, when employed hesitantly, to dramatize it. In Mather's defence it may be argued that by his time the Puritan project on the frontier had come to seem, in retrospect, so melodramatic as to warrant turning the anxious wrath of another person to the purposes of racial and cultural propaganda, and furthermore to use the words of Holy Writ for the purpose. Even so, the modern reader is entitled to argue that doubt, rather than strident assertion, should be the proper (if not the probable) response to the margins of experience, especially when encountered at second hand.

In any case, it was Bradford's and Mrs Rowlandson's narrative model that was taken up by the great experimenters of classical American fiction. Properly read, *The Confidence Man* (1857) is not the story of what happened, and then what happened next, on a Mississippi paddle steamer, but a drama of the disguising and uncovering of meaning, and the reader's energy is aroused chiefly to the work of interpreting the events in the plot. Similarly, *The Scarlet Letter* and *The House of the Seven Gables* (1850 and 1851) are neither interesting nor accurate in their details of the Puritans' speech and manners (Arthur Miller's *The Crucible* of 1952 comes much closer), but very 'realistic' in prompting the question of how we are to interpret the behaviour of these strange people – of whether any of their odd beliefs can be salvaged and redeployed in a 'modern' ethical system. Melville and Hawthorne also felt themselves to be in the advance guard of a new cultural experiment; only this time it was the explicitly aesthetic project of a new literature specific to the new world. Fortunately they allowed the inevitable uncertainty of such a venture to find free play at the very heart of the narrative procedures.

References

Rosenmeier, Jesper (1974), '"With my owne Eyes": William Bradford's *Of Plymouth Plantation*', in Sacvan Bercovitch (ed.), *The American Puritan Imagination*, Cambridge: Cambridge University Press.

Further reading

TEXTS

William Bradford, *Of Plymouth Plantation*, ed. Samuel Eliot Morison, New York: Knopf, [1952].

Anne Bradstreet, *Works*, ed. John Harvard Ellis, Gloucester, Mass.: P. Smith, 1962.

Edward Johnson, *Wonder-working Providence of Sions Savior in New England*, ed. J. Franklin Jameson, New York: Scribner's, 1910.

Nathaniel Morton, *New Englands Memoriall* [facsimile of the 1669 edition], ed. Howard Hall, New York: Scholar's Facsimiles and Reprints, 1937.

[Mourt's Relation], *A Journal of the Pilgrims at Plymouth*, ed. Dwight Heath, New York: Corinth Books, 1963.

Mary Rowlandson, *The Soveraignty & Goodness of God . . . Being a Narrative of the Captivity and Restauration of Mrs Mary Rowlandson*, Fairfield, Wash.: Ye Galleon Press, 1974.

Samuel Sewall, *The Diary*, ed. M. Halsey Thomas, New York: Farrar, Strauss & Giroux, 1973.

Edward Taylor, *The Poems*, ed. Donald Stanford, New Haven, Conn.: Yale University Press, 1960.

Roger Williams, *A Key into the Language of America . . .*, [vol. i of] *The Complete Writings*, New York: Russell & Russell, 1963.

John Winthrop, *Journal* [also called: *The History of New England from 1630 to 1649*], ed. James Savage, 2 vols, Boston, Mass.: Little, Brown, 1853.

CONTEXTS

Loren Baritz, *City on a Hill; a History of Ideas and Myths in America*, New York: Wiley, 1964.

Daniel Boorstin, *The Americans* [vol. 1]; *the Colonial Experience*, New York: Random House, 1958 / Harmondsworth: Penguin, 1965.

Perry Miller, *The New England Mind* [vol. 1]; *the Seventeenth Century*, New York: Macmillan, 1939.

Samuel Eliot Morison, *Builders of the Bay Colony*, revised edn, Boston, Mass.: Houghton Mifflin, 1964.

Ernest Tuveson, *Redeemer Nation; the Idea of America's Millennial Role*, Chicago, Ill.: University of Chicago Press, 1968.

Larzer Ziff, *Puritanism in America; New Culture in a New World*, New York: Viking, 1973.

PART TWO

'Rise, Wash and Address *Powerful Goodness*'

4

Benjamin Franklin
(1706-90)

In 1751 Dr Thomas Bond, a particular friend of mine, conceived the idea of establishing a hospital in Philadelphia, for the reception and cure of poor sick persons, whether inhabitants of the province or strangers. A very beneficent design, which has been ascribed to me, but was originally his. He was zealous and active in endeavouring to procure subscriptions for it; but the proposal being a novelty in America, and at first not well understood, he met with small success. At length he came to me, with the compliment that he found there was no such thing as carrying a public spirited project through, without my being concerned in it; 'for, says he, I am often asked by those to whom I propose subscribing, Have you consulted Franklin upon this business? and what does he think of it? And when I tell them that I have not, (supposing it rather out of your line) they do not subscribe, but say they will consider of it.' I enquired into the nature, and probable utility of his scheme, and receiving from him a very satisfactory explanation, I not only subscribed to it myself, but engaged heartily in the design of procuring subscriptions from others. Previous however to the solicitation, I endeavoured to prepare the minds of the people by writing on the subject in the newspapers, which was my usual custom in such cases, but which he had omitted.

The subscriptions afterwards were more free and generous, but beginning to flag, I saw they would be insufficient without some assistance from the Assembly, and therefore proposed to petition for it, which was done. The country members did not at first relish the project. They objected that it could only be serviceable to the city, and therefore the citizens should alone be at the expense of it; and they doubted whether the citizens themselves generally approved of it: my allegation on the contrary, that it met with such approbation as to leave no doubt of our being able to raise £2000 by voluntary donations,

they considered as a most extravagant supposition, and utterly impossible. On this I formed my plan; and asking leave to bring in a bill, for
incorporating the contributors according to the prayer (of their)
petition, and granting them a blank sum of money, which leave was
obtained chiefly on the consideration that the House could throw the
bill out if they did not like it, I drew it so as to make the important
clause a conditional one, viz. 'And be it enacted by the authority afore-
said that when the said contributors shall have met and chosen their
managers and treasurer, *and shall have raised by their contributions a capital
stock of £2000 value* (the yearly interest of which is to be applied to the
accommodating of the sick poor in the said hospital, free of charge for
diet, attendance, advice and medicines) *and shall make the same appear to
the satisfaction of the Speaker of the Assembly* for the time being; that *then* it
shall and may be lawful for the said Speaker, and he is hereby required to
sign an order on the Provincial Treasurer for the payment of two
thousand pounds in two yearly payments, to the treasurer of the said
hospital, to be applied to the founding, building and finishing of the
same.' This condition carried the bill through; for the Members who
had opposed the grant, and now conceived they might have the credit of
being charitable without the expense, agreed to its passage. And then in
soliciting subscriptions among the people we urged the conditional
promise of the law as an additional motive to give, since every man's
donation would be doubled. Thus the clause worked both ways. The
subscriptions accordingly soon exceeded the requisite sum, and we
claimed and received the public gift, which enabled us to carry the
design into execution. A convenient and handsome building was soon
erected, the institution has by constant experience been found useful,
and flourishes to this day. And I do not remember any of my political
manoeuvres, the success of which gave me at the time more pleasure. Or
that in after-thinking of it, I more easily excused myself for having made
some use of cunning.

The Autobiography (1771–90)

*   *   *

This passage from Benjamin Franklin's autobiography encapsulates
much of what people have found both maddening and admirable in the
personality projected in that book. There is a degree of pomposity in the
redundant phrases ('reception and cure', 'zealous and active'). There is
the self-regard filtered through the *oratio obliqua* ('he came to me,

with the compliment that . . .'), for though he admits that the proposal came sugar-coated in flattery, he does not neglect to repeat the praise, word for word, for his shrewd judgement. And there is that absolutely characteristic last sentence, in which he forgives himself for a 'cunning' he seems smugly certain his reader will approve. Above all, Franklin's concern in the project seems strongly coloured by material interest, even if not his own.

On the other hand, the redundant phrases are more than space fillers; they echo the parallelism of biblical rhetoric, as though to suggest that to provide a hospital is also to do the Lord's work. At least one of them – 'whether inhabitants of the province or strangers' – not only reinforces this sense of practical charity but also, through its legalistic expression, gives a hint of difficulty to come – of distributing support for the hospital among various constituencies, not all of which stood to benefit equally from it. And there is no doubting Franklin's interest in the politics of public finance. Whereas the purpose of the project is briefly sketched as 'a very beneficent design', and the result – the physical building itself and the institution to maintain it – is mentioned as only a short coda in the passive mode, the *means* by which the end was achieved absorbs by far the greater part of the story's space and energy. And even if Franklin exaggerates his role in the project, he shows remarkable political acumen: a well-developed sense of how to appeal to various interests, considerable expertise in the psychology of fundraising and public relations in general, and a practised skill in working the Assembly. What this passage shows is how complex and sophisticated a democracy Philadelphia had become by the middle of the eighteenth century, and how much colonial America had developed from the zealous Puritan settlements intent on searching out signs of election to which good works were irrelevant. And no one represents that shift from the predestinarian to the 'beneficent' community – the society for which the standards of behaviour had become both 'nature' and 'probable utility' – better than Benjamin Franklin himself.

That Franklin typified his age better than any of his contemporaries in the crucial half-century leading to the American War of Independence was a statement that received his full assent. Indeed self-consciousness in his exemplary role was one of the most typical things about him. Although it was his friend Benjamin Vaughan, writing to Franklin in 1783 to praise the first part of his autobiography and to urge him to continue it, who first suggested that 'all that has happened to you is also connected with the detail of the manners and situation of a *rising people*',

Franklin was so willing to be represented as being thus representative that he included the complete text of Vaughan's letter at the beginning of the second part of the book.

In making himself a model of his time and place, Franklin was conforming to an old pattern of American autobiography, going back at least to the writings of Cotton Mather, in which private lives were made to dramatize public issues. In the words of Sacvan Bercovitch (1975, 185), 'From Mather through Emerson, auto-American-biography served rhetorically to resolve the conflicts inherent in the very meaning of "free-enterprise": spiritual versus material freedom, private versus corporate enterprise, the cultural "idea", expressed by the country's "purest minds", versus the cultural fact, embodied in a vast economic-political undertaking.'

In fact, there are echoes in Franklin's autobiography of American narrative procedures even older than Mather's. Franklin's text has a way with business competitors which recalls William Bradford's with sectarian rivals in the colonial enterprise. When a printer named Keimer, Franklin's first employer in Philadelphia, begins to fail, has to sell up and decides to move to Barbados, his apprentice sets up on his own. Fearing a powerful competitor in the new business, Franklin proposes a partnership in his own printing works, 'which [the rival], fortunately for me, rejected with scorn. He was very proud, dressed like a gentleman, lived expensively, took much diversion and pleasure abroad, run into debt, and neglected his business, upon which all business left him; and finding nothing to do, he followed Keimer to Barbados.' There the rival apprentice employs his former master, but they fall to quarrelling, fail, and have to sell up again, the apprentice to return to 'his country work' in Pennsylvania, and Keimer to work for another printer in Barbados; 'in a few years he died' (126). Though this kind of petty, spuriously moralistic gloating is uncommon in the autobiography, it is very like Bradford's treatment of Lyford and Morton – the perceived threat, the late revelation of misdeeds, the appropriate catastrophe – except that here the violated canons of behaviour bear directly on matters of trade, and the 'providential plan' exemplified is the inevitable movement of market forces.

The larger-scale organization of the narrative, too, harks back in places to a feature of Puritan prose. Not the first part, roughly one half the total, which tells the story of Franklin's youth in Boston, his removal to Philadelphia as a penniless journeyman, and his early success as a printer and man of affairs in that city. This section, intended as a memoir for the edification of his son, has been called a kind of secular *Pilgrim's Progress*, and reads quite like a novel of the time. The effect was no doubt intended, because Franklin expresses his admiration for these modern narratives in the text of the first part: 'Honest John [Bunyan] was the first that I know of who mixes narrative and dialogue, a method of writing very engaging to the reader, who in the most interesting parts finds himself as it were, brought into the company and present at the discourse. Defoe in his *Crusoe*, his *Moll Flanders* . . . and other pieces has imitated it with success; and Richardson has done the same in his *Pamela*, etc.' (72). But the second half of the autobiography, especially the early pages occasioned by Vaughan's letter alerting Franklin to the portentousness of his career, adhere to a pattern much more like the Puritan spiritual autobiography in the form of diary or journal entries than the novel – more like *Grace Abounding* than *Pilgrim's Progress*. Here the indications of time – whether frankly vague, as in the often reiterated 'about this time', or even (as in the passage selected) when mentioning specific dates – serve not as chronological markers in a continuing narrative but as rhetorical openers to brief episodes organized so as to illustrate single moral points. For intance, Franklin finances one of his journeymen to open a printing works in Charleston, South Carolina. 'He was a man of learning and honest, but ignorant in matters of account', so that Franklin 'could get no account from him nor any satisfactory state of our partnership while he lived'. When he dies (characteristically, the little story has nothing to say about why or in what circumstances), his widow, 'being born and bred in Holland, where, as I have been informed, the knowledge of accounts makes a part of female education,' renders Franklin his regular share and 'managed the business with such success that she not only brought up reputably a family of children but at the expiration of the term was able to purchase of me the printing house and establish her son in it' (166). 'I mention the affair', continues Franklin, 'chiefly for the sake of recommending that branch of education for our young females as likely to be of more use to them and their children in case of widowhood than either music or dancing.'

Another long paragraph outlines Franklin's education in languages: his father had been able to afford only one year for him at the Boston Latin school, but he 'had begun in 1733 to study languages', and 'soon' mastered French, Italian and Spanish, after which labours he 'was surprised to find, on looking over a Latin Testament, that I understood so much more that language than I had imagined'. Renewing his study of Latin, he found that he made quick progress with it, because of his knowledge of the related vernacular languages. This experience too he turns into an educational principle: that children should begin with French, 'proceeding to the Italian, etc.' so that even if they should never progress to Latin, 'they would, however, have acquired another tongue or two that being in modern use might be serviceable to them in common life' (168–9).

These are public lessons, of course – nothing to do with the private progress of the soul – but they are organized like the entries in the journals of Samuel Sewall and William Bradford: the 'novelistic' details of setting and event are absent, and the personal element is made subservient to the elucidation of a general rule. The most extreme example of this procedure in the autobiography is a paragraph of only eighty-eight words in which Franklin tells of the death by smallpox of 'one of my sons, a fine boy of four years old': 'I long regretted bitterly, and still regret, that I had not given it to him by inoculation. This I mention for the sake of parents who omit that operation on the supposition that they should never forgive themselves if a child died under it – my example showing that the regret may be the same either way, and that therefore the safer should be chosen' (170).

Yet Benjamin Franklin would not have been called, or thought himself, typical of his age if he were nothing more than an old Puritan divine warmed over. The autobiography is really 'modern' – or rather, contemporary – in ways both superficial and fundamental. To see why and how, it will be necessary to outline, however briefly, the major shifts in American colonial religious experience, and particularly habits of moral analysis, between Franklin's time and that of the early settlers in the New England in which he was born and brought up. The first fact to register, often overlooked in intellectual histories of early America, is that the theological establishment of Massachusetts was only one of many such institutions in the pre-revolutionary colonies. Rhode Island soon became a refuge for professing Christians theologically to the left of the Massachusetts Bay divines, like the antinomian Anne Hutchinson and the leveller Roger Williams. Quakers, also persecuted in Massachusetts, went there too, but settled in greater numbers in North Carolina, and even greater in Pennsylvania, when that colony was granted to their leader, William Penn, in 1781. Virginia was Anglican; New York, Maryland, the Carolinas and Georgia, nominally so, but without much force behind the establishment. Other colonies, including Delaware and New Jersey, never had state churches. In the first half of the eighteenth century the population of the American colonies multiplied six times, and with them the number and variety of Protestant sects. According to Richard Hofstadter, who provides a fuller account of these developments than can be attempted here, there were 423 parishes of Congregationalists (or Puritans) in 1740, but also 246 of Anglican, 160 Presbyterian, 96 Baptist, 95 Lutheran, 78 Dutch Reformed, 51 German Reformed, and about the same number of Quaker meetings as of Baptist or Lutheran congregations. But there were also 'a number of pietistic sectarians – Mennonites, Schwenkenfelders, Dunkers, Seventh-Day Adventists, and the like, as well as tiny groups of Jews' in the seaboard cities (1973, 183).

As relations with the mother country began to force the colonies into more and more communal projects, as communications and trade improved between the American regions, so it became increasingly difficult for separate settlements to avoid a sense of alternative religions and cultures. Franklin's own physical and social mobility would have made it impossible for him to follow the career of a narrow sectarian, even though he was born and brought up in a family whose 'forefathers continued Protestants through the reign of Queen Mary, when they were sometimes in danger of trouble on account of their zeal against Popery' (*Autobiography*, 50–1). Born in Puritan Boston, he moved to Philadelphia, the city of the Quakers, to seek his fortune, build a business and start a public career. Later he served as agent in London for Pennsylvania, Georgia, New Jersey and Massachusetts, and as deputy postmaster general for the whole of North America, not to mention his better-known role in the history of the new Republic – helping to compose the Declaration of Independence, going to Paris as minister-plenipotentiary of the United States to the French court, signing the treaty of 1783 ending the Revolutionary War, and acting as delegate to the Constitutional Convention of 1787. And there were many Americans like him, if not as industrious, ingenious, likeable or long-lived, whom the affairs of the emerging nation drew into ever more cosmopolitan contacts.

The rapid growth in size and complexity of the colonies would have been sufficient to encourage toleration of religious difference, if not of no religion at all, but of course there were influences working in England to promote it as well, from the limited legal provisions of the Toleration Act of 1689 to the more pervasive growth of the idea of 'nature' as the fundamental criterion of human judgement in all matters from the theological to the scientific. What 'nature' meant (in fact, it meant many things) was less important than the assumption of a common basis for enquiry. The greater the variety of faith and opinion, the greater the search for criteria shared by all of them. In matters of religion, the grounds for this intellectual synthesis was the search for an 'ethical' Christianity.

In theory, ethics were not the strongest suit of a New England Calvinism whose doctrine of salvation denied the efficacy of works, yet even in Massachusetts the governing faith had become softened and liberalized in the sixty years following the first settlements at Plymouth and Boston. Hofstadter says that the history of New England Puritans centres around their 'long, slow tormenting transition from being sects into being churches' (209); or, to put the idea in other words, from comprising tiny nuclei of self-appointing élites to representing the entire community. Even the first waves of New England settlement contained a minority of church members, and while the criteria for membership remained fixed, the proportion of 'saints' to 'strangers' actually declined. To belong to the Puritan congregation, one had to be convinced of election, to test that conviction against the possibility of spiritual pride (works might be admitted as evidence, but were no certain agent of salvation or damnation) and to persuade the assembled congregation, through a personal account or 'relation', that the experience of conversion was genuine. Many immigrants could not be convinced, or bothered about it when there was so much to do in the way of settling and planting. The catch was that the right to vote for delegates to the House of Deputies in the General Court of Massachusetts was restricted to church members, and since membership was not inherited, but a matter for each individual's conscience, even the élite of the 'saints' might fear to see their children disenfranchised.

To meet this objection the Puritan ministers met in 1662 to devise a compromise they called the Halfway Covenant, which allowed those unable or unwilling to make a 'relation' into membership of the church, including the right to vote and hold office, excluding them from only the sacrament of the Lord's Supper. Fifteen years later, Solomon Stoddard, one of the strongest advocates of the Halfway Covenant, began to admit allcomers even to the Lord's Supper in his church in Northampton, Massachusetts. There should be no test of any kind for admission to the church, he wrote in his *The Doctrine of Instituted Churches* (1700); the Lord's Supper was a 'converting ordinance', not a confirmation of sanctity already achieved. By this time

Thomas and William Brattle (the one a businessman, astronomer and mathematician who had graduated from Harvard and spent several years in England, and the other a minister in Cambridge and tutor at Harvard) had established a breakaway congregational church in Boston, in which 'relations' were abolished altogether and baptism offered to the children of all professed Christians. Communion was available to persons of visible sanctity – that is, to those whose works declared them worthy of it – and sermons concentrated on a practical approach to moral problems of secular affairs.

This summary of the transition from predestinarian sect to 'ethical' church ignores not only the strenuous opposition to such developments but also the later reaction of Jonathan Edwards (1703–58), who tried to re-establish a Calvinism even more severe in its doctrine of salvation than the covenantal theology of the early settlers, but it will serve to show what could happen in a country rapidly developing in wealth and complexity, even to a faith for which works were irrelevant to salvation, in a little over half a century. Even the career of Cotton Mather shows something of this transition. Though a conservative who opposed the reforms of both Stoddard and the Brattles, Mather was also a Fellow of the Royal Society of London who advocated inoculation for the smallpox and wrote the earliest known account of plant hybridization. Though he believed in devils and witches (if they could be made to vanish, he said in a sermon, then so could the whole of the 'invisible world', and then 'we shall come to have no Christ but a light within, and no Heaven but a frame of mind' – cited Hansen, 1969, 27), he had doubts about the willingness of the prosecution at the Salem witchcraft trials to accept 'spectral evidence' – that is, the assertions of the girls that the spirit of the alleged witch had haunted them even though her person was known to have been elsewhere at the time. Though his *Magnalia Christi Americana* (1702) mixes marvels and 'special providences' with historical documents to prove the great things done of Christ in America, his *Christian Philosopher* (1721) argues the need for scientific research to unfold the beauties of God's creation – a position reconcilable with the principles of deistic philosophy and the founding purpose of the Royal Society. Finally, in his *Bonifacius* (1710), frequently reprinted as *Essays to do Good*, the great proponent of apocalyptic Calvinism issued a modest, practical guide to personal and social behaviour, every bit as though works mattered and the world would last for ever.

The Boston of Mather's later years was the Boston of Franklin's early life. Franklin heard Mather preach there more than once, and the auto-biography mentions the impact on him of the *Essays to do Good*, which Franklin read in his father's library and 'which perhaps gave me a turn of thinking that had an influence on some of the principal future events of my life'. The convergence of the two men was more than an accident of history, however. As Daniel Boorstin writes,

> It is misleading to separate Mather and Franklin by the academic anti-theses between 'Calvinism' and 'the Enlightenment'. The similari-ties in the interests and achievements of these two great men reveal distinctive features of American culture in the provincial age: an un-discriminating universality of interest surprisingly unconfined by a priori theories; a lack of originality; an intense practicality; an un-systematic and random approach to philosophy; and, above all, a willingness to be challenged by New World opportunities.
>
> (1965, 249)

For all their kinship, however, Franklin took Mather's late stirrings of ethical Christianity much further. How much further can be judged by his plan for moral improvement outlined at the beginning of Part II of the autobiography. 'It was about this time', he writes, 'that I conceived the bold and arduous project of arriving at moral perfection.' A scheme of moral *perfection* goes a good way beyond Mather, even at his most pro-gressive. Was Franklin serious? Up to a point, but he admits, with what must be at least a degree of irony, that 'I soon found I had undertaken a task of more difficulty than I had imagined. While my attention was taken up in guarding against one fault, I was often surprised by another' (148). Still, the adjectives 'bold and arduous' imply a serious attempt, and he does go on to present the scheme at some length.

First it was necessary to reinvent the cardinal virtues. The traditional seven had been divided customarily into three 'divine' (faith, hope and charity) and four 'natural' qualities (prudence, justice, fortitude and temperance). Characteristically, Franklin dispensed with the first three altogether, and found the 'natural' four too few for his purpose: 'I proposed to myself, for the sake of clearness, to use rather more names with fewer ideas annexed to each.' He subdivided prudence into 'Frugality', 'Silence' and 'Sincerity'; although justice stood alone, fortitude became 'Resolution' and 'Industry', and temperance was joined by no less than 'Order', 'Moderation', 'Cleanliness', 'Tranquil-lity', 'Chastity' ('Rarely use venery but for health or offspring . . .') and 'Humility' ('Imitate Jesus and Socrates') (149–50).

The next stage was to de-mythologize the deity; in Franklin's scheme he (or it) became 'Powerful Goodness', and he wrote a prayer beginning 'O Powerful Goodness! bountiful Father! merciful Guide! Increase in me that wisdom which discovers my truest interests.' Next, he entered each virtue on a sort of balance sheet, with ticks in squares to represent days when the virtue was observed. Finally he drew up a schedule ('The precept of order requiring that every part of my business should have its alloted time') allocating 'the twenty-four hours of a natural day' each to its improvement. From 5 to 7 a.m. he would 'rise, wash, and address Powerful Goodness; contrive [the] day's business and take the resolution of the day; prosecute the present study; and breakfast'. From 8 to 11 he would work. From 12 to 2 he would 'read or overlook [his] accounts, and dine'. More work from 2 to 6 p.m., then from 6 until bedtime at 10 he would 'put things in their places, [have] supper, [then] music, or diversion, or conversation'. Every morning he would ask himself 'What good shall I do this day' and every evening 'What good have I done this day?'

It is a jolly synthesis of faiths and philosophies stripped of the transcendence of God. Mather, despite *Essays to do Good*, would surely have hated it as much as did a later apostle of the apocalypse, D. H. Lawrence, whose passionate and humane attack on Franklin forced him again to revise the catalogue of virtues by putting the gods back in:

1

TEMPERANCE

Eat and carouse with Bacchus, or munch dry bread with Jesus, but don't sit down without one of the gods. . . .

6

INDUSTRY

Lose no time with ideals; serve the Holy Ghost; never serve mankind. . . .

12

CHASTITY

Never 'use' venery at all. Follow your passional impulse, if it be answered in the other being; but never have any motive in mind, neither offspring nor health nor even pleasure, nor even service. . . .

(1924, 23–4)

On the other hand, what characterizes Franklin's 'faith' — and that of his generation of Americans — is (1) the willingness to throw over old authority, even in this most authoritarian of human institutions, in order to invent one's own salvation; and (2) the utilitarian criterion of the enterprise. 'Salvation' in what sense, and 'utility' to what end? The careless answer is, to get rich. This is wrong. It has been a truism, ever since Max Weber's *The Protestant Ethic and the Spirit of Capitalism* (1904–5) became established in university courses of history and sociology, that the Puritans tried to be good in order to be rich — that God was thought to show His favour to His elect in terms of immediate material rewards. Weber (whom Lawrence knew well, of course) erects Franklin as the *daimon* of 'the spirit of capitalism', for whom 'the increase of his capital . . . is assumed as an end in itself' (trans. Parsons, 1958, 51). But even allowing that Weber was right about the motives of the Puritans, he underestimated the degree to which Franklin diverged from their mentality. Franklin's materialism was more profound than Weber's version of the Protestant ethic; for he tried to be rich in order to be good — or, as he put it himself, when reviewing his reasons for publishing *Poor Richard's Almanack* for twenty-five years, to 'inculcate industry and frugality as the means of procuring wealth *and thereby securing virtue*' (my italics, 164).

Franklin knew as well as any of his contemporaries that progress, from local public improvements to the founding of a whole nation, needed a financial base. The enormous success of his printing business and its associated periodicals was itself a means, not an end. By 1748, when he was 42, he was able to retire from it, leaving its management to his partner and taking an annual stipend of around £500 — enough to support what might seem, in the lives of ordinary men, two further careers as an experimental scientist and successful diplomat. Yet Weber's mistake is understandable, for in the autobiography the various 'ends' are more often assumed than stated, and it is the means that occupy the centre of the narrative. In the passage selected, 'charity' has been deconsecrated from saving love to the technology of good works. What conditions prevailed before the charity hospital was built? What arguments were advanced in its favour? What moral or spiritual imperatives were served? Perhaps the answers are obvious; Franklin, in any case, seems to have felt the simple formulation of 'poor sick persons' sufficient to trigger assent in his readers to the 'beneficent design'. What interests him are the arguments by which he placated the country members of the Assembly, the exact language in which the necessary bill was drafted, and the mechanism of fund raising, considered (most modernly) in the tactics of its finance and the strategy of mass psychology.

And that is how he tells his stories, repeatedly. When the English Methodist, George Whitfield, began his American tour in 1739, moving hundreds and thousands of tears and conversion (moving even Franklin, it should be added, to empty his pockets, 'Gold and all' into the collection plate), what Franklin noted was his oratorical technique. 'His delivery . . . was so improved by frequent repetitions, that every accent, every emphasis, every modulation of voice, was so perfectly well turned and well placed, that without being interested in the subject, one could not help being pleased with the discourse' (180). While Whitfield was speaking one evening at the corner of Market and Second Streets in Philadelphia, Franklin walked slowly backwards to determine how far the famous voice would carry:

> I found his voice still distinct till I came near Front Street, when some noise in that street obscured it. Imagining then a semicircle, of which my distance should be the radius, and that it were filled with auditors, to each of whom I allowed two square feet, I computed that he might well be heard by more than thirty thousand. (179)

This is a long way from Calvinism, or even from the evangelistic fervour felt by Whitfield's other 'auditors'; no trace here of the conviction of election, much less conversion of the soul. Where once works were inefficacious, now 'the works' are everything. Message had become medium, the Word dissolved into an experiment with acoustics. If this seems unduly materialistic from a post-romantic point of view — say, that of Matthew Arnold or D. H. Lawrence — it follows from the revolution in ideas about the relationship between God and the universe. Franklin revised the Puritans' divine plan as the deistic mechanism of nature. If God is here, He is immanent, not transcendent. 'Nature' in the excerpt has been stripped of its moral presuppositions. In the sentence beginning 'I enquired into the nature . . . of his scheme', the word stands for a neutral condition, instead of the positive, generative force governing the whole sub-lunary world — the principle that medieval theologians used to pose against 'fortune'. This is like the change in emphasis in the revised *Macbeth*, first published in 1674 and performed until well into the eighteenth century as the accepted version of the play, in which the dramatist Davenant changed Lady Macbeth's terrible prayer 'That no compunctious visitings of nature / Shake my fell purpose' to 'Empty my nature of humanity / And fill me up with cruelty'.

As for Franklin's concern with money, his apparent confusion of material with spiritual values, this follows from his belief that the laws of economics were as much a part of the natural mechanism as were the laws of science, which, though not yet perfectly discovered, could be applied, where their practical operations were clear, to the improvement of material circumstances. And this material progress would entail, or at least promote, moral improvement. What *kind* of moral improvement is not stated – assuredly not that which Whitfield hoped to inspire in all his listeners, which Franklin would have thought no improvement at all. The 'system' is imperfect; many of its causes and effects are unknown; only some of its operations are clear. Human progress is assumed, not argued. So is the potential of each individual to work out his own 'philosophy', drawing eclectically on whatever systems of knowledge and natural fact seem to suit his purpose. But the necessary corollary to this way of thinking is a rhetoric that now seems at best amateurish, or at worst (as Weber said of Bunyan's comparison of the relationship of sinner to God with that of customer to shopkeeper) 'characteristically tasteless' (124) – a jumbling of categories that have since become separate academic specialities, or levels of reference.

Franklin's science, for instance, though it won him numerous international honours and involved him in correspondence in nine languages with all the major scientific societies of Europe, now appears a hopeless confusion of disciplines, whether 'pure' or 'applied'. At one moment he might struggle to induce the most fundamental theories from a few facts (as when, after a few experiments with an 'electric tube' sent him from England by his Quaker friend, Peter Collinson, he produced the still valid theory that electricity was a 'single fluid' polarized positively and negatively), and at the next he might apply his mind with the same degree of attention to the problem of smoking chimneys. (His letters to Collinson on his electrical experiments, published first in 1751, later reissued in revised form and translated into Latin, Italian, French and German, and his *On the Causes and Cure of Smoky Chimneys*, republished in 1787, were two of his most popular works.) An account of his 'New-Invented Pennsylvanian Fire-places' (the description of the Franklin stove, published in 1744) mixes practical information with a good deal of 'theory', like: '1. Air is rarified by heat, and condensed by cold, i.e. the same quantity of air takes up more space when warm than when cold. This may be shown by several very easy experiments. Take any clear glass bottle (a Florence flask stript of its straw is best), place it before the fire, and. . . .' Not exactly what the chilly artisan needs to know.

As for his many projects, he made no distinction in either the degree of attention he gave to them, or the linguistic register in which he relates the event. Plans for lighting and paving the streets of Philadelphia, the establishment of a 'junto' to discuss both the issues of the day and general philosophical questions, projects for schools, academies, subscription libraries, a fire-engine company, the invention of bi-focal spectacles and the lightning rod — all received the same enthusiasm in his life and writing as his plans for his personal moral development, and his diplomatic ventures on behalf of his adopted state or his country. All tended toward 'improvement'; that was what mattered.

In other words, for all his interest in mechanism, Benjamin Franklin was anything but systematic. This comes as something of a surprise to those who, like Lawrence, have come to think of him as a snuff-coloured little prig with his eye on the main chance. But in truth a good number of his projects, and particularly those announced for the development of his private morality, remained incomplete. When he was about sixteen, he came upon a book recommending a vegetarian diet, and 'determined to go into it' (63). A year later on his first trip from Boston to Philadelphia, when his ship was becalmed off Block Island, the crew began to fish for cod. Franklin had learned from his book that 'the taking of every fish [is] a kind of unprovoked murder', but then again, he 'had formerly been a great lover of fish' and the meal in the frying pan 'smelled admirably well':

> I balanced some time between principle and inclination till I recollected that when the fish were opened, I saw smaller fish taken out of their stomachs. Then, thought I, if you eat one another, I don't see why we mayn't eat you. So I dined upon cod very heartily and have since continued to eat as other people. (87–8)

In 1731 he resolved to establish 'a united party for virtue' which he would call the 'Society of the Free and Easy'. Its creed would consist of a few simple headings, such as 'That there is one God who made all things. That he governs the world by his providence. That he ought to be worshipped by adoration, prayer, and thanksgiving. But the most acceptable service to God is doing good to man. . . .' The society should be made up, in the first case, of young, single men who would assent to the creed and follow the thirteen virtues of Franklin's moral scheme. But it came to nothing; 'this is as much as I can now recollect of the project, except that I communicated it in part to two young men who adopted it with some enthusiasm' (162–3).

Even his scheme of virtues persisted only for a season or two. For a time he addressed himself to one virtue per week, entering a spot in a square representing a day whenever he transgressed. In this way he could go through the whole 'course' (his word, suggesting a medical prescription) in thirteen weeks, and repeat the process three times again in a year. 'After a while', however, he 'went though one course only in a year, and afterwards only one in several years, till at length [he] omitted them entirely, being employed in voyages and business abroad with a multiplicity of affairs that interfered' (155). Another intention, to write a short commentary on the virtues, went unfulfilled (158).

There is little hypocrisy in this. After all, it is Franklin himself telling the story, and had he been as cunning as he has sometimes been taken, he could easily have avoided such embarrassing juxtapositions of project and result. There is a degree of self-mockery too. Following the fish episode he comments, 'So convenient a thing it is to be a reasonable creature, since it enables one to find or make a reason for everything one has a mind to do.' The real subject is not the project, much less its intended result, but the limitations of human endeavour. He makes fun of his own resolve, showing the rationality (or at least the common sense) of what looks at first like a failure to persist.

So in Franklin's writing, as in his life, nothing lacked its utility; he had the ingenuity to turn even his failure — or rather, lack of complete success — into a moral topic, even if the 'moral' is not always clear. Virtue number 3, 'Order', gave him particular trouble, he admits. 'In truth, I found myself incorrigible with respect to *Order*; and now . . . I feel very sensibly the want of it.' Here, though, he offers himself the palliating qualification that at least 'by the endeavor' he was 'a better and a happier man' than if he had not wrestled with his fault.

This is the point, really: if the end cannot always be achieved, or even identified, then at least the process will be worth while. It is in connection with his troubles with 'Order' that Franklin tells a little story that has since become famous, the anecdote of the speckled axe. A man, having bought a rusty axe head from a blacksmith, asks to have it ground clean. The smith agrees, providing the man will turn the crank on the grindstone. After much time and laborious turning, the axe is only partly clean. '"No," says the smith, "turn on, turn on; we shall have it bright by and by; as yet 'tis only speckled." "Yes," says the man, "*but I think I like a speckled axe best*," ' Franklin's comment on this is very puzzling indeed:

> For something that pretended to be reason was every now and then suggesting to me that such extreme nicety as I exacted of myself might be a kind of foppery in morals, which if it were known would make me ridiculous; that a perfect character might be attended with the inconvenience of being envied and hated; and that a benevolent man should allow a few faults in himself to keep his friends in coun-
> tenance.
> (156)

What exactly *is* the moral of the story: that we settle too easily for compromises? Is reason's message a diabolical temptation because it comes from one pretending? Possibly, but the pejorative terms correspond so exactly to what Franklin hated, in other contexts ('extreme', 'foppery', 'ridiculous', 'inconvenience') that the temptation must be accounted a very insidious one. In the event, Franklin does not close the *oratio obliqua* so in a sense his moral self disappears from the speckled axe story, and the reader is left to take it as he will. What Franklin goes on to argue is the utility of his having, at least, *tried* to perfect the virtue of 'Order' (cited above). It is the application of the method, not the final result, with which the narrative culminates. In case the reader should remain unconvinced, Franklin anticipates and deflects skepticism with a self-deprecating joke about his inability to maintain even the method in all the details of its design. Nor is this just self-defence. The joke buried in the autobiography, overlooked by the English moralists, is that such imperfections involve us all.

References

Bercovitch, Sacvan (1975), *The Puritan Origins of the American Self*, New Haven, Conn.: Yale University Press.

Boorstin, Daniel (1965), *The Americans* [vol. 1]; *the Colonial Experience*, Harmondsworth; Penguin.

Hansen, Chadwick (1969), *Witchcraft at Salem*, New York: Braziller.

Hofstadter, Richard (1973), *America at 1750; a Social Portrait*, New York: Random House (Vintage Books).

Lawrence, D. H. (1924), *Studies in Classical American Literature*, London: Secker.

Max Weber (1958), *The Protestant Ethic and the Spirit of Capitalism*, trans. Talcott Parsons, New York: Scribner's.

Further reading

TEXTS

Leonard Labaree *et al.*, then William B. Willcox *et al.*, (eds), *The Papers of Benjamin Franklin*, 22 vols (up to 27 Oct. 1776) completed to date, New Haven, Conn.: Yale University Press, 1959–   .

Leonard Labaree, *et al.* (as above) (eds), *The Autobiography*, New Haven, Conn.: Yale University Press, 1964.

CONTEXTS

Sacvan Bercovitch, *The Puritan Origins of the American Self*, New Haven, Conn.: Yale University Press, 1975.

G. Thomas Couser, *American Autobiography: the Prophetic Mode*, Amherst, Mass.: University of Massachusetts Press, 1979.

Richard Hofstadter, *America at 1750: a Social Portrait*, New York: Random House (Vintage Books), 1973.

Henry May, *The Enlightenment in America*, New York: Oxford University Press, 1976.

Perry Miller, *The New England Mind* [vol. 2]; *From Colony to Province*, Cambridge, Mass.: Harvard University Press, 1953.

Vernon Parrington, *Main Currents in American Thought* [vol. 1]; *The Colonial Mind, 1620–1800*, New York: Harcourt, Brace & World, 1927.

Daniel Shea, Jr, *Spiritual Autobiography in Early America*, Princeton, N.J.: Princeton University Press, 1968.

CRITICAL AND BIOGRAPHICAL

Carl Becker, *Benjamin Franklin: a Biographical Sketch*, Ithaca, N.Y.: Cornell University Press, 1946 (reprints his entry on Franklin in the *Dictionary of American Biography*).

Bruce Granger, *Benjamin Franklin: an American Man of Letters*, Ithaca, N.Y.: Cornell University Press, 1964.

5

Thomas Paine (1737–1809)

To the evil of monarchy we have added that of hereditary succession; and as the first is a degradation and lessening of ourselves, so the second, claimed as a matter of right, is an insult and an imposition on posterity. For all men being originally equals, no one by birth could have a right to set up his own family in perpetual preference to all others for ever, and though himself might deserve some decent degree of honors of his contemporaries, yet his descendants might be far too unworthy to inherit them. One of the strongest natural proofs of the folly of hereditary right in kings, is, that nature disapproves it, otherwise she would not so frequently turn it into ridicule by giving mankind an ass for a lion.

Secondly, as no man at first could possess any other public honors than were bestowed upon him, so the givers of those honors could have no power to give away the right of posterity, and though they might say 'We choose you for our head,' they could not, without manifest injustice to their children, say 'that your children and your children's children shall reign over ours for ever.' Because such an unwise, unjust, unnatural compact might (perhaps) in the next succession put them under the government of a rogue or a fool. Most wise men, in their private sentiments, have ever treated hereditary right with contempt; yet it is one of those evils, which when once established is not easily removed; many submit from fear, others from superstition, and the more powerful part shares with the king the plunder of the rest.

This is supposing the present race of kings in the world to have had an honourable origin; whereas it is more than probable, that could we take off the dark covering of antiquity, and trace them to their first rise, that we should find the first of them nothing better than the principal ruffian of some restless gang, whose savage manners or pre-eminence in subtilty obtained him the title of chief among plunderers; and who by increasing in power, and extending his depredations, over-awed the quiet and defenceless to purchase their safety by frequent contributions. Yet his electors could have no idea of giving hereditary right to his descendants, because such a perpetual exclusion of themselves was incompatible with the free and unrestrained principles they professed to live by. Wherefore, hereditary succession in the early ages of monarchy could not take place as a matter of claim, but as something casual or complimental; but as few or no records were extant in those days, and traditionary history stuffed with fables, it was very easy, after the lapse of a few generations, to trump up some superstitious tale, conveniently timed, Mahomet like, to cram hereditary right down the throats of the vulgar. Perhaps the disorders which threatened, or seemed to threaten on the decease of a leader and the choice of a new one (for elections among ruffians could not be very orderly) induced many at first to favor hereditary pretentions; by which means it happened, as it hath happened since, that what at first was submitted to as a convenience, was afterwards claimed as a right.

England, since the conquest, hath known some few good monarchs, but groaned beneath a much larger number of bad ones, yet no man in his senses can say that their claim under William the Conqueror is a very honorable one. A French bastard landing with an armed banditti, and establishing himself king of England against the consent of the natives, is in plain terms a very paltry rascally original. – It certainly hath no divinity in it. However, it is needless to spend much time in exposing the folly of hereditary right, if there are any so weak as to believe it, let them promiscuously worship the ass and lion, and welcome. I shall neither copy their humility, nor disturb their devotion.

Yet I should be glad to ask how they suppose kings came at first? The question admits but of three answers, viz. either by lot, by election, or by usurpation. If the first king was taken by lot, it establishes a precedent for the next, which excludes hereditary succession. Saul was by lot yet the succession was not hereditary, neither does it appear from that transaction there was any intention it ever should. If the first king of any country was by election, that likewise establishes a precedent for the next; for to say, that the right of all future generations is taken away, by the act of the first electors, in their choice not only of a king, but of a family of kings for ever, hath no parallel in or out of scripture but the doctrine of original sin, which supposes the free will of all men lost in Adam; and from such comparison, and it will admit of no other, hereditary succession can derive no glory. For as in Adam all sinned, and as in the first electors all men obeyed; as in the one all mankind were subjected to Satan, and in the other to Sovereignty; as our innocence was lost in the first, and our authority in the last; and as both disable us from re-assuming some former state and privilege, it unanswerably follows that original sin and hereditary succession are parallels. Dishonourable rank! Inglorious connexion! Yet the most subtile sophist cannot produce a juster simile.

Common Sense (1776)

* * *

'Can then Mr Burke produce the English Constitution? If he cannot, we may fairly conclude, that though it has been so much talked about, no such thing as a constitution exists, or ever did exist, and consequently that the people have yet a constitution to form.' Thomas Paine was always asking awkward questions. This one comes in the first chapter of *Rights of Man* (1791-2), his masterful reply to Edmund Burke's *Reflections on the Revolution in France* (1790). Now the English constitution was something of an object of veneration, though not an object at all, of course. Even the enlightened Montesquieu, no respecter of tradition for its own sake, had praised its fine balance of opposing interests in King, Lords and Commons (*De l'Esprit des Lois*, 1748, Book XI). The standard answer to Paine's question is that the English rejoice in a constitution that lies all around them – in a thousand statutes and precedents going back at least to Magna Carta – and that it is all the better for being both invisible and flexible.

Paine's challenge to Burke is a powerful combination of debating-society rhetoric and serious moral sense. Here the rhetoric consists both of a spurious allusion to the method of the new experimental sciences, by which a phenomenon was tested against the physical evidence of what could be held, seen and experienced, and also in the appeal to logic and common consensus ('If he cannot, we may fairly conclude . . .'), by which he proceeds to his demonstration. Yet, more seriously, if the constitution is invisible to ordinary people without the connections, time or money to pursue their enquiries through the courts, it really does not 'exist' in practical terms for them. The common man, especially if he has the vote, needs a ready access to his rights and duties if he is to make a useful contribution to a democratic society. And the real difference between Paine and his more traditional opponents was that he wanted such a society and they did not.

This tension between surprising, sometimes even shocking rhetoric and a residual 'common sense' – that is, a meaning understood by all, as it were, by natural reason, and also a sense of the issue applicable to ordinary people – is a formidable tactic in the prose of Tom Paine. Again and again the reader catches his breath at the cheekiness of the assault, only to find himself acquiescing to a truth newly revealed by the altered perspective. In this passage excerpted from Paine's earlier *Common Sense*, the predominant trope is that of meiosis, or the belittling 'disabler', as the sixteenth-century rhetorician Puttenham called it. The attack on hereditary monarchy seems almost to foretell the popular nineteenth-century American newspaper sketch in which a common-sensical humourist (Mark Twain, for instance) visits the grand opera. Respect for the traditional iconography of the British monarchy, the lion and the unicorn, is reduced to idolatrous 'worship' of 'the ass and lion'; William the Conqueror (with a gesture towards the antipathy, widely shared by English revolutionaries from the seventeenth century onwards, to the 'Norman yoke') is revealed as nothing more than 'a French bastard landing with an armed banditti'. The last word completes the process; it sounds both foreign and unpleasant, but retains enough of its English equivalent to remain comprehensible. On this hallowed precedent the sanctity of the British monarchy depends: an opportunistic incursion by a band of foreign outlaws.

Yet was the truth any different from the rhetoric? What *was* the argument for hereditary succession? It is not easy, now or perhaps ever, for common sense to follow it. In *Leviathan* (1651) Thomas Hobbes had argued that the true commonwealth was founded on a contract between king and subject by which succeeding generations were bound. For although men die, the institution of government must be preserved in an 'Artificial Eternity'; otherwise the state would 'return to the condition of War in every age' (Part II, Chap. 19). Medieval jurists had fixed this 'Artificial Eternity'; in the person of the monarch, in the legal fiction that the king had 'two bodies': one that pertained to his own personal life and that died when 'he' did, and the other that survived as an institution. 'The King is dead; long live the King.' Though John Locke repudiated the notion of hereditary political power in his first *Treatise on Civil Government* (1689), Burke would reaffirm it in his *Reflections on the Revolution in France*, and Paine attack it again in *Rights*. Here, in *Common Sense*, he puts his case succinctly: 'no one by birth could have the right to set up his own family in perpetual preference to all others for ever.' But at this point rhetoric and truth converge in aphorism. Put like this, the case is almost impossible to answer.

Thomas Paine was born in Thetford, Norfolk, of Quaker parents, in 1737. His father was a corset maker who apprenticed his son to the business. Like Franklin, Paine ran away from home in his late teens, but there the parallel between them diverges. In the next twenty years of his life he worked at a number of occupations – staymaker, excise man, tobacconist, teacher and itinerant preacher – and lived in London, Dover, Sandwich, Diss in Norfolk, London again, and Lewes, Sussex. He was married twice. His first wife died within a year, and the second marriage ended in divorce. By the time he was 37, he had yet to find a calling, let alone establish a 'financial base' for good works; by the same age Franklin had amassed the better part of a life's sufficiency from his printing business, married and had two children, founded the junto and the Philadelphia library, begun *Poor Richard's Almanack*, established the fire company, invented the Franklin stove, been made a member of the Pennsylvania Assembly and been appointed postmaster of Philadelphia.

Yet within two years of the two men meeting in London in 1774, Paine had emigrated to America, become editor of the *Pennsylvania Magazine*, and published *Common Sense*, a pamphlet so forcefully argued, so persuasively phrased in the language of ordinary people, that it was read within a year by something over one fifth of the entire colonial population, and precipitated the American War of Independence just as surely as *Uncle Tom's Cabin* prepared the mood of the North for the Civil War eighty-five years later.

Paine's sudden success as a propagandist was not wholly unpredictable. In Lewes he had participated actively in a sort of Franklinian 'junto', a debating society called the Headstrong Club. He had taken an early interest in the pay and conditions of his fellow excise men, had published a pamphlet in their defence, and gone to London to lobby the government on their behalf (it was on this trip that he met Franklin). Also the most plausible reason for at least one of his 'failures' in employment was that the government dismissed him from his job with the Excise for being an agitator.

Still, even granted that Franklin saw enough promise in him to provide him a letter of introduction to his son in Pennsylvania, it is hard to find in Paine's education and experience convincing explanations for the rhetorical power of *Common Sense* – let alone for the articulacy of the substantial works that followed, *Rights of Man* and *The Age of Reason* (1794–5). In *The Making of the English Working Class*, E. P. Thompson suggests that for Paine the change of environment was all important: '[In England] the context was hopeless, politics seemed a mere species of "jockeyship". Within one year of his arrival in America . . . he had published *Common Sense* and the *Crisis* articles which contain all the assumptions of *Rights of Man*. . . . The seed of *Rights of Man* was English; but only the hope brought by the American and French Revolution enabled it to strike' (1968, 40).

The question of 'influences', in the sense of that term as adduced by historians of literature or ideas, goes unanswered in Paine's case. What did he read, whom did he meet, before coming to America? The famous association with Blake, William Godwin and Mary Wollstonecraft would not occur until the 1790s, after the appearance of *Rights of Man*. There are traces in *Common Sense* of the idea to be found in Locke (but also in Adam Smith's *The Wealth of Nations*, published in the same momentous year of 1776) that the only legitimate purpose of government is to protect the natural rights of the subject. But the idea of 'natural rights', like the assumption on which it is based that once a happy state of 'nature' existed before all governments began, is very old. Locke's first *Treatise on Government* was an answer to Sir Robert Filmer's *Patriarcha; or the Natural Power of Kings* (1680), which had deprecated the 'common opinion' that 'mankind is naturally endowed and born with freedom from all subjection'; so it appears that for all its radicalism, *Common Sense* was assuming some ideas that were indeed 'common' and had been around for some time, even if not in that stratum of discourse normally cited by historians as influences. 'Common' sense was what everyone felt to be the case,* and also the 'good sense' of the common people.

'It is repugnant to reason, to the universal order of things, to all examples from the former ages, to suppose that this continent can longer remain subject to any external power' (*Common Sense*, 89). This triad of terms neatly expresses the basis of Paine's argument: a continuum of truth extending outwards in space (into 'the universal order of things') and backwards in time, through the examples of the past. But what could 'the former ages' have to do with a revolutionary programme for the future? This is a common paradox of apocalypses, and the immediate source of the idea for Paine, together with his confident expression of it and his near certainty that it would move his American audience, can be located in his non-conformist background, where sermons, tracts and

---

* Paine wanted to call the pamphlet *Plain Truth*, but his friend, fellow expatriate and another protégé of Franklin, Dr Benjamin Rush, suggested *Common Sense*. The idea of a universal moral sensibility can be traced, via Rush's education at Edinburgh, according to Garry Wills (1978, 303, 198), to the moral aesthetics of the Scottish enlightenment. It is exemplified in *Essays on the Principles of Morality and Natural Religion* (1751) by Henry Home, Lord Kames.

discussions provided underground conduits running back to religious and political disputes of at least two hundred years' duration.

The purest vision of sixteenth-century Protestants was the establishment of a millennial community of saints in mystical communion with each other and their God. But this revolution of affairs and the spirit was imaged as a stripping away of the accretions of history – the wordly deposits of man-made liturgy, canon law and the episcopal polity of bishops and parish priests licensed to interpret Christ's Word for the ordinary worshipper. The Millennium would not be a reckless adventure into an uncharted future, but a return to the simple structures of the primitive Christian Church, when small groups of the faithful met in upstairs rooms to work out their own salvation.

This idea, which might be called the palindromic model of revolution, could be adopted into spheres of thought and behaviour other than the spiritual, from the enterprise of physical exploration (as when the journey to America was imagined and even 'seen' as the return to a golden age) to the politics of private privilege and state power, in which, for example, the radical sects of the Interregnum projected a return to the state of the English commonwealth before the advent of kingly government in the form of the 'Norman yoke'. 'What is kingly government or monarchy?' asked the Digger, or 'True Leveller', Gerrard Winstanley, in his pamphlet, *The Law of Freedom in a Platform* (1652): 'Kingly government governs the earth by that cheating art of buying and selling, and thereby becomes a man of contention, his hand is against every man, and every man's hand against him.' The government of kings ('alias conquerors') 'may well be called the government of highwaymen, who hath stolen the earth from the younger brethren by force, and holds it from them by force'.

The biblical echoes in words like 'brethren', phrases like 'his hand is against every man' and ideas like elder brothers stealing birthrights from younger, is no accident. Later Winstanley puts in the names, in case they were not already reverberating in the heads of his readers: 'for this is Cain who killed Abel: and because of this, he is called the *great red dragon* . . . and so one Scripture calls this *the power and government of the Beast*, another Scripture calls it *the god of this world or the devil*.'

'Commonwealth's government', on the other hand,

> Is within the laws of common freedom, whereby there is a provision for livelihood in the earth both for elder and younger brother . . . both living in plenty and freedom. . . .

This government depends not upon the will of any particular man or men; for it is seated in the spirit of mankind, and it is called the *light, or son of righteousness and peace.* The tyrants in all ages have made use of this man's name, while he hath lain buried, to cover their cheating mystery of iniquity. . . .

This commonwealth's government may well be called the *ancient of days*: for it was before any other oppressing government crept in.

It is the moderator of all oppression; and so is like Moses and Joseph in Pharaoh's court, and in time will be the restorer of long lost freedoms to the creation, and delights to plant righteousness over the face of the whole earth.

(ed. Hill, 1973, 306–12)

Here a political programme is welded to the expectations of an audience used to hearing sermons on the Last Things, through apocalyptic trigger words like 'beast' and 'dragon' (from the Book of Revelation) and 'the ancient of days' (from the Apocalypse in the Book of Daniel), and through the evocation of a future that restores the past. Yet the weld is not seamless. Odd things happen to the references. Just as an institution (kingly government) is predicated as a person ('becomes a man of contention') so biblical people (Christ, via the punning movement from 'light' [sun] to 'son', and 'the ancient of days', who is an old man in Daniel) become institutions to be desired. Christ is re-invented, 'made new' to serve the vision of a 'common-wealth' that is spiritual as well as material; he is 'seated', not at the right hand of God, as in the Creed, but 'in the spirit of mankind' – available to all in a new, vernacular incarnation. Christopher Hill says that Winstanley used the Bible as Marx did the philosophy of Hegel – 'he found it standing on its head and set it the right way up' – and adds that 'We should read Winstanley as we read a poet, as we read William Blake, and as Winstanley himself read the Bible: concerned not too pedantically with the letter, but with the spiritual content which the myths have, or can be given' (Winstanley, ed. Hill, 1973, 53–4).

To put the case conservatively, Paine is extremely unlikely to have read Winstanley. In any case, his bourgeois liberalism was a long way from Winstanley's radical communism, and his use of the Bible much more a matter of local rhetorical tactics. Nevertheless, the comparison shows the extent to which these ideas were shared by ordinary people with a common Protestant background. For the American colonists, despite their graduation to a religion of works based on reason, could still be moved by apocalyptic sermons, as the enormous success of Jonathan Edwards's Great Awakening (1734 to 1750) and George Whitefield's seven missions to America (from 1738 to 1770) demonstrate.

No doubt this is why Paine began *Common Sense* by reminding his readers that 'Government, like dress, is the badge of lost innocence; the palaces of kings are built on the ruins of the bowers of paradise' (65) and referred to monarchy as 'the Popery of government' (76). It is also why, though he was to devote most of the second part of *The Age of Reason* to discrediting the Old Testament as historical authority, he prefaced the passage selected here with instances to support his argument drawn from 'scripture chronology'. 'Government by kings', he writes in a careful selection of loaded words, 'was first introduced into the world by the Heathens, from whom the Children of Israel copied the custom. It was the most prosperous invention the Devil ever set on foot for the promotion of idolatry' (72). The Jews went for nearly three thousand years without kings, during which time their government, '(except in extraordinary cases, where the Almighty interposed) was a kind of republic administered by a judge and the elders of the tribes'. He then goes on to give examples from the Old Testament – at great length, considering the brevity of *Common Sense* as a whole – to show that the state of kingship was not a natural one, but imposed by selfish men who had turned away from God. As for the inconvenient instance of King David, 'the high encomium given of [him] takes no notice of him *officially as a king*, but only as a *man* after God's own heart' (75).

With this Paine concludes what might be called his argument from revelation. It is doubtful if he really believed it. The evidence of *The Age of Reason* suggests otherwise, and even here his laborious and inefficient repetition of the same point, heavily illustrated over four pages out of forty-eight in the modern text of the first edition, suggests that his heart was not wholly in the argument. But in the passage selected, which follows the discussion of kingship in the Bible, Paine's prose comes alive. His assault on the theory of the king's two bodies is like the child's view of the emperor's new clothes. Repeatedly Paine measures the exalted doctrine against common experience. Suppose history and tradition were only a 'superstitious tale, conveniently timed' to serve the interests of the powerful; then the institution of kingship might be nothing more than an elaborate confection to justify the posterity of 'the principal ruffian of some restless gang'. Reduce the occasion to what everyone has suffered at the hands of a bully in childhood, and the 'honourable' institution collapses into absurdity. The use of the word 'some' is a superbly understated throwaway, indicating a trifling occurrence selected at random from many others like it, rather than the signal event to which a hereditary monarchy liked to trace its origins. By reducing the relationship between king and subject to a matter of a family in a community, Paine compounds the satire; forget what you have heard about the institution of monarchy, he implies, and think of the king as an ordinary man looking after his 'own'. From that perspective, he is only too distastefully familiar, as the local squire or the village-merchant grandee.

In the doctrine of the king's two bodies, imperfections in the personal character of the king would only affect his constitutional position if they hampered his institutional function. But since he wants to dissect the Siamese twins of person and institution, Paine does not shrink from the vigorous *argumentum ad hominem*, the suppressed pun by which the legitimacy of the line of English kings is dismissed along with that (in another sense) of its founder, William the Conqueror. William may have been a bastard, in the popular as well as the technical sense, for all we know, but according to Hobbes's theory, if the English accepted his sovereignty at the time of the Conquest, they bound their successors to his descendants. William's children, and their children, had to be 'legitimate'; he did not. Logic is also slighted in another pun, the quibble on 'natural' and 'nature' in 'One of the strongest *natural* proofs on the folly of hereditary right in kings, is, that nature disapproves it'. The first term is an adjective signifying 'orderly' and the second a word for the decidedly disorderly accidents of the mutable world. (Shakespeare 'slights logic' on the same topic in *King Lear*.)

Yet there is a great pretence of reason in the passage, not only through the repeated appeal to common sense, everyday experience, but also in the careful parallelism giving the impression that all possibilities have been fairly considered. If the 'principal ruffian' did not get his start through 'savage manners', then perhaps by his 'pre-eminence in subtlety', and no doubt common, contemporary instances could be found for this too, as when a small-town builder, or a politician playing favourites, trick their way to wealth and prestige. 'Increasing in power' is balanced by 'extending his depredations'; 'casual' by 'complimental'. Latinisms reinforce the sense of disinterested judgement. Then ordinary words break through, blowing a raspberry at the balanced phrases. The best instance of this device is the long period beginning 'Wherefore, hereditary succession . . .' and ending, after a long suspension, a final balance of words and rhythm ('superstitious tale // conveniently timed') and a climax of stresses ('Mahŏmet like'), with a rush of unstressed syllables and a vivid concrete action: 'to cram hereditary right down the throats of the vulgar.'

Thus the British constitution is dismissed as a nonsense founded on plunder and maintained by superstition. To overcome the great weight of admiration for the object of his scorn, Paine adduces the test of his readers' common experience – their knowledge of the vernacular scriptures and their sense of what is 'naturally' fit and right. He flatters them that, however, unlearned, they have in the stuff of their ordinary lives the solvent, the antidote to all the elaborate theories foisted on them by the upholders of the divine right, the sanctity of empire, and the unchallengeable prerogative of tradition. He appeals to the old Protestant conviction (which Ralph Waldo Emerson would later enshrine in his essay 'Self Reliance') that the individual consciousness, unaided by experts, can be the test of truth.

Next in *Common Sense*, following the passage selected here, Paine turns his attention to the relationship of the American colonies to the mother country. Again, the mood is meiotic. Here the main thrust of the argument is a critique of argument itself, especially as advanced by interested parties: 'Volumes have been written on the subject. . . . Men of all ranks have embarked in the controversy, from different motives and with various designs; but all have been ineffectual, and the period of debate is closed' (82). The issue is too great for parish politics: ''Tis not the affair of a city, a country, a province, or a kingdom, but of a continent. . . . 'Tis not the concern of a day, a year, or an age; posterity are virtually involved in the contest. . . . Now is the seed time of continental union, faith and honor.' These are the urgent periods of the apocalyptic sermon. Time is at an end; the Norman yoke and the pre-varications of tradition that support it are about to be swept aside in the onrush of the republican millennium.

One by one Paine dismisses the arguments for continued union between England and her colonies. Did not America 'flourish under her former connexion with Great Britain'? The answer comes as a maxim: 'We may as well assert, that because a child has thrived upon milk, that it is never to have meat.' Has Britain not protected us? Call it by another name: 'That she has engrossed us is true, and defended the continent at our expense as well as her own'; then, following this mag-nanimous admission, a string in the tail: 'and she would have defended Turkey from the same motive, viz. the sake of trade and dominion' (83).

But is not England the mother country? Suppose we turn the argument from 'nature' back on Paine; is there not something 'unnatural' in matricide? He answers with another maxim, and of course one drawn from nature: 'Even brutes do not devour their young, nor savages make war upon their families' (84). Besides (more seriously), 'Not one third of the inhabitants, even of this province [i.e. Pennsylvania], are of English descent' (85). That, at least, was hard to counter.

And so it goes on, now attacking, now feinting, now confronting the issue, now redefining it – and always that brilliant shift of perspective, characteristic of strong satire, that subjects the object of attack to ridicule. Yet *Common Sense* was not entirely negative. Part of its appeal must have lain in the series of practical suggestions that now followed, for, as he said, 'If there is any true cause of fear respecting independence, it is because no plan is yet laid down' (95). He offered a series of 'hints' on how a Continental Congress and a President might be elected, and the size of majority needed to pass legislation. He outlined a 'CONTINENTAL CHARTER . . . (answering to what is called the Magna Carta of England) fixing the number and manner of choosing members of Congress . . . securing freedom and property to all men, and above all things the free exercise of religion, according to the dictates of conscience' (97), and he pointed out the need for a 'manifesto' of independence to be published, for the practical purpose of establishing America as a sovereign nation able to treat with European countries for sympathy and material support (111–12).

The first edition of *Common Sense* appeared anonymously in Philadelphia on 10 January 1776, and the second, enlarged by an appendix, just over a month later. To understand its impact, one has only to recall that the American colonies were already teetering on the cusp of war with the mother country. Ever since the end of the French and Indian War in 1763, the British had been trying to find ways of making the Americans pay their share of the war debt. Parliament would devise a tax, the colonists would object, and the tax would be repealed only to be replaced by another. Further resistance was met by reprisals against American trade. Violent skirmishes had already occurred at points of friction, particularly in the Boston area: the Boston Massacre of 1770, when British troops fired into a protesting mob, killing five civilians, the Boston Tea Party in 1773, when colonists disguised as Indians stole aboard a ship and dumped 342 cases of East India Company tea into the harbour; the engagements at Lexington and Concord in April 1775, when American irregulars turned a march of 1000 British troops into a disorderly retreat, and the Battle of Bunker Hill, two months later, when the British captured an American fort after being repulsed twice. A Continental Congress had already met twice, the first in 1774, and the second after Bunker Hill to establish a Continental Army with George Washington as commander. In August 1775, George III issued a proclamation declaring that the colonies were in a state of rebellion, and the following October he opened Parliament with a bellicose address referring to their 'rebellious war . . . manifestly carried on for the purpose of establishing an independent empire'.

Yet by the turn of the year they were not at war. What was lacking can be summarized in the modern cliché (never more fitting in this early instance of the phenomenon) 'a national will'. Washington himself was against independence as late as May 1775: 'If you ever hear of my join-ing in any such measures', he said to an acquaintance, 'you have my leave to set me down for everything wicked.' Jerome Wilson and William Ricketson, who quote this remark in their recent critical biography of Paine (1978, 30–1), go on to cite testimonies to the con-temporary force of *Common Sense*. General Charles Lee wrote Washing-ton, 'I never saw such a masterly, irresistible performance. . . . I own myself convinced by the arguments, of the necessity of separation.' The next day Washington wrote Joseph Reed that the 'sound doctrine and unanswerable reasoning contained in the pamphlet "Common Sense," will not leave numbers at a loss to decide upon the propriety of separation'. In April a New York news correspondent said *Common Sense* had 'converted thousands to independence that could not endure the idea before'. On 7 June Richard Henry Lee, a delegate from Virginia, presented to Congress his resolution: 'That these United Colonies are, and of right ought to be, free and independent States, that they are absolved from all allegiance to the British Crown, and that all political connection between them and the State of Great Britain is, and ought to be, totally dissolved.' After some debate, the resolution was passed on 2 July, and the Declaration of Independence, the manifesto for which Paine had called, issued to the world.

Common Sense, in other words, galvanized the 'national will'. The fact is a salutary corrective to the received wisdom that 'books' have no effect on 'life'. Yet Paine's practical involvement did not stop with *Common Sense*. He joined the army. He wrote the *Crisis* papers at crucial points right through the course of the war (the first of them, beginning with the resonant sentence, 'These are the times that try men's souls'. Washington ordered to be read to his troops, and it did much to reinforce both morale and recruiting during that bleak first winter of the struggle). He served as secretary to the congressional committee on foreign affairs, and clerk to the Pennsylvania Assembly. In 1781 he went to France to negotiate a loan, returning with $2.5 million in silver and two shiploads of military stores.

The timeliness and practical applicability of Paine's pamphleteering is in no way better illustrated than by his disengagement from American affairs after the Revolution. When the war was over a grateful State of New York granted him a farm near New Rochelle, where he lived for three years designing an iron bridge. After that his active life is more a matter of European history than American. He returned to England in 1787 to promote his bridge, where he met Burke and Charles Fox. *Rights of Man* was a defence of the French Revolution against the attack of an Englishman, and it was for that book (not *Common Sense*, which was equally scornful of the rights of the hereditary monarchy, but of which the authorities had little fear of a domestic, working-class readership radicalized by the Jacobin example) that the English tried him *in absentia* and convicted him of seditious libel. His main contribution to public affairs after his role in the American Revolution was to the political life of France, where he was made a citizen and elected to the National Convention in 1792, only to have these honours revoked and to be put in jail a year later, when he opposed the execution of Louis XVI and defended moderate revolutionary elements during the Terror. After this disillusionment with politics he turned his mind to philosophical matters. His great exposition of popular rationalistic deism, *The Age of Reason*, was written during this time of doubt and disfavour, before and after his imprisonment in France, while he was exiled from England and all but forgotten in America.

To put it another way, *Common Sense* was directed almost exclusively toward the American situation, and its effect – in both time and place – was very local, so much so that it tells the attentive reader something about the nature of American radicalism at the time. For instance the pamphlet says nothing about the distribution of land and wealth. This is not because Paine lacked either courage (the very act of publication, once the author was known, put his head in the noose) or a radical vision, in today's sense of the phrase. An essay published shortly after he arrived in Philadelphia called for the abolition of slavery, a cause already advanced by Jefferson, among others, and the second part of *Rights of Man* would offer practical suggestions for redistributing the wealth of the English landed gentry: graduated taxation, family allowances, free public education, old-age pensions, and even maternity benefits. *Rights of Man*, as E. P. Thompson has shown (108 and *passim*), dominated English popular radicalism of the 1790s and would be picked up, again and again, by English political reformers in the nineteenth century, but it was *Common Sense* that spoke to the immediate American need − not for more taxes or further inroads on property and wealth, not for an egalitarian system of social justice, not even (just yet) for an end to black slavery − but for a fundamental break with the metropolitan centre.

Whether this impulse was more or less radical than (say) Winstanley's programme for Christian socialism depends on the definition of radical. From one point of view it seems absurd (and certainly un-Marxist) to object to hereditary political power without also arguing against inherited land and property, from which so much power flows. Yet not even the most radical of European revolutionaries could effect a separation from his country's major concentrations of population and institutional power, and thanks to the gravity of geography and tradition, the bureaucracies of France and Russia are as centralized today as ever they were under the Bourbons and Romanovs. And in a sense even Winstanley's re-invention of the Bible is less 'radical' than Paine's, in whose manifesto the Scriptures are torn up from their roots and arranged as the dead flowers of rhetoric. For finally, Paine's revolution was not a palindrome, but a cusp − a sharp peak over which his readers, having crossed it in risk of their lives, could never return.

Which may be why, when Paine moved on to other countries and other concerns, he was so quickly forgotten in his adopted country − except (once he had declared his hand on the validity of biblical history in *The Age of Reason*) as an atheist. The ironies of his last days are painful and well rehearsed: how he returned to America in 1802 after quarrelling with Washington, how he came to be reviled for his free-thinking, how he took to drink, and how, after his death in 1809, he was buried on his New Rochelle farm after the Quakers had denied his request to be laid to rest in one of their cemeteries. Six people came to his funeral. Ten years later William Cobbett, repenting of his attacks on Paine for his support of the French Revolution, took his bones back to England, where he proposed to give them a proper burial under a suitable monument. He never got around to it, and the mortal remains of Tom Paine disappeared for ever.

References

Thompson, E. P. (1968), *The Making of the English Working Class*, Harmondsworth: Penguin.

Wills, Garry (1978), *Inventing America; Jefferson's Declaration of Independence*, New York: Random House.

Wilson, J. D. and Ricketson, W. F. (1978), *Thomas Paine*, Boston, Mass.: Twayne (United States Authors Series, 301).

Winstanley, Gerrard (1973), *The Law of Freedom in a Platform, and Other Writings*, ed. Christopher Hill, Harmondsworth: Penguin.

Further reading

TEXTS

Philip Foner (ed.), *The Complete Writings of Thomas Paine*, 2 vols, New York: Citadel Press, 1969; originally published 1945.

Isaac Kramnick (ed.), *Common Sense*, Harmondsworth: Penguin, 1976.

Henry Collins (ed.), *Rights of Man*, Harmondsworth: Penguin, 1969.

CONTEXTS

Bernard Bailyn, *The Ideological Origins of the American Revolution*, Cambridge, Mass.: Harvard University Press, 1967.

E. P. Thompson, *The Making of the English Working Class*, London: Gollancz, 1963; revised edition, Harmondsworth: Penguin, 1968.

CRITICAL AND BIOGRAPHICAL

David Hawke, *Paine*, New York: Harper & Row, 1974.

Jerome Wilson and William Ricketson, *Thomas Paine*, Boston, Mass.: Twayne (United States Authors Series, 301), 1978.

6

The Declaration of Independence

In Congress, July 4, 1776.
A DECLARATION
By the Representatives of the
UNITED STATES OF AMERICA,
In General Congress Assembled.

When in the course of human events, it becomes necessary for one people to dissolve the political bands which have connected them with another, and to assume among the powers of the earth, the separate and equal station to which the laws of nature and of nature's God entitle them, a decent respect to the opinions of mankind requires that they should declare the causes which impel them to the separation.

We hold these truths to be self-evident, that all men are created equal, that they are endowed by their creator with certain unalienable rights, that among these are life, liberty, and the pursuit of happiness—that to secure these rights, governments are instituted among men, deriving their just powers from the consent of the governed, that whenever any form of government becomes destructive of these ends, it is the right of the people to alter or to abolish it, and to institute new government, laying its foundation on such principles, and organizing its powers in such form, as to them shall seem most likely to effect their safety and happiness. Prudence, indeed, will dictate that governments long established should not be changed for light and transient causes; and accordingly all experience hath shewn, that mankind are more disposed to suffer, while evils are sufferable, than to right themselves by abolishing the forms to which they are accustomed. But when a long train of abuses and usurpations, pursuing invariably the same object, evinces a design to reduce them under absolute despotism, it is their right, it is their duty, to throw off such government, and to provide new guards for their future security. Such has been the patient sufferance of these colonies; and such is now the necessity which constrains them to alter their former systems of government. The history of the present King of Great-Britain is a history of repeated injuries and usurpations, all having in direct object the establishment of an absolute tyranny over these States. To prove this, let facts be submitted to a candid world.

He has refused his assent to laws, the most wholesome and necessary for the public good.

He has forbidden his governors to pass laws of immediate and pressing importance, unless suspended in their operation till his assent should be obtained; and when so suspended, he has utterly neglected to attend to them.

He has refused to pass other laws for the accommodation of large districts of people, unless those people would relinquish the right of representation in the legislature, a right inestimable to them, and formidable to tyrants only.

He has called together legislative bodies at places unusual, uncomfortable, and distant from the depository of their public records, for the sole purpose of fatiguing them into compliance with his measures.

He has dissolved representative houses repeatedly, for opposing with manly firmness his invasions on the rights of the people.

He has refused for a long time, after such dissolutions, to cause others to be elected; whereby the legislative powers, incapable of annihilation, have returned to the people at large for their exercise; the State remaining in the mean time exposed to all the dangers of invasion from without, and convulsions within.

He has endeavoured to prevent the population of these States; for that purpose obstructing the laws for naturalization of foreigners; refusing to pass others to encourage their migrations hither, and raising the conditions of new appropriations of lands.

He has obstructed the administration of justice, by refusing his assent to laws for establishing judiciary powers.

He has made judges dependent on his will alone, for the tenure of their offices, and the amount and payment of their salaries.

He has erected a multitude of new offices, and sent hither swarms of officers to harrass our people, and eat out their substance.

He has kept among us, in times of peace, standing armies, without the consent of our legislatures.

He has affected to render the military independent of and superior to the civil power.

He has combined with others to subject us to a jurisdiction foreign to our Constitution, and unacknowledged by our laws; giving his assent to their acts of pretended legislation:

For quartering large bodies of armed troops among us:

For protecting them, by a mock trial, from punishment for any murders which they should commit on the inhabitants of these States:

For cutting off our trade with all parts of the world:

For imposing taxes on us without our consent:

For depriving us, in many cases, of the benefits of trial by jury:

For transporting us beyond seas to be tried for pretended offences:

For abolishing the free system of English laws in a neighbouring province, establishing therein an arbitrary government, and enlarging its boundaries, so as to render it at once an example and fit instrument for introducing the same absolute rule into these colonies:

For taking away our charters, abolishing our most valuable laws, and altering fundamentally the forms of our governments:

For suspending our own legislatures, and declaring themselves invested with power to legislate for us in all cases whatsoever.

He has abdicated government here, by declaring us out of his protection and waging war against us.

He has plundered our seas, ravaged our coasts, burnt our towns, and destroyed the lives of our people.

He is, at this time, transporting large armies of foreign mercenaries to complete the works of death, desolation, and tyranny, already begun with circumstances of cruelty and perfidy, scarcely paralleled in the most barbarous ages, and totally unworthy the head of a civilized nation.

He has constrained our fellow citizens taken captive on the high seas to bear arms against their country, to become the executioners of their friends and brethren, or to fall themselves by their hands.

He has excited domestic insurrections amongst us, and has endeavoured to bring on the inhabitants of our frontiers, the merciless Indian savages, whose known rule of warfare, is an undistinguished destruction, of all ages, sexes and conditions.

In every stage of these oppressions we have petitioned for redress in the most humble terms: Our repeated petitions have been answered only by repeated injury. A prince, whose character is thus marked by every act which may define a tyrant, is unfit to be the ruler of a free people.

Nor have we been wanting in attentions to our British brethren.

We have warned them from time to time of attempts by their legislature to extend an unwarrantable jurisdiction over us. We have reminded them of the circumstances of our emigration and settlement here. We have appealed to their native justice and magnanimity, and we have conjured them by the ties of our common kindred to disavow these usurpations, which, would inevitably interrupt our connections and correspondence. They too have been deaf to the voice of justice and of consanguinity. We must, therefore, acquiesce in the necessity, which denounces our separation, and hold them, as we hold the rest of mankind, enemies in war, in peace, friends.

We, therefore, the representatives of the UNITED STATES OF AMERICA, in GENERAL CONGRESS, assembled, appealing to the supreme judge of the world for the rectitude of our intentions, do, in the name, and by authority of the good people of these colonies, solemnly publish and declare, that these United Colonies are, and of right ought to be, FREE AND INDEPENDENT STATES; that they are absolved from all allegiance to the British Crown, and that all political connection between them and the State of Great-Britain, is and ought to be totally dissolved; and that as FREE AND INDEPENDENT STATES, they have full power to levy war, conclude peace, contract alliances, establish commerce and to do all other acts and things which INDEPENDENT STATES may of right do. And for the support of this declaration, with a firm reliance on the protection of divine Providence, we mutually pledge to each other our lives, our fortunes, and our sacred honor.

Signed by ORDER *and in* BEHALF *of the* CONGRESS,
JOHN HANCOCK, PRESIDENT.

ATTEST.
CHARLES THOMSON, SECRETARY.

The Declaration of Independence (1776)

* * *

Americans think of the Declaration of Independence as the founding statement of their nation. It is the first entry in countless popular collections of documents relating to the constitutional history of the United States. To its authors, though, it must have seemed more like the end of a long process – the final term in a prolonged series of anxious arguments punctuated by fragmentary propositions, uneasy compromises and partial solutions. But now, in the words of *Common Sense*, 'the period of debate [was] closed' and the time had come to issue the manifesto for which Paine had called, 'setting forth the miseries we have endured, and the peaceable methods we have ineffectually used for redress; declaring, at the same time, that not being able, any longer to live happily or safely under the cruel disposition of the British court, we had been driven to the necessity of breaking off all connection with her' (111–12).

America decided on independence on 2 July 1776, when a majority of the delegates to the second Continental Congress carried the motion of Richard Henry Lee, of Virginia, 'That these United Colonies are, and of right ought to be, free and independent States'. The signing of the Declaration followed this act by two days, on the date now revered, by an accident of history, as America's *jour de gloire*. Though its title suggested a legal document – a deposition in a civil suit, for example – and though the argument resembled that of earlier papers setting out the rights of the people and their representatives in the constitutional process, the Declaration was not an instrumental document, or what the Oxford philosopher J. L. Austin would later term a 'performative utterance' like naming a ship at its launch (see Austin, 1962, *passim*). It 'declared' the independence of the United States only in the sense of advertising or justifying it, not effecting it. It was a statement to a 'candid' world – that is, a world 'free from bias' and 'free from malice' (*OED*, 3 and 4), not to mention 'frank' and 'open' – that America was now a free nation, open to alliance and trade with any suitable country that might be interested. 'Such a memorial', said Tom Paine (*Common Sense*, 112), 'would produce more good effects to this Continent, than if a ship were freighted with petitions to Britain.' So it was both written and intended to be read primarily as a work of persuasion, and its first audience lay outside as well as within the boundaries of the new country.

The proper analysis of the Declaration, therefore, will attend not only to what it says, but how it says it. On the first question there is, by now, a voluminous literature, reflecting both the continuing interest in the document as a repository of ideas, and also a lively debate as to the sources of the ideas themselves. On the second, very little has been written. Yet the rhetorical orchestration of the Declaration's arguments is as much a part of the paper's meaning as is its paraphrasable content. Consider, for example, the way in which the complaints against the king – the paragraphs beginning with 'He . . .' – are arranged. Taken separately, these vary widely in their validity and importance. Some, as we will see, could be answered easily by English critics of the

Declaration; other could not. Some were substantial, others trivial. Among the serious charges was that of the dissolution of 'representative houses', which refers to the treatment of the Virginia House of Burgesses in 1769, 1773 and 1774, and of the General Court of Mass-achusetts in 1768 and 1774.* Equally unanswerable was the king's attempt 'to prevent the population of these States' by refusing assent to naturalization acts, such as that passed by Georgia (1766) and North Carolina (1771) offering specially favourable conditions to immigrants. Again, 'He has made judges dependent on his will alone, for the tenure of their offices' reflected a crucial departure from practice in England, where judges were (and still are, as many have cause to complain) appointed for life, subject to good behaviour. On the other hand, the claim that the king had 'called together legislative bodies at places unusual, uncomfortable, and distant from the depository of their public records' refers to several instances, in the first of which, at least, the Crown was acting at the behest of the colonists. When members of the Massachusetts Assembly objected that the presence of British troops in Boston in 1769 might overshadow its deliberation, the governor obliged by moving the Assembly across the Charles River to Cambridge. Still others of the charges, like 'He has plundered . . . ravaged . . . burnt . . .' and 'He is, at this time, transporting large armies of foreign mercenaries to compleat the works of death . . .' were consequences of the rebellion itself – not unwarranted or unprecedented in time of war.

Yet look at the charges against the king from criteria established within the text itself, and they add up to an overwhelming denunciation of the character and administration of George III. If one forgets, for a moment, the king's myriad transgressions against the rights of Englishmen, Americans and Man himself as set out in everything from Magna Carta to the law of nature, and thinks instead in the more literary polarities, posed by the text, of chaos and order, it becomes clear that the king is being arraigned as an emperor of dullness fit to stand in the ranks of Alexander Pope's great goddess of anarchy in *The Dunciad*. And just as dullness in *The Dunciad* progresses from the lower classes to the irresponsible aristocracy, from the minor hacks of Grub Street to scientists and philosophers, from the particulars of eighteenth-century London to the universals of time and place, so the Declaration's paragraphs accusing the king are arranged in a series of raids on order,

---

* Dumbauld (1950), 102–3; for a most useful summary of the contexts of and responses to the various charges against the king, see Dumbauld, 87–147.

increasingly serious in their implications. Step by step, the king undoes American civilization in the wilderness. First he refuses to assent to the laws they have made for themselves; then he forbids the passing of laws, both those 'of immediate and pressing importance', and others 'for the accommodations of large districts of people'. Next he turns his attention to the Assemblies that pass the laws, first moving them about, then dissolving them, finally preventing them from being formed at all, thus opening the community to the threat of chaos from within and without. Then he prevents the immigration of fresh populations to make new laws, and for whom new laws might be made. Finally he unravels 'the law' itself, in the form of the guardians of the law, the judiciary – first by preventing their appointment, and then (most serious of all) by undermining their independence.

This completes the indictment of what might be called the king's passive assault on civilized order in America. Thus far the catalogue of complaints has dealt with what he has 'refused', 'forbidden', 'suspended', 'dissolved', 'obstructed' and 'endeavoured to prevent' – as it were, the things he has not done that he ought to have done. But Pope added an important note to Book I of *The Dunciad* to remind the reader that dullness is not just a negative quality:

> I wonder the learned Scriblerus has omitted to advertise the reader, at the opening of this poem, that dullness here is not to be taken contractedly for mere stupidity, but in the enlarged sense of the word, for all slowness of apprehension, shortness of sight, or imperfect sense of things. It includes . . . labour, industry, and some degree of activity and boldness: a ruling principle not inert, but turning topsy-turvy the understanding, and inducing an anarchy or confused state of mind. (I, 15n)

So the Declaration also indicts the king for what he has 'erected', 'excited' and 'combined with others' to do to create the confusion of 'arbitrary government', violent attacks by the Indians and open warfare between fraternal nations. Now his resistance to beneficent innovation gives way to malignant productivity. As within the negative list, the positive abuses are graduated according to seriousness. The difference is that, being active, aggressive assaults on American order, they proceed from outside inwards, from the remote to the immediate. At first the king operates from afar, creating 'swarms' of officers to consume the time, patience and physical substance of the colonists. Then he sends armies to displace them from their homes and supplant their government with instruments of his arbitrary will. Finally exploding in frenetic activity, he causes myriad laws to be passed in London to the direct harm of the colonies. Several of the paragraphs beginning with 'For . . .' express negative action, like 'cutting off', 'depriving', 'taking away' and 'suspending', but all are subsumed under the decidedly active 'combined with others to subject us' and 'giving his assent to their acts of pretended legislation'. For this is not good law prevented, but bad law propagated to negative ends.*

At the end, the king moves in on America, as it were in his physical presence (though his personal body remained safely at home), plundering first the American seas, then coasts, and finally towns (even this subset moves the action inward, step by step, to the civilized centre). Having destroyed property he takes life. But if these are the accidents of armed conflict, he is also cruel by intention. Whereas men must expect to fight other men in any war, the king sets, not one country against another, but friend against friend, brother against brother. Finally, in case the frontal assault should prove ineffectual, he stirs up revolt and prepares to 'bring on' the Indians to perform the bloody work behind the lines.

The 'domestic insurrections' and the mention of the Indians refer, respectively, to the threat of Lord Dunmore in 1775 to free and arm the black slaves 'and reduce the city of Williamsburg to ashes' if he was harmed by the Virginia colonists, and to several British attempts to form alliances with the Indians against the settlers in the same year (see Dumbauld, 146–7). Thomas Jefferson's rough draft of the Declaration divided these accusations into two paragraphs, each beginning with 'He . . .', and added a third (the last of his list of grievances) attacking the slave trade:

> He has waged cruel war against human nature itself, violating it's [sic] most sacred rights of life and liberty in the persons of a distant people who never offended him, captivating and carrying them into slavery in another hemisphere or to incur miserable death in their transportation thither. . . . And that this assemblage of horrors might want no fact of distinguished die, he is now exciting those very people to rise in arms among us . . . thus paying off former crimes

---

* Dumbauld (137) explains the paragraph on the 'neighbouring Province' as referring to the Quebec Act of 1774, which 'provided that the boundaries of Quebec, as proclaimed in 1763, should be extended to include all the country west of the Alleghenies and south to the Ohio River. This would hamper westward migration, and curtail the territory governed by the common law under free institutions, while extending the area where Roman law would prevail.'

committed against the liberties of one people, with crimes which he urges them to commit against the lives of another.

(See Wills, 1978, 377, or Ginsberg, 1967, 264)

In deleting this paragraph, Congress nevertheless retained a ghost of the charge and (more to the point) kept something of Jefferson's culmination in the king's general assault on nature. To the antipenultimate paragraph they added 'scarcely parallel in the most barbarous ages' and in what was now the final clause, they allowed to stand 'an undistinguished destruction of all ages, sexes and conditions'. This retains the effect of bringing the grievances to a climax, because although it refers to the alleged conditions of Indian warfare, it also widens the king's depravity in space and time ('all ages', of course, can also suggest all times) and, through the adjective 'undistinguished' (that is, both 'indistinct' and 'confused'), dramatizes his tendency to 'induc[e] an anarchy or confused state of mind'. The Dunce has undone all, first to barbarism and now to the primal chaos.

The point of all this is not to suggest *The Dunciad* as a source of the Declaration, though Jefferson certainly read Pope and recommended his nephew to read him 'in order to form your style in your own language' (letter to Peter Carr, 19 August 1785, ed. Koch and Peden, 1944, 375), but to show the extent to which the document disposed its argument according to the conventions of eighteenth-century satire. At first sight, this seems a strange context for a revolutionary paper. Augustan satire, after all, was almost invariably conservative. From an implied preference for unity of polity and belief, it attacked the increasing diversity of opinions, sects, political parties (and the texts by which they were promulgated) which its authors so feared and deplored in England after 1688. A recurrent image for all this confusion was a swarm of insects – tiny, many and noisome. As the momentum of disintegration builds in Book IV of *The Dunciad*, so the references to insects accumulate: 'The buzzing Bees . . . The gath'ring number as it moves along, / Involves a vast involuntary throng' (IV, 80–2); 'Then thick as Locusts black'ning all the ground, / A tribe, with weeds and shells fantastic crown'd' (IV, 397–8).

But according to the Declaration, it is the very symbol and fact of the unitary state, the king, who destroys order and disseminates dissension with his 'multitude of new offices' and 'swarms of officers'. This reversal of the reader's expectation is a neat turn in what might have been taken, after all, as the most factious paper imaginable – arguing as it does, not for a new faith or party, but for a new *country* to be split off from the old. Yet this intertextual reference to Augustan satire is the rhetorical equivalent of the Declaration's appeal to natural law. For all the exaggeration of 'plundered' and 'ravaged' (even the 'swarm' amounted to only thirty or forty customs officers), the rhetoric of the Declaration takes the argument over the heads of the immediate antagonists into the disinterested criteria of order and chaos.

In its appeal to an order above the quotidian, the Declaration strikes yet another kind of balance. In all the literature on the document some-one must surely have pointed out (though I have not discovered where) that the list of grievances against the king is arranged numerologically, in groups of nine, or three times the numinous number of three com-mon to most 'traditionary' systems of religion, philosophy and cos-mology. There are nine 'passive' and nine 'active' grievances, and nine sub-paragraphs under the fourth of the 'active' headings. Indeed some, though not many, of the paragraphs beginning with 'He . . .' are grouped by subject in triads. Thus the first three deal with laws and the second three with legislatures, and paragraphs six, seven and eight of the 'active' transgressions express the effects of the war. It might be a coincidence, of course, though a series comprising three sets of three times three expressions does not, at first sight, look accidental. Another possibility is that Congress discerned the potential of a numerological system in Jefferson's rough draft and made its alterations at least partly in order to perfect this emergent form. Perhaps this is another reason for the reduction of Jefferson's grievances in the rough draft from twenty (nine 'passive' and eleven 'active') to eighteen. Admittedly the deletion of Jefferson's slave-trade clause is a matter of considerable substance (usually attributed to the sensitivity of the Virginia colonists), but the combination of his two paragraphs relating to the incitement of slave revolts and attempted alliance with the Indians seems to proceed from a concern more for form than content.

In any case redundant clauses were allowed to stand. The paragraph about preventing immigration might well have been subsumed under paragraphs one or two, since it instances a refusal to 'assent to laws' and to pass others 'of immediate and pressing importance'. 'Active' para-graph four, sub-paragraph five ('suspending our own legislatures') repeats the accusation (paragraph five on the 'passive' list) that 'He has dissolved representative houses repeatedly'.

On the matter of the Declaration's philosophical and legal context there is much written but little (surprisingly enough, even in its own time) agreed. What *is* agreed is that the document is chiefly the work of Thomas Jefferson, as amended by Franklin, John Adams and other delegates to the second Continental Congress; that it draws on earlier statements of rights in various English and American confrontations with the executive power going back to Magna Carta; and that its immediate argument is grounded in the eighteenth-century premise of natural rights common to all mankind.

Carl Becker traced the history of the idea of natural rights to Newton and Locke. Newton's effect on his age, says Becker (1922, 41), was similar to Darwin's on his: that is, he was concerned to deduce rules about the physical operations of nature from his particular observations and experiments, but his intellectual contemporaries were quick to draw analogies with 'nature' in less verifiable processes such as human 'nature', and the 'nature' of society and political institutions. In other words, Newton's prestige imparted a sense of objectivity and candour to issues that had been shrouded in the mystery of theological assertion and counter-assertion based on *a priori* assumptions. As for Locke, his *Essay Concerning Human Understanding* (1690) attacked the unverifiable 'truth' of Scripture and innate ideas in favour of knowledge accumulated through experience in the minds of individual men. As Becker summarizes the argument:

> God has not revealed the truth that is necessary for man's guidance, once for all, in holy writ, or stamped upon the minds of all men certain intuitively perceived intellectual and moral ideas which correspond to the truth so revealed; on the contrary, all the ideas we can have come from experience, are the result of the sensations that flow in upon us from the natural and social world without, and of the operations of the reflecting mind upon these sensations; from which it follows that man . . . is part and parcel of the world in which he lives, intimately and irrevocably allied to that Universal Order which is at once the work and will of God. (56)

Up to a point, the Declaration can indeed be glossed according to Locke. The notion of a 'self-evident' truth, for instance, comes from Locke's attempt to find a middle term between (on the one hand) the idea of 'innate principles', or 'characters, as it were stamped upon the mind of man', which he thought the cause of a great deal of intellectual bullying throughout the ages, and (on the other) his idea of knowledge as built up through the imprint of experience properly sorted and associated in the mind. For if the philosophy of innate ideas was self-contradictory ('to imprint anything on the mind without the mind's perceiving it, seems to me hardly intelligible', he wrote in Book I, Chapter ii of the *Essay*), there were maxims or axioms, like those in Euclidean geometry such as 'the whole is greater than one of its parts', to the demonstration of which no amount of experiment would be relevant but which were still useful and valid to anyone knowing the meaning of the related terms. These Locke called 'self-evident propositions' (*Essay*, Book IV, Chapter vi).

One of these self-evident truths was the principle that 'all men were created equal'. 'There [is] nothing more evident', wrote Locke in his *Treatise on Civil Government* (1689, Chapter II, paragraph 4), 'than that creatures of the same species and rank, promiscuously born to all the same advantages of nature, and the use of the same faculties, should also be equal one amongst another without subordination or subjection'. What made the proposition 'self-evident' was the accepted use of terms like 'species' (that it was a category including 'man', for example) and 'nature' (as applied to the physical attributes of the world); once you agreed on the meaning of the terms, you could not, Locke felt, escape the conclusion.

That argument might serve as a philosophical basis for the statement that 'We hold these truths to be self-evident, that all men are created equal', but where Lockeian ideas appear in the Declaration, they seem to have undergone a metamorphosis. The best-known example is the alteration from Locke's triad of natural rights, as stated in *Civil Government* (Chapter IX, paragraph 123) of 'lives, liberties and estates, which I call by the general name, property' to the Declaration's 'life, liberty, and the pursuit of happiness'. As late as 1774 the First Continental Congress had issued a Declaration of Rights ennumerated as 'life, liberty and property'; so the Declaration of 1776 must surely have been striking out in a new direction. Vernon Parrington (1927, 350) certainly thought so: 'in Jefferson's hands the English doctrine was given a revolutionary shift. The substitution of "pursuit of happiness" for "property" marks a complete break with the Whiggish doctrine of property rights that Locke had bequeathed to the English middle class . . . and it was this substitution that gave to the document the note of idealism which was to make its appeal so perennially human and vital.'

Yet there was nothing new about the idea of the pursuit of happiness; Wills (240–3), following Ganter (1936) locates it in Pope, Johnson, Laurence Sterne and Locke himself, where (in Book II, Chapter xxi of the *Essay*) 'pursuit' is given the sense of an inevitable natural force, like magnetism or gravitation. On the other hand, where the Declaration seems to follow Locke almost to the letter, it may be a long way from him in spirit. Recent commentators on the Declaration, like Morton White (1978) and especially Wills, have leaned toward another source for the ideas in the paper, the Scottish-enlightenment philosophy of the 'moral sense' as advanced by Francis Hutcheson, Thomas Reid and Henry Home, Lord Kames. This intellectual context might impart a quite different meaning to a phrase used also by English rationalists like Locke. For example, when Jefferson wrote Henry Lee in 1825 that he wrote the Declaration 'to place before mankind the common sense of the subject' (ed. Ford, 1899, x, 343), did he mean by 'common sense' the 'plain truth' (as Paine's first title had it) accessible to all rational men, or a common intuition of the good *not* accessible to reason? Or, to borrow from another famous title, did he mean 'sense' or 'sensibility'?

The same kind of question might be raised over 'self-evident'. Locke's *Essays on the Laws of Nature*, written shortly after 1660, suggests that only a minority of people can be expected to perceive self-evident truths; others may be too dull, never trained, or too depraved to think. 'Not the majority of people should be consulted but those who are more rational and perceptive than the rest' (Chapter I, ed. and tr. von Leyden, 1954, 115). As to moral reasoning, there seem few universal values throughout the world in history: 'there is almost no vice, no infringement of natural law, no moral wrong, which anyone who consults the history of the world and observes the affairs of men will not readily perceive to have been not only privately committed somewhere on earth, but also approved by public authority and custom' (Chapter v, 167).

But the common-sense philosopher Thomas Reid thought that 'moral truth', at least, could be intuited by every normal adult, even if he did not possess the training to generalize from the impulse: 'Moral truths, therefore, may be divided into two classes, to wit: such as are self-evident to every man whose understanding and moral faculty are ripe, and such as are deduced by reasoning from those that are self-evident' (cited Wills, 181). Reid's 'egalitarian epistemology' was therefore much more optimistic than Locke's, and it might account for what Wills (185) calls 'one of Jefferson's most celebrated assertions: "State a moral case to a ploughman and a professor. The former will decide it as well and often better than the latter, because he has not been led astray by artificial rules".'

In addition, there are expressions in the Declaration that yield little or no sense without recourse to the philosophy of the Scottish enlightenment. What, for instance, is meant by 'unalienable' rights? Both White and Wills trace the idea to Francis Hutcheson, who distinguished, in his *An Inquiry into the Original of our Ideas of Beauty and Virtue* (1725), between alienable and unalienable rights. By this he meant, not those rights that could, or could not be taken from us, but those we could, or could not give away, sell or otherwise transfer to another owner. Hutcheson based his distinction, not as a philosopher of the social contract (say, Hobbes or Locke) might have done, on a trade-off between the rights an individual kept for himself and those he allowed the state to assume, but on the individual's feelings of social obligation, as prompted by the overriding moral sense. The question was not, what must I keep to retain my integrity? but, what must I keep to retain my ability to do good? The answer was, life and liberty. These were the unalienable rights. So Wills summarizes the idea (217), 'Life and liberty are the principal rights in Hutcheson's scheme of things. They are also the principal duties. . . . Men have a duty to stay alive and to stay free in their thoughts and actions. Duty is simply one's right considered from another aspect.'

This explains why 'property' was dropped from the triad of rights mentioned as unalienable in the Declaration. In the first place, property clearly was alienable; in fact an individual in a capitalist system of ownership might claim the right precisely to alienate his property. Secondly, property was a condition of the social contract – necessary and defensible, no doubt, but not grounded in nature. Hutcheson called the right to retain property 'adventitious', not unalienable – that is, literally, coming from abroad, or added from without, not essentially inherent (*OED*).

Reference to the Scottish enlightenment certainly makes better sense of the Declaration than an appeal exclusively to Locke and Newton, and it also goes a long way towards harmonizing the document with Jefferson's work and writing in other spheres of his multifarious activities. But one must not suppose that even the best recent books have unlocked a code available to Jefferson's contemporaries; those who read the Declaration in 1776 without the benefit of modern scholarship seem to have been as confused as everyone else over the last 200 years. For not even the promptings of the adversarial posture can account for the widespread contemporary confusion (at least among the learned) over the meaning and worth of the document, or even as to whether its ideas were revolutionary or hackneyed. 'From the date of its original publication down to the present moment [wrote Moses Coit Tyler in his two-volume *The Literary History of the American Revolution* (1897, I, 499)] it has been attacked again and again, either in anger or in contempt, by friends as well as by enemies of the American Revolution, by liberals in politics as well as by conservatives. It has been censured for its substance, it has been censured for its form . . . for its audacious novelties and paradoxes, for its total lack of all novelty . . . even for its downright plagiarisms.'

Many of these objections were made to points of substance in the Declaration's list of grievances. Thus John Lind, a propagandist for the North administration, wondered how the king could stand accused of 'taking away our charters' when the charters themselves were nothing more than acts repealing earlier charters (*An Answer to the Declaration of the American Congress*, 1776, 82, cited Dumbauld, 138). Thomas Hutchinson, the brilliant but unpopular last royal civilian governor of the Massachusetts Bay Colony, challenged the description of the king as 'a tyrant . . . unfit to be the ruler of a free people': 'Have these men given an instance of any one act in which the king has exceeded the just powers of the crown as limited by the English constitution?' (*Strictures upon the Declaration of the Congress at Philadelphia . . ., 1776*, cited Dumbauld, 148). Both Lind and Hutchinson agreed in dismissing the complaint that the king had 'combined with others to subject us to a jurisdiction foreign to our constitution . . . giving his assent to their acts of pretended legislation'. Who were these 'others', they responded, but the Lords and Commons of the British Parliament (cited Dumbauld, 120).

But it was the preamble of the Declaration, the philosophical generalizations with which it began, that drew the heaviest fire. How can someone already living also claim the *right* to life? asked an anonymous article in the *Scots Magazine* for August 1776 (see Ginsberg, 7). Perhaps, suggested Lind helpfully, they meant 'the right to *enjoy* life'* (Ginsberg, 10). American critics, too, got in on the act. Later, but no less laboured was the contribution to Joseph Dennie's conservative *Port Folio*, published in Philadelphia from 1801 to 1827: 'No man ever before considered *life* as a *right*, still less as an *unalienable* right. Life is a state of being, without which a man has no rights, and when that state is changed, when the man is dead, his rights are gone. He has indeed,

---

* This was a shrewd guess; Jefferson's rough draft of the Declaration read 'the preservation of life, and liberty, and the pursuit of happiness'.

so long as he lives, a right to defend his life; and he has also a right to defend his property, his parents, his wife, his children, his country' (*Port Folio*, 1801, 99).

Then there was liberty. All law is a restraint of liberty, said the critics, so you cannot have the one without a measure of the other. Thus Hutchinson: 'Every restraint which men are laid under by a state or government, is a privation of part of their natural rights' (cited Dumbauld, 61). And thus the *Port Folio*: 'the first question is, to what liberty? Is it the liberty of a soldier in the French army, of a sailor in the British fleet, of a German boor, or a Mohawk Indian? If the last was in contemplation, will it not follow, that all legal restraint is tyranny?' (99) But a positive riot of heavy-handed humour exploded over the claim that all men were created equal. Does this mean equal in size, asked the *Scots Magazine*, or in strength, intelligence, accomplishments? 'Every ploughman knows that they are not created equal in any of these' (Ginsberg, 6). Can they really be suggesting, asked Lind (cited White, 75–6), that 'a child, at the moment of his birth, has the same quantity of *natural* power as the parent, the same quantity of *political* power as the magistrate?' 'It is true [rejoined the *Port Folio*] that [men] are all equally born, except those who are brought forth by the Caesarian operation, but that (when born) they are equal to each other is a matter not so clear. Setting aside the difference between a healthy and an unhealthy, a strong and a weak child, it seems somewhat questionable whether (in Virginia) a black child be equal to a white child.'

When the American revolutionists claimed that all men are created equal they were twitching a line of legal reasoning that ran through Locke all the way back to the Roman concept of the *jus naturale*. Dumbauld (56n) cites and translates a passage from the jurist Ulpian in Justinian's Digest that answers the *Port Folio* over one and a half millennia before that paper's critic strained his wit over the slave's case: 'In so far as pertains to civil law, slaves are considered as being nonentities; but it is not so by natural law, since, in so far as pertains to natural law, all men are equal.' Locke himself – as was well known to every reader of *Civil Government* – qualified his claim to man's equality under the law of nature, to pre-empt the obvious objection still thought valid by the Declaration's critics a century later: 'Though I have said above, chap. II, "that all men by nature are equal," I cannot be supposed to understand all sorts of equality: age or virtue may give men a just precedency; excellency of parts and merit may place others above the common level . . . the equality I there spoke of . . . [is] that equal right, that every man hath, to his natural freedom, without being subjected to the will or authority of any other man' (*Civil Government*, Chapter VI, paragraph 54).

It seems, therefore, that whatever its effect on the common man, the Declaration of Independence could not – or would not – be decoded by its more educated contemporary critics as a philosophical statement. It did not activate any single line of thought already laid down in their – or their readers' – experience. Since this problem has also been a feature of later analysis, it seems at least worth considering whether the Declaration would not be more accurately described as something of a synthesis of contemporary ideas. After all, a well-known feature of Jefferson's mental processes was his search for the common thread in diverse traditions of thought and belief. His Christianity, for example, was founded on admiration for Jesus as a reformer who had stripped away the mystery and literalism of the Scribes and Pharisees to reveal the universal truths of human nature which had always lain beneath them. As Daniel Boorstin (1948) summarizes his ideas, Jefferson might almost have seen himself in Christ's image:

> Jesus had been a great 'philosopher' – in the strict Jeffersonian sense. He was not a system builder, but a reformer . . . he corrected some of the crude Jewish ideas of the attributes of God; he improved the moral doctrines of the ancients regarding kindred and friends, and went beyond these to a universal philanthropy. . . . Jesus' ethics were thus eclectic and progressive, combining the best tenets of his predecessors, and improving them by bold reforms.   (157–8)

Indeed Jefferson carried the synthesizing process further when he made his 'wee-little book [as he called it in a letter written in 1816 to the secretary of the Continental Congress, Charles Thompson] which I call the Philosophy of Jesus; it is a paradigma of His doctrines, made by cutting the texts out of the book, in a certain order of time or subject. . . . And I wish I could subjoin a translation of Gosindi's Syntagma of the Doctrines of Epicurus [another such epitome], which, notwithstanding the calumnies of the Stoics and caricatures of Cicero, is the most rational system remaining of the philosophy of the ancients' (ed. Lipscomb and Bergh, 1903–4, XIV, 386).

This habit of synthesis was characteristic of American thought about the cultural premises of a nation that had made itself new. Cut off from 'the tradition' of the mother country, Americans have felt free, in their religion, their education system and their literature, to select the best of what many countries and ages had to offer – to make anthologies, as it were, of world culture. Was the Declaration the first of such anthologies? Does it, too, epitomize various branches of enlightenment philosophy without adhering ideologically to any one school of thought?

The question can first be considered in the context of the debate between the colonies and the metropolis leading up to the *act* which severed the two. It is an enormously complicated subject, but it can be reduced to this issue: what were the rights and duties of a citizen of a British colony? Were they the same as those of someone living at home, as set out in state papers from Magna Carta down to the Bill of Rights of 1689? Or were they weakened by practical disadvantages such as the transatlantic distance and the lack of American representation in Parliament? Or were they equal but separate – perhaps even strengthened – by virtue of the several charters granted the colonial companies, and of the local assemblies that had arisen since the early seventeenth century to deal with pressing matters close at hand?

In his *The Rights of the Colonies Examined* (1764), the governor of Rhode Island, Stephen Hopkins, claimed that all colonies in ancient as well as modern times had enjoyed as much freedom as the mother state. But the issue was really too novel for such an appeal to precedent. Samuel Adams, though a fierce opponent of British moves to tax the colonies and the guiding spirit of the Boston Tea Party, tried to work out a mediating formula in which, as he said in a letter in 1769 (cited Becker, 98–9), the colonies would be 'subordinate' but not 'subject' to Parliament. The distinction was not clear to Benjamin Franklin, who wrote in 1768, 'I know not what the Boston people mean by the "subordination" they acknowledge in their Assembly to Parliament, while they deny its power to make laws over them. . . . The more I have thought and read on the subject, the more I find . . . that no middle ground can be well maintained. . . . Parliament has a power to make *all* laws for us, or . . . it has a power to make *no laws* for us; and I think the arguments for the latter more numerous and weighty, than those for the former' (cited Becker, 101–2).

When it came to particular issues, the debate grew even more confusing. Did Parliament have the power to tax the colonies? Not as long as we are unrepresented in Parliament, said the Americans. Ah, but you are represented there, said the MP and commissioner to the Board of Trade Soame Jenyns, in a widely circulated pamphlet published in 1765 – at least as much as the citizens of Birmingham and Manchester (who, of course, were quite unrepresented in the House of Commons until the

Reform Bill of 1831). In any case the Americans had been paying a heavy duty on rum, sugar and molasses imported from non-British dependencies since 1733; why were they now (in 1765) objecting to the Stamp Tax on legal documents, newspapers and playing cards? Oh, those are *external* taxes, said the Americans; Parliament has the right to levy external taxes on the colonies, but not internal ones. George Grenville, Chancellor of the Exchequer, told the House of Commons (14 January 1766) that he did not understand the distinction, but what he did understand was that 'this kingdom has the sovereign, the supreme legislative power over America . . . and taxation is a part of that sovereign power' (see Beloff, 1960, 97–8).

The immediate problem, then, was taxation, and the more general issue was whether the rights and obligations of the Americans were focused on Parliament or the colonial assemblies. It was not a question on which the precedents set by the British constitution offered a clear answer. Besides, the colonists were losing the legal debate. In an impasse like this the best tactic is a knight's move into a different category – say, into the implications of membership, not of the British Empire but of the human race. Hence the American recourse to the natural law.

This point must be made absolutely clear: the colonists both believed in the natural law and used it as an argumentative tactic. The need to do both had been growing as the inevitable contradictions had become manifest between the metropolitan and colonial legislative bodies. The conflict had been sharpened by increased meddling from London after the Restoration, and not really much dulled after the Glorious Revolution. Genuine antitheses tend to produce syntheses. The perspective of distance from the centre of empire began to give the colonists a sense of alternative procedures of government, and the comparison between Parliament and the colonial Assemblies (as comparisons often do) began to put the Americans in mind of the imperfections of both, and of the possibility of a higher order than the prerogative of any particular legislative body.

Though derived from Whig doctrine, the idea of a fundamental law to which even Parliament was subject is seen by one influential British historian of government as characteristically American. Max Beloff (24–6, 45–69) cites the speeches and pamphlets of James Otis dating from 1761 to show that the idea 'was for some time indeed the major element in political thinking on the American side' of the debate leading up to the Revolution (24–5). But that it was also a tactic for escaping from a tight corner must not be doubted. Becker quotes revealingly from a passage in John Adams's *Autobiography* about the discussions in the first Continental Congress leading to the Declaration of Rights of 1774. Two points, according to Adams, occupied the Congress above all others. The first was 'Whether we should recur to the law of nature, as well as to the British Constitution, and our American charters and grants. Mr Galloway and Mr Duane were for excluding the law of nature. I was very strenuous for retaining and insisting on it, as a resource to which we might be driven by Parliament much sooner than we were aware' (cited Becker, 119–20).

Adams's discussion of the second point suggests something of the mood of the meeting:

> After several days deliberation, we agreed upon all the articles excepting one, and that was the authority of Parliament, which was indeed the essence of the whole controversy; some were for a flat denial of all authority; others for denying the power of taxation only; some for denying internal, but admitting external, taxation. After a multitude of motions had been made, discussed, negatived, it seemed as if we should never agree upon anything.　　　　　　　(ibid.)

The feeling communicated here is clearly one of frustration, of patience running out. The longer the Americans stayed on the ground of constitutional legalism, the more firmly Parliament would fence them in with quotations from Blackstone or references to constitutional precedent. And the longer the colonists fussed over terminological quibbles or other partial solutions to the tax issue, the more they would obscure their primary impulse not to pay taxes of any description to London. The time had come to be clear. So, the Declaration of 1774 reserved the right of American taxation exclusively to the 'several provincial legislatures . . . subject only to the negative [or veto] of their sovereign', and it claimed every possible authority for the Declaration – 'the immutable laws of nature, the principles of the English constitution, and the several charters or compacts [of the colonies]'. This touches all the bases. And it was from this mood of exasperation, and this impulse to synthesize an argument from the various elements available, that the Declaration of Independence would take its start.

The two years between the Declaration of 1774 and the Declaration of Independence witnessed the crucial events of the Revolution: the skirmishes at Lexington and Concord, Ethan Allen's capture of Fort Ticonderoga, the Battle of Bunker Hill. In May 1775 the second

Continental Congress established the Continental Army and appointed George Washington commander-in-chief of the American forces. On 23 August the king, rejecting a final petition by Congress desiring to maintain union with Great Britain but upon 'terms of just and equal liberty', proclaimed the colonies in 'open and avowed rebellion'. Two months later he opened Parliament with a speech repeating the charge and accused the Americans of seeking to establish 'an independent empire'.

So the Declaration of Independence could not open with an appeal to the British constitution. Now the act of synthesis was not an *omnium gatherum* of various rights of which the Americans could be assured as British subjects, but an elaboration of the rights of humanity under the natural law as interpreted under several branches of eighteenth-century philosophy. The point was precisely not to be specific – not to appeal (say) to Lockeians as opposed to Hutchesonians – and the formulations 'certain unalienable rights', and 'among these are . . .' were surely meant to be inclusive. Having moved its argument to the more general category, the Congress was not about to engage in ideological dispute with philosophers about what *kind* of natural rights they had in mind. This was indeed the 'common sense of the subject', but also in that it was the common denominator of any expression of the natural law that would support its sonorous general propositions: 'Governments are instituted among men', 'whenever any form of government becomes destructive of these ends', 'Prudence . . . will dictate.'

The Declaration was synthetic also in its complaints against the king. Here it imitated – without being – two kinds of legal and constitutional document, the declaration and the humble petition. A declaration can be any kind of explanation, but in diplomatic or legal procedures it becomes an instrumental document, as when a country declares war or the plaintiff involves the defendant in a civil suit by making a declaration of his case. In constitutional confrontations both declarations and petitions commonly affirmed rights and grievances (the rights might be listed separately or implied in the grievances); the difference was that the former announced or effected the remedy, while the latter appealed for redress to a superior body – say, either house of Parliament or the monarch himself.

Thus, the English Bill of Rights, titled An Act Declaring the Rights and Liberties of the Subject and Settling the Succession of the Crown, accused James II (among other things) of attempting 'to subvert and extirpate the Protestant religion' by the 'suspending of laws and the execution of laws', of 'levying money for and to the use of the Crown', and 'raising and keeping a standing army . . . in time of peace' – all without the consent of Parliament. As 'the only means for obtaining a full redress and remedy' for these and other grievances, it resolved 'that William and Mary, prince and princess of Orange, be and be declared king and queen of England, France and Ireland and the dominions thereunto belonging'.

One of the rights declared in the English Bill of Rights was that of petition. Humble petitions were not instruments of the law, though the important Petition of Right (1628), in which Parliament addressed Charles I with a statement of the rights and liberties of the people, would come to have the force of law in time. Petitioners shifted the burden of redress to the executive to whom the appeal was made, thus implying their allegiance to it. Almost until the final break with London the American colonists thought of themselves as petitioners – no doubt partly for tactical reasons but also out of a genuine reluctance to sever themselves from the British Empire.

Congress continued to petition the king through 1775. Indeed the entire *raison d'être* of the first Congress, as Wills argues convincingly (57–64), was to petition for redress. The Declaration of 1774, though it enacted the agreement between the colonies not to trade with the mother country, also reiterated the right to petition and resolved 'to prepare a loyal address to his Majesty'. Thus the Declaration was not the end of the business of Congress in 1774, but part of the process by which the humble petition to the king could be uttered. Even Jefferson's 'A Summary View of the Rights of British America', considered too radical by the Virginia delegation to the first Congress for whom it was intended as a brief, ended with a humble-sounding appeal to the king's better nature, allowing him the excuse (always tactful in such appeals) that he had been misled by evil counsellors: 'Open your breast, Sire, to liberal and expanded thought. Let not the name of George the Third, be a blot on the page of history. You are surrounded by British counsellors, but remember that they are parties. . . . It behooves you, therefore, to think and act for yourself and your people' (Koch and Peden, 310).

But once the king had proclaimed the Americans in a state of rebellion and the colonists had severed their allegiance to the Crown, a petition was no more possible than the recourse to rights under the British constitution. The Declaration of Independence made no plea to the king, now disallowed even the power of veto and referred to throughout the document in the third person; nor did it address Parliament. The implied reader was now an open-minded, disinterested member of the human race — possibly in England, certainly in another country, probably in times to come. 'The Declaration of Independence announced the failure of reform by petition,' says Wills (65). And it did so by recapitulating earlier texts in the struggle for independence, as though to remind its readers of the long series of declarations, petitions, pamphlets, debates in Parliament and Congress — all of which had come to nothing. The rhetorical stance was to recall these earlier texts without becoming just another one of them (the Declaration, remember, asked for nothing and enacted nothing) in order both to dramatize the colonists' patience in pursuing all the constitutional remedies and also to emphasize that the constitutional process had run its course.

To recapitulate a text, though, is not simply to repeat or recall it. Recapitulation summarizes headings in order to epitomize or bring out the inherent meaning of a discourse. The theological sense of the word (sometimes expressed in the exact Greek equivalent, *anakephalaiosis*, or 'again-head-ship') expresses the role of Christ as fulfilment or perfection of the various fragmentary statements of God's Word in the Old Testament. The Declaration (if one dare say so of a paper that has been so often described as a document of the Enlightenment) has at least this in common with the Gospels: that it gives a new shape to, or uncovers a latent structure in, the texts on which it draws — re-forms them, in fact.

By contrast to the Declaration, the grievances in earlier bills of rights exhibit little concern for rhetorical accumulation, let alone numerological tidiness. The Resolutions of the first Continental Congress which formed the Declaration of 1774 are much more businesslike; using the proper notation, they cite fourteen Acts of Parliament, beginning with '4 Geo.3.ch.15', which they claim violate the colonists' rights. The English Bill of Rights lists thirteen specific grievances against James II. As befits a Bill which is also an Act, it too proceeds purposefully with exact legal terminology and little drama. But the Declaration of Independence is qualitatively distinct from these earlier documents. Where they are specific as to rights under the constitution and the natural law, the Declaration is general. Where the Declaration is particular as to grievances, it arranges those particulars so that the words on the page take on a power only partly derived from the events to which they refer. If the Declaration of Independence draws on these and other earlier documents of right and petition, it also rounds them off, perfects and (in both the printer's sense and the theological use of the term) justifies them. It is pertinent to call the Declaration the gospel of the American nation. It is the American gospel not only in the loose sense of something to be revered and to which (occasional) reference might be made in the course of an argument, but also in that it fulfilled all the fragmentary wisdom 'spake by the prophets', put an end to debate, compromise and imperfect accommodation to the truth. The Declaration of Independence was the secular scripture for a country whose time had come.

References

Austin, J. L. (1962), *How to Do Things with Words*, Oxford: Clarendon Press.

Becker, Carl (1922), *The Declaration of Independence, a Study in the History of Political Ideas*, New York: Harcourt, Brace.

Beloff, Max (1960), *The Debate on the American Revolution, 1761–1783*, 2nd edn, London: Black.

Boorstin, Daniel (1948), *The Lost World of Thomas Jefferson*, New York: Henry Holt / Boston, Mass.: Beacon Press, 1960.

Dumbauld, Edward (1950), *The Declaration of Independence and What it Means Today*, Norman, Okla.: University of Oklahoma Press.

Ginsberg, Robert (1967), *A Casebook on the Declaration of Independence*, New York: Crowell.

Jefferson, Thomas (1899), *The Works*, ed. Paul Leicester Ford, 10 vols, New York and London: Putnam's.

Jefferson, Thomas (1903–4), *The Writings*, ed. Andrew Lipscomb and Albert Ellery Bergh, 20 vols, Washington.

Jefferson, Thomas (1944), *The Life and Selected Writings*, ed. Adrienne Koch and William Peden, New York: Modern Library.

Locke, John (1954), *Essays on the Law of Nature*, ed. and trans. W. von Leyden, Oxford: Clarendon Press.

Parrington, Vernon (1927), *Main Currents in American Thought; The Colonial Mind, 1620–1800*, New York: Harcourt, Brace.

Port Folio (1801), '[Letter to] Mr. Oldschool', *Port Folio*, 13 (I) (28 March 1801) 93–100.

Tyler, Moses Coit (1897), *The Literary History of the American Revolution, 1763–1783*, 2 vols, New York: Barnes & Noble (Facsimile Library, 1941).

White, Morton (1978), *The Philosophy of the American Revolution*, New York: Oxford University Press.

Wills, Garry (1978), *Inventing America; Jefferson's Declaration of Independence*, New York: Random House.

Further reading

TEXT

'A Declaration by the Representatives of the United States of America, in General Congress Assembled', Philadelphia: John Dunlap, 4 July 1776 (the 'Dunlap Broadside', or first public, official text of the Declaration, widely reproduced).

DOCUMENTS

Julian Boyd, *The Declaration of Independence; the Evolution of the Text as Shown in Facsimiles of Various Drafts by its Author, Thomas Jefferson*, Princeton, N.J.: Princeton University Press, 1945.

Andrew Browning (ed.), *English Historical Documents, vol. VII, 1660–1714*, London: Eyre & Spottiswoode, 1953 (for the English Bill of Rights, 1689).

Henry Steele Commager (ed.), *Documents of American History*, 9th edn, New York: Appleton-Century-Crofts, 2 vols, 1973 (for the Declaration of the first Continental Congress, 1774).

SECONDARY

Carl Becker, *The Declaration of Independence; a Study in the History of Political Ideas*, New York: Harcourt, Brace, 1922.

Edward Dumbauld, *The Declaration of Independence and What it Means Today*, Norman, Okla.: University of Oklahoma Press, 1950.

Garry Wills, *Inventing America; Jefferson's Declaration of Independence*, New York: Random House, 1978.

PART THREE

Retrospective Revolutions

7

Hector St John de Crèvecoeur (1735–1813)

My father left me three hundred and seventy-one acres of land, forty-seven of which are good timothy meadow, an excellent orchard, a good house, and a substantial barn. It is my duty to think how happy I am that he lived to build and to pay for all these improvements; what are the labours which I have to undergo, what are my fatigues when compared to his, who had everything to do, from the first tree he felled to the finishing of his house? Every year I kill from 1500 to 2000 weight of pork, 1200 of beef, half a dozen of good wethers in harvest: of fowls my wife has always a great stock; what can I wish more? My negroes are tolerably faithful and healthy; by a long series of industry and honest dealings, my father left behind him the name of a good man; I have but to tread his paths to be happy and a good man like him. I know enough of the law to regulate my little concerns with propriety, nor do I dread its power; these are the grand outlines of my situation, but as I can feel much more than I am able to express, I hardly know how to proceed.

When my first son was born, the whole train of my ideas was suddenly altered; never was there a charm that acted so quickly and powerfully; I ceased to ramble in imagination through the wide world; my excursions since have not exceeded the bounds of my farm, and all my principal pleasures are now centred within its scanty limits; but at the same time there is not an operation belonging to it in which I do not find some food for useful reflections. This is the reason, I suppose, that when you were here, you used, in your refined style, to denominate me the farmer of feelings; how rude must those feelings be in him who daily holds the axe or the plough, how much more refined on the contrary those of the European, whose mind is improved by education, example, books, and by every acquired advantage! Those feelings, however, I will delineate as well as I can, agreeably to your earnest request.

When I contemplate my wife, by my fireside, while she either spins, knits, darns, or suckles our child, I cannot describe the various emotions of love, of gratitude, of conscious pride, which thrill in my heart and often overflow in involuntary tears. I feel the necessity, the sweet pleasure, of acting my part, the part of an husband and father, with an attention and propriety which may entitle me to my good fortune. It is true these pleasing images vanish with the smoke of my pipe, but though they disappear from my mind, the impression they have made on my heart is indelible. When I play with the infant, my warm imagination runs forward and eagerly anticipates his future temper and constitution. I would willingly open the book of fate, and know in which page his destiny is delineated. Alas! where is the father who in those moments of paternal ecstasy can delineate one half of the thoughts which dilate his heart? I am sure I cannot; then again I fear for the health of those who are become so dear to me, and in their sicknesses I severely pay for the joys I experienced while they were well. Whenever I go abroad it is always involuntary. I never return home without feeling some pleasing emotion, which I often suppress as useless and foolish. The instant I enter on my own land, the bright idea of property, of exclusive right, of independence, exalt my mind. Precious soil, I say to myself, by what singular custom of law is it that thou wast made to constitute the riches of the freeholder? What should we American farmers be without the distinct possession of that soil? It feeds, it clothes us; from it we draw even a great exuberancy, our best meat, our richest drink; the very honey of our bees comes from this privileged spot. No wonder we should thus cherish its possession; no wonder that so many Europeans who have never been able to say that such portion of land was theirs cross the Atlantic to realise that happiness. This formerly rude soil has been converted by my father into a pleasant farm, and in return, it has established all our rights; on it is founded our rank, our freedom, our power as citizens, our importance as inhabitants of such a district. These images I must confess I always behold with pleasure, and extend them as far as my imagination can reach; for this is what may be called the true and the only philosophy of an American farmer.

Pray do not laugh in thus seeing an artless countryman tracing himself through the simple modifications of his life; remember that you have required it; therefore with candour, though with diffidence, I endeavour to follow the thread of my feelings, but I cannot tell you all. Often when I plough my low ground, I place my little boy on a chair which screws to the beam of the plough—its motion and that of the horses please him; he is perfectly happy and begins to chat. As I lean over the handle, various are the thoughts which crowd into my mind. I am now doing for him, I say, what my father formerly did for me; may God enable him to live that he may perform the same operations for the same purposes when I am worn out and old! I relieve his mother of some trouble while I have him with me; the odoriferous furrow exhilarates his spirits and seems to do the child a great deal of good, for he looks more blooming since I have adopted that practice; can more pleasure, more dignity, be added to that primary occupation? The father thus ploughing with his child, and to feed his family, is inferior only to the emperor of China ploughing as an example to his kingdom. In the evening, when I return home through my low grounds, I am astonished at the myriads of insects which I perceive dancing in the beams of the setting sun. I was before scarcely acquainted with their existence; they are so small that it is difficult to distinguish them; they are carefully improving this short evening space, not daring to expose themselves to the blaze of our meridian sun. I never see an egg brought on my table but I feel penetrated with the wonderful change it would have undergone but for my gluttony; it might have been a gentle, useful hen leading her chickens with a care and vigilance which speaks shame to many women. A cock perhaps, arrayed with the most majestic plumes, tender to its mate, bold, courageous, endowed with an astonishing instinct, with thoughts, with memory, and every distinguishing characteristic of the reason of man. I never see my trees drop their leaves and their fruit in the autumn, and bud again in the spring, without wonder; the sagacity of those animals which have long been the tenants of my farm astonish me; some of them seem to surpass even men in memory and sagacity. I could tell you singular instances of that kind. What, then, is this instinct which we so debase, and of which we are taught to entertain so diminutive an idea? My bees, above any other tenants of my farm, attract my attention and respect; I am astonished to see that nothing exists but what has its enemy; one species pursues and lives upon the other: unfortunately our king-birds are the destroyers of those industrious insects; but on the other hand, these birds preserve our fields from the depredation of crows which they pursue on the wing with great vigilance and astonishing dexterity.

Letters from an American Farmer (1782)

*   *   *

At first sight there seem to be few barriers to a reading of this passage. A simple American farmer, Farmer James, an uncultivated cultivator (he insists on his position as 'artless countryman' not only here but more elaborately in an introductory chapter) expresses the pleasure of possession: of his land, his son, 'his' wife, even his bees. America has freed him from the European feudal system; in the new world he is part of a growing class of happy, independent freeholders, improving his lot (in two senses) because it is his to enjoy and pass on to his wife and children. Thus contented and at ease, he is able to look around him, at every natural thing from the smallest insects to the largest governing forces which his economic status has allowed him to exploit, to comment on the universal laws of action and reaction, of predator and counter-predator – in short, of the 'natural' balance of things. The passage moves effortlessly – indeed, apparently 'artlessly' – from autobiography to general proposition. Little seems to trouble the surface. Granted, the boy's perch on the plough seems a bit precarious, and there is the anxiety, common to all family men of property, that illness or some other power of nature will lay waste to all he owns; but even these worries are part of that balanced scheme – another aspect of his prudential and productive responsibility.

Yet when *Letters from an American Farmer* first appeared in 1782, the reviews could not agree on what kind of discourse it was, or whether it represented the actual experiences of a real man. Samuel Ayscough (1783) attacked the *Letters* as a 'new species of forgery' designed to attract emigrants to America. The *Gentleman's Magazine* called it 'absurd and romantic'. An anonymous notice in the *European Magazine and London Review* (1782) said the style was too refined to be that of a real farmer, and suggested the book was the product of two authors: one who lived in and observed the American setting and another who wrote up his rough notes. The French, on the other hand, found the writing convincingly naive and untutored. The *Courier de l'Europe* (1783) said that if it were fiction, it would be agreeable fiction. Writing in the *Mercure de France*, Pierre-Louis Lacretelle claimed that Crèvecoeur was a natural poet who made up in fidelity to local detail whatever he lacked in training as a descriptive writer. (For a review of the contemporary criticism, see Cutting, 1976, 107 ff.)

The confusion is pardonable. Crèvecoeur *was* an American farmer, for a while, but he had been born in Caen in 1735, the son of a Norman petty nobleman. Educated by the Jesuits, he lived a year in England, served in the Canadian colonial militia as a surveyor and cartographer, was wounded when the English captured Quebec, then cashiered from the French forces in circumstances he kept hidden for the rest of his life. From Canada he went south to New York, where he worked as a surveyor and Indian trader, became a naturalized citizen, married a New England girl named Mehitable Tippet, and bought 120 acres of land in Orange County about ten miles south-east of what is now Middletown, New York. This was the farm he cleared and worked, where his three children were born, and which forms the setting for part of the *Letters*. But he enjoyed his peace for only five or six years. The Revolutionary War swept Orange County with raids from royalist guerrillas and their Indian allies, while local revolutionary committees used threats and coercion to keep the population loyal to the American cause. In an attempt to escape the turmoil, Crèvecoeur left Mehitable and the two younger children (again, the circumstances remain obscure), taking his elder son to New York City, where he was imprisoned briefly by the British as an American spy, then left for Dublin, London and finally France. In his absence his farm was burned by Indians, his wife died and his children were taken in by neighbours.

Crèvecoeur returned to France to retrieve his inheritance, both material and cultural. His experience as an adventurer and settler in America made him a diverting *ingénu* to the upper reaches of French society, and the English publication of the *Letters* in 1782 fixed his reputation as a literary figure. The Marquis de Turgot, brother of the Physiocrat economist, became his patron. Madame d'Houdetot, once Rousseau's lover, played Old Lady to his Babar, introducing him to d'Alembert, Friedrich-Melchior Grimm, and many others. Now considered something of an expert on America, Crèvecoeur was appointed French Consul in New York, Connecticut and New Jersey. His return to America gave him a chance to retrieve his two younger children. He produced a French version of the *Letters*, and then another, expanded with heightened expressions of the kind of 'sentiment' made so popular by the many French editions of Sterne's *A Sentimental Journey*. He returned to France in 1790, only to be overtaken by another revolution, from which he escaped to Germany during the Reign of Terror. Back in France from 1796, he wrote an ambitious, three-volume work of pseudo-travel he called *Le Voyage dans la haute Pennsylvanie et dans l'état de New York* (1801). He lived his last years with his daughter and her husband, an influential diplomat, and died in 1813.

Crèvecoeur's life, marked by shifts and flights from one role to another, therefore spanned three careers and, in a sense, three nationalities. He spent barely one tenth of his life as an American farmer. Even his name changed to suit the mask: from Michel-Guillaume-Jean de Crèvecoeur to the anglified J. Hector St John and to various permutations of these names. The first edition of the *Letters* gives the author's name as J. Hector St John, and is prefaced by a dedication to the Abbé Raynal (about whom more later) written as from 'Carlisle, in Pennsylvania'; so the author, whose first name begins with J., might be supposed the narrator, Farmer James. Only about the same proportion of the book as Crèvecoeur actually lived as a farmer is devoted to conditions on the narrator's farm. The rest consists of an essay (subsequently much anthologized and even reprinted as a separate pamphlet) called 'What is an American?', no fewer than five chapters on life on the islands off the Massachusetts coast, Nantucket and Martha's Vineyard, a traveller's description of conditions on the slaveholding plantations of South Carolina, an essay 'On Snakes; and on the Humming-bird', another account – supposedly written by a Russian traveller, 'Mr Iw—n Al—z', about his visit to the celebrated botanist John Bartram, and a final letter as from the book's original narrator-correspondent, Farmer James, expressing his distress at the danger posed by the Revolutionary War to his family and property, and declaring his intention (as Huck Finn would say) to 'light out' for a peaceful Indian settlement beyond the frontier.

So what kind of discourse is *Letters from an American Farmer* and what is it really about? Its contexts are as mixed as Crèvecoeur's life itself. To take the immediate American setting first, the word 'farmer' in the title announced the book as another of those plain comments on public events by honest men, like John Dickinson's attack on the Stamp Act, *Letters from a Farmer in Pennsylvania* (1768) and Richard Henry Lee's anti-federalist pamphlets 'Letters of the Federal Farmer' (1787–8). 'When Jefferson referred to himself as a farmer [writes Garry Wills, 366], he was not indulging in false modesty. "Letters of a Farmer" was a basic literary form in his time – the voice of an independent and reflective man, of the Country Party in England.'

But the 'letters' of the title could signal more fictional forms as well; American and European readers might have been put in mind of popular epistolary novels like Richardson's *Pamela* (1740) and *Clarissa* (1747–8), the French translations of which inspired Rousseau's *Julie, or the New Heloïse* (1761). More generally, imaginary voyages, whether epistolary, as with Montesquieu's *Persian Letters* (1721) or expressed in another pseudo-documentary form like a diary or a ship's log, as in *Robinson Crusoe*

(1719, three French editions by 1770), were also common vehicles for philosophical, sociological and economic speculation.

Sometimes the popular theme of sentiment so widespread in the epistolary novels — that is, the ideal of refined and tender emotion — was married to the travel fiction; the very title of Sterne's *A Sentimental Journey* (1768) proclaims the best-known example of the kind. A translation appeared in France in 1769 (to be followed by half a dozen reprints within fifteen years), where the book was admired, as was Crèvecoeur's *Letters*, for its beguiling formlessness (see Howes, 1974, 388–9).

So much for what might be called the generic context of *Letters from an American Farmer*. As for the intellectual setting, one might turn first to European accounts of real-life travels in America. Crèvecoeur treats at least three subjects regularly mentioned in these books: the whale industry in Nantucket, Quakerism in Nantucket and Pennsylvania, and (above all) southern slavery (see Philbrick, 1970, 42–55). The last of these topics was almost invariably condemned, the second treated to curious, sometimes amused debate for and against, and the first admired for its advanced technical and financial methods.

Secondly, there was the lively interest taken by European intellectuals in the polity of the Swiss Cantons, a counterpart of the republican theme advanced by propagandists of the American cause, like Paine and Franklin. The case for Swiss democracy had been set out in D'Alembert's article on Geneva in the great *Encyclopaedia* (VII, 1757), which praised the beauty of the city's setting, the vigour of its independent government, the simplicity of its church practice and tolerance of the clergy, and the equality of opportunity enjoyed by its citizens. He had only one substantial criticism — that there were no theatres. This complaint was answered by a famous native of the city. In his *Letter to D'Alembert* (1758), Rousseau argued that theatres, where the wealthy sit passively in dark caverns to watch spectacles of bondage and inequality, were more appropriate to large cities; small, self-governing cities and towns could make their own entertainment in the form of festivals of folk art, celebrating in the open air the natural social bonds to which their happy form of government had already given expression. The *Letter to D'Alembert* also contained digressive descriptions of country life in the valleys around Neuchâtel, where small farmers and their families lived happily on their freehold plots. *The New Heloïse* is set in the same physical and intellectual environment.

In European literature of the late eighteenth century, therefore, agriculture – as the means by which the latent powers of soil and human talent were made to flourish – became a recurrent symbol of the natural man in his proper environment. As happens so often, a 'scientific' theory soon sprang up to validate the widespread feeling. In this case it was professed by the French school of economists called the Physiocrats. This was the notion, expressed by François Quesnay, court physician to Louis xv, Anne-Robert-Jacques Turgot, French minister of finance from 1774, and others, that only agriculture could be deemed the true source of national wealth, since it alone offered a 'real' (because natural) surplus over the cost of production – the *produit net* or net increase produced by the fertility of the soil itself. Other kinds of surplus – say, those of manufacturing or trade – were 'sterile', because in these processes only the value of labour was added to the product. This idea was to have many reverberations in the United States, not only among Jefferson and the Anti-federalists (who could also be described as the physiocratic party, opposed to the mercantilist Federalists) but also in some ideas of the nineteenth-century populists (and later Ezra Pound, that son of a populist who discerned the blessed pattern in the founding principles of the Siena bank, the Monte dei Paschi). 'And the voice is not yet silent,' adds the economist John Kenneth Galbraith (1977, 18). 'When politicians campaign for the few farm votes that remain, the message of physiocracy may still be heard. "Yours, my friends, is the basic industry; the farmer is the man who feeds them all."'

All these ideas come together in the work of the Abbé Guillaume Thomas François Raynal, to whom Crèvecoeur's *Letters* are dedicated. His *Histoire . . . des Européens dans les deux Indes* (1770), from which an extract on North America was translated into English as *History of the British Settlements and Trade in North America* (1779), also bases its investigations on physiocratic assumptions, 'celebrating agriculture as the basis of human happiness and prosperity. . . . Both [the *History* and the *Letters*] identify the family as the basic source of legitimate pleasure and social stability. Both . . . champion the Quakers as models of simplicity and humanitarianism. Both fervently condemn Negro slavery as well as all other forms of injustice and exploitation. . . . At almost every point, Raynal offers a striking parallel to the ideas which find expression in the *Letters*' (Philbrick, 67–8).

Set within these various literary and intellectual contexts, the passage from Crèvecoeur's *Letters* seems less evasive and haphazard in form and reference. When the author 'lies' about his father, claiming he settled in America before him to clear the farm he now works, he is constructing a fictional narrator along the same lines, though not as fully developed, as Robinson Crusoe. The same may be said for the statement that he was content to stay at home, when we know, from the internal evidence of the remaining nine tenths of the book alone, that the fictional narrator James travelled widely in America. The incident of the boy on the plough, though it might have had some basis in actual life, is clearly announced as an example, and may be taken as a tableau symbolic of the value, proclaimed throughout the book, and taken very seriously, of cultivation. The ideas are related through the etymology of the French word *cultiver*, 'to plough', and the English word for 'ploughshare', *coulter* or *colter*. Cultivation is what the small freeholder does to improve his land, the means by which he produces – or perhaps *educes* would be a better word – his physical well-being from nature. The process is validated by physiocratic economics, but the result is not just physical. The proximity of the words 'education' and 'plough' contrasts his mode of 'improvement' with that of the European. Improvement is of the sensibility as well as of the soil; yet in this passage the theme of the improvement of nature, grounded as it must be in the virtues of physical cultivation, inverts the European model of distant travel. When his work is done, even here he has the ease, the leisure for casual encounter of the young aristocrat on the Grand Tour, time even to observe the tiniest insects, themselves 'improving' their short space and time. His very narrative method is one of easeful meditation on the natural tendencies and forms that can evolve only in the absence of business and authoritarian structures. The urge to improve may seem to undercut the idea of leisure, but this improvement works with nature, not against it. So confident is he of the equation that later in the same 'letter' he can bring them together in the reflection that 'the whole *economy* [my emphasis] of what we proudly call the brute creation is admirable in every circumstance' (56).

So pervasive is the figure of cultivation in the *Letters* that it gives the book its shape. At first sight the narrative seems to have very little sense of direction, with its meanderings between local observation and general principle, from the middle colonies like New York and Pennsylvania to the islands off the coast of Massachusetts, then down south, and finally back to the middle colonies in the visit to John Bartram. Yet it is informed by a moral geography in which a region is judged by how well it cultivates its environment.

The middle colonies, with their rich soil and temperate climate, their local government (Crèvecoeur describes the intervention of London as a trivial matter of a few customs officers) and their equitable distribution of wealth in the form of countless freehold plots worked by yeoman farmers, constitute the most favoured of the American environments. Out west in the great forests of the frontier, on the other hand, the men

> are regulated by the wildness of the neighbourhood. . . . This surrounding hostility immediately puts the gun into their hands [and] . . . they soon become professed hunters; this is the progress; once hunters, farewell to the plough. The chase renders them ferocious, gloomy, and unsocial. . . . In a little time, their success in the woods makes them neglect their tillage. They trust to the natural fecundity of the earth and therefore do little.   (70)

Meanwhile, in South Carolina, the maniacal division of labour, wealth and happiness has undone all the fecundity that nature can offer. 'Here [in Charleston] the produce of this extensive territory concentrates. . . . The inhabitants are the gayest in America; it is called the centre of our beau monde' (160). Here live the lawyers, planters and merchants luxuriating in the sequestered goods of the community, while the slaves work on the plantations, unnoticed, unconsidered:

> The cracks of the whip urging these miserable beings to excessive labour are far too distant from the gay capitol to be heard. The chosen race eat, drink, and live happy, while the unfortunate one grubs up the ground, raises indigo, or husks the rice, exposed to a sun full as scorching as their native one, without the support of good food, without the cordials of cheering liquor.   (162)

Against the two marginal regions of the South and frontier is set another, much less favoured in soil and climate, in which good government has made good 'tillage'. The inhabitants of the sandy, windswept island of Nantucket do practise some literal cultivation: 'salt grasses . . . carefully fenced, yield a considerable quantity of . . . wholesome fodder' (108); a parson is paid in seaweed with which to fertilize his land 'which he tills himself: for nothing will grow on these hungry soils without the assistance of this extraordinary manure' (118). But their real strength is their ability to improve a poor environment by other sorts of ploughing: 'If these people are not famous for tracing the fragrant furrow on the plain, they plough the rougher ocean' (104). The sea is 'a great nursery of seamen' (118): as for the land, 'It is but seldom that vice grows on a barren sand like this. . . . How could the common follies of society take root in so despicable a soil?' Such is the 'rotation of those different scenes of business which fill the measure of their days' (119) – their fishing, their whaling, their trading – that even the poverty of their soil is turned to economic and moral advantage, and Crèvecoeur's metaphors of cultivation expand to accommodate their non-agricultural activities. Meanwhile, so sane is their local polity and so healthy their bodies untroubled by excess consumption, that the Nantucketers provide a poor soil for the professions (145). They have only two doctors and but a single lawyer (and he thrives only because he married money): 'Here, happily, unoppressed with any civil bondage, this society of fishermen and merchants live without any military establishments, without governors or any masters but the laws; and their civil code is so light that it is never felt' (146).

Thus each excursion from the normative centre of the middle colonies, where he makes his home, involves Crèvecoeur's narrator in an experiment to determine the true relationship between soil and society. He finds that rich natural resources do not alone produce a happy community (they may even discourage it) and that in every case man must so organize his society as to improve his surroundings. Cultivation may be actual ploughing or another form of productive activity (though fishing is preferred to trade, and manufacturing is not mentioned). The environment itself, in other words, is institutional as well as physical. He learns the truth in fact of what he has set out as a general proposition in the essay 'What is an American?':

Men are like plants; the goodness and flavour of the fruit proceeds from the peculiar soil and exposition [i.e. position, aspect] in which they grow. We are nothing but what we derive from the air we breathe, the climate we inhabit, the government we obey, the system of religion we profess, and the nature of our employment.　　(65)

The penultimate chapter of the book, the visit of 'Mr Iw—n Al—z' to John Bartram, 'The Celebrated Pennsylvanian Botanist', is a summary – indeed, itself an extended tableau – of all the themes developed thus far in the book. The real John Bartram was the first native American botanist to achieve an international reputation. He established the first American botanical garden (now preserved as a city park in Philadelphia), and wrote accounts of several 'experimental' journeys, of which his best known was *Observations on the Inhabitants, Climate, Soil, etc. . . . in . . . travels from Pennsylvania to . . . Lake Ontario* (1751). (His son William was even more celebrated as a travel writer and describer of flora and fauna.) When one adds that he was a Quaker, his attractiveness as an epitome of values advanced in the *Letters* will be obvious.

Bartram's career is firmly established within the theme of cultivation. 'Pray, Mr Bertram [*sic*], when did you imbibe the first wish to cultivate the science of botany?' asks Mr. A—z. It turns out he began while actually ploughing:

> Well, then, I'll tell thee; one day I was very busy in holding my plough (for thou see'st that I am but a ploughman), and being weary, I ran under the shade of a tree to repose myself. I cast my eyes on a daisy; I picked it mechanically and viewed it with more curiosity than common country farmers are wont to do, and observed therein very many distinct parts, some perpendicular, some horizontal. 'What a shame,' said my mind, or something that inspired my mind, 'that thee shouldest have employed so many years in tilling the earth and destroying so many flowers and plants without being acquainted with their structures and their uses!' (188)

Bartram is important to the *Letters* not only because of his simple mode of life, his decent treatment of his black slaves, his improvement by dike and drain so that 'an amazing number of cattle now feed on solid bottoms, which but a few years before had been covered with water' and an 'orchard, formerly planted on a barren, sandy soil' was now 'converted into one of the richest spots in that vicinage' (186) – but above all for the leisure he has made to cultivate things of the mind and spirit. Throughout the chapter the idea of aimless discovery is much insisted upon: 'Thence we *rambled* through his fields, where the right-angular fences, the heaps of pitched stones, the flourishing clover, announced the best husbandry' (186); the Quaker service is apparently formless, but 'every one had his head reclined and seemed absorbed in profound meditation' (192); Mr. A—z summarizes his visit to the Bartrams: 'Thus I passed several days in ease, improvement, and pleasure' (189). It is this triad – ease, improvement and pleasure – which governs the mood and thought of Crèvecoeur's other narrator, James, when discussing life on his own farm. It is how Bartram began his career, how Crèvecoeur pursued his, and how most of *Letters from an American Farmer* is made.

Except that the book ends very differently. The Bartram chapter is not only a tableau but a distinctly 'framed' picture, portraying a mode of life already passing into the status of impossible ideal. Around it the discourse of the *Letters* has turned dark and foreboding. How has it changed? In the first place, the narrator has begun to think of the 'economy' of nature as really a balance of terror. The chapter immediately preceding the one on Bartram, 'On snakes; and on the humming-bird', is full of images of nature at war with itself. As the narrator is 'sitting solitary and pensive in [his] primitive arbour' (178) his attention is caught by two snakes fighting ferociously, 'biting each other with the utmost rage' (179), wrestling, writhing, in and out of a muddy ditch, until one of them succeeds in drowning the other. A tiny humming-bird (in a description based on a passage in Raynal's *History of . . . North America*) looks enchanting in its plumage of 'the most perfect azure, the most beautiful gold, the most dazzling red', but 'when it feeds . . . from what motives I know not, it will tear and lacerate flowers into a hundred pieces', and two of its kind will 'often fight with the fury of lions until one of the combatants falls a sacrifice and dies' (178).

In the last 'letter', immediately following the visit to Bartram, the savagery spreads to the world of man. Now even the narrator's 'primitive arbour', his secure vantage point from which to observe the savagery of nature, is overrun by the events of the Revolutionary War. The threat of Indian raids interrupts the farming, making it dangerous to go into the fields for any length of time, and breaks their sleep with nightmare. Even their 'very appetite proceeding from labour and peace of mind is gone; we eat just enough to keep us alive' (196). Caught between two factions, neither caring much for the property of the peaceful farmer, they become 'necessarily involved in the dark wheel of fortune'. Who will win? Will it be the right side? Who is right? One might as well ask which of the two snakes was 'right':

> What one party calls meritorious, the other denominates flagitious. These opinions vary, contract, or expand, like the events of the war on which they are founded. . . . And after all, who will be the really guilty? Those most certainly who fail of success. (199)

At the climax of the snake battle 'the black one gained an unexpected superiority; it acquired two great folds likewise, which necessarily extended the body of its adversary in proportion as it had contracted its own' (179–80).

Who can imagine Crèvecoeur's feelings as he wrote this long, vehement 'letter', as he took it to Europe to be published knowing that he had left his wife and two of his children to face the very danger he so feelingly described? Yet it would be a misreading of the *Letters* to seek to explain this last chapter entirely as the result of a sudden impulse from 'real life' cutting across an otherwise sunny fiction. Danger is latent even in the happy passage about the boy on the plough ('I fear for the health of those who are become so dear to me') and so is the natural law that one animal must die to feed another ('I never see an egg brought on my table but I feel penetrated with the wonderful change it would have undergone but for my gluttony'). And on the frontier things have already begun to come apart. 'There, remote from the power of example and check of shame, many families exhibit the most hideous parts of society. They are a kind of forlorn hope' (66). The narrator brings in his imagery of cultivation to judge them: '[their] new manners being grafted on the old stock produce a strange sort of lawless profligacy' (71); 'Thus our bad people are those who are half cultivators and half hunters; and the worst of them are those who have degenerated into the hunting state. As old ploughmen and new men of the woods, as Europeans and new-made Indians, they contract the vices of both' (71–2).

Here the narrator is touching on perhaps the deepest fear of the early American immigrant – that his removal from the metropolitan centre will cause him to degenerate into a state of savagery. Raynal's *History of . . . North America*, from which Crèvecoeur took so many of his ideas, gives 'scientific' support to this concern. That book is not just a favourable report on the success of Quakers in Pennsylvania and freehold farmers in New York, though Raynal certainly praises these aspects of America, but is posed as a desperate struggle between the forces of progress and regress, the outcome of which remains uncertain. In particular Raynal was concerned to question the likelihood of productive increase, in people, animals and crops, in the American environment. For example, was America attracting the right kind of immigrant? He noted that the first American settlers 'were Englishmen who had been persecuted at home' (255; citations are from the first edition in English, 1779); nothing wrong with that, but the persecution was short-lived, and the British 'are so strongly attached to their native soil, that nothing less than civil wars or revolutions can induce those among them that have any property, character, or industry, to a change of climate and country' (255–6). In any case, 'the English . . . were ill-adapted to the business of clearing the grounds' (256). Then there was the fact that many of the early colonists were 'malefactors which the mother country transported after condemnation to America', and that 'these have been replaced by indigent persons, whom the impossibility of subsisting in

Europe has driven into the new world' (258–9). And British immigrants were only part of the problem. Others came too: 'Irishmen,
Jews, Frenchmen, Switzers, Palatines, Moravians, and Saltzburghers,
who, having been worn out with the political and religious troubles
they had experienced in Europe, have gone in search of peace and quiet-
ness in distant climates' (266). Could these disparate elements be
worked into a single people, increasing in numbers and strength,
cultivating the land to provide for that increase? Or, as Raynal himself
asks the question:

> Has nature . . . punished them for having crossed the ocean? Are
> they a race of people degenerated by transplating, by growth, and by
> mixture? Will not time be able to reduce them to the nature of their
> climate? Let us beware of pronouncing on futurity, before we have
> the experience of several centuries. . . . Let us wait till education may
> have corrected the unsurmountable tendency of the climate towards
> the enervating pleasures of luxury and sensuality. Perhaps we shall
> then see that America is propitious to genius and the arts, that give
> birth to peace and society. A new Olympus, an Arcadia, an Athens, a
> new Greece, will produce, perhaps . . . another Homer, a Theo-
> critus, and especially an Anacreon.   (258)

Perhaps. 'Indeed!' Franklin (or even we) might chime. But for
Raynal the issue was still in doubt. And the reason why is contained in
that curious phrase 'degenerated by transplanting'. Raynal was one of
those, like Georges-Louis Leclerc, Count Buffon (who developed the
theory in no fewer than 44 volumes of his *Histoire Naturelle*, 1749) who
believed that animals degenerated when removed from one physical
environment to another. Because the Bible history of the Creation
precluded the proposition that any species were native to the American
continent, there were fewer species there, and each individual was
smaller than in the old world. The American Indians, wrote Raynal, are
refugees from the Flood. 'They are a species of men degraded and
degenerated in their natural constitutions, in their stature, in their way
of life, and in their understandings, which have made little progress in
all the arts of civilization' (*History*, 17). As for domestic animals
brought over by the Europeans, 'all of them, excepting the hog, whose
whole merit consists of fattening himself, have lost much of that
strength and size which they enjoyed in those countries from whence
they were brought' (245).

This idea posed a serious problem for the physiocrat. For what would become of the *produit net* in a country in which nature was undoing the natural increase on which the prestigious theory of economics was based – in which nature fought against itself? Cultivation, education, 'improvement' might overcome the deterioration, but then again it might not. In any case, the progress was no longer inevitable – no longer a matter of 'science'. There were ways of answering this pessimistic hypothesis. One was the joke Benjamin Franklin played on Raynal and others at a dinner party he gave to various *philosophes* at his home in Passy. This is Jefferson's version of the occasion:

> During the dinner [Raynal] got on his favorite theory of the degeneracy of animals, and even of man, in America, and urged it with his usual eloquence. The Doctor [Franklin] at length, noticing the accidental stature and position of his guests at table, 'Come,' says he, 'M. l'Abbé, let us try this question by the fact before us. We are here one half Americans, and one half French. . . . Let both parties rise, and we will see on which side nature has degenerated.' It happened that his American guests were . . . of the finest stature and form; while those of the other were remarkably diminutive, and the Abbé himself particularly, was a mere shrimp.
>
> (Jefferson, 1903–4, xviii, 170 ff)

Jefferson himself answered Buffon and Raynal by patient argument, statistics and scientific geographical description in his *Notes on the State of Virginia* (1782 [sc. 1784]).

For Crèvecoeur's narrator, whose very style is 'American Farmer', for whom the theme of cultivation pervades his entire narrative, the challenge to the very basis of cultivation itself is both more direct and more difficult to answer. As a man of feeling, not a scientist, he can attempt to counter the anxiety by metaphor. That is why his father is said to have developed the farm before him and why he is remembered again in the symbolic arrangement of man, boy and plough: 'As I lean over the handle, various are the thoughts which crowd into mind. I am now doing for him, I say, what my father formerly did for me.' The idea is not just to establish the narrator's *bona fides* as an American but to reinforce the idea of orderly generation – three successive generations grouped around the plough that not only sustains them but *improves* their natural environment. But the image is precarious – as much so, at least, as the boy's seat on the moving beam. The next sentence is a desperate prayer: 'My God enable him to live that he may perform the same operations for the same purposes when I am worn out and old!'

Out on the edges of this settled community – particularly on the western frontier – nature is busy undoing centuries of cultivation, and by the end of the book, savagery has encroached on the civilized centre itself.

So the narrator has to 'light out'. At every level, save one, the end of the book is an evasion. In the first place, the author who wrote it was not, himself, lighting out but 'lighting in', back to the metropolis to sell his book and become a great literary man. Secondly, he was abandoning the better part of his family. Thirdly, his narrator cannot really convince either his readers or himself that moving towards the frontier is any sort of solution to his predicament. In terms of the book's narrative, it just will not work. What will become of his cultivation, the education of his children, their 'improvement'? He tries to invoke the glamour of the exotic primitivism – 'Without temples, without priests, without kings, and without laws, [the Indians] are in many instances superior to us. . . . They most certainly are much more closely connected with Nature than we are' (209) – but the qualifying and intensifying phrases betray it as a vain attempt to convince himself, and us. 'Perhaps my imagination gilds too strongly this distant prospect,' he admits (219). Yes, it does.

But in this very projection of uncertainty the chapter does have a kind of honesty. What Crèvecoeur discovered, through actual experience and real pain sharpened by a wholly preposterous theory, was (as we will see) what Philip Freneau would realize when he reworked Joseph Wharton's ode 'To Fancy': that the American artist who truly faces his awesome situation runs the grave risk of alienation. Even if he turns back to the east, or Europe, or the big city (as Mark Twain later did, after all), he has to finish his story, to complete the deeper logic of what he has confronted, by at least *miming* the escape from civilization. And Crèvecoeur discovered too (and in this respect he may have been the first) that the most effective narrator for such a fiction is one who also moves in and out of the story, like Herman Melville's Ishmael, in *Moby Dick*, and Fitzgerald's Nick Carraway, in *The Great Gatsby*, now the author's voice and now part of the fiction. It is this unstable point of view, this refusal to commit themselves, that characterizes so many American narrators. The tactic is elusive, but it implies such a frank admission of the difficulties facing the American writer that it cannot be called wholly evasive.

References

Cutting, Rose Marie (1976), *John and William Bartram, William Byrd II and St John de Crèvecoeur: a Reference Guide*, Boston, Mass.: G. K. Hall.

Galbraith, John Kenneth (1977), *The Age of Uncertainty*, London: BBC/Deutsch.

Howes, Alan B. (1974), *Sterne: the Critical Heritage*, London: Routledge & Kegan Paul.

Jefferson, Thomas (1903–4), *The Writings*, ed. Andrew Lipscomb and Albert Ellert Bergh, 20 vols, Washington: Thomas Jefferson Memorial Association.

Philbrick, Thomas (1970), *St John de Crèvecoeur*, New York: Twayne (United States Authors Series, 154).

Further reading

TEXTS

Hector St John de Crèvecoeur, *Letters from an American Farmer and Sketches of Eighteenth-Century America*, with a foreword by Albert E. Stone Jr, New York: New American Library, 1963.

Journey into Northern Pennsylvania and the State of New York, translated by Clarissa Spencer Bostelmann, Ann Arbor, Mich.: University of Michigan Press, 1964.

CONTEXTS

Daniel Boorstin, *The Lost World of Thomas Jefferson*, New York: Henry Holt, 1948.

Abbé Raynal, *A Philosophical and Political History of the British Settlements and Trade in North America*, Edinburgh: C. Denovan, 1779.

Jean-Jacques Rousseau, *The Indispensable Rousseau*, ed. John Hope Mason, London: Quartet, 1979.

CRITICAL AND BIOGRAPHICAL

Robert de Crèvecoeur, *Saint Jean de Crèvecoeur: Sa vie et ses ouvrages*, Paris: Librairie des Bibliophiles, 1883.

Thomas Philbrick, *St John de Crèvecoeur*, New York: Twayne (United States Authors Series, 154), 1970.

Howard C. Rice, *Le Cultivateur Américain: Étude sur l'oeuvre de Saint John de Crèvecoeur*, Paris: Champion, 1932.

8

Philip Freneau (1752–1832) and Joel Barlow (1754–1812)

Philip Freneau (1752–1832)

PICTURE XVII.

Columbus in Chains

Are these the honours they reserve for me,
Chains for the man that gave new worlds to Spain!
Rest here, my swelling heart! – O kings, O queens,
Patrons of monsters, and their progeny,
Authors of wrong, and slaves to fortune merely!
Why was I seated by my prince's side,
Honour'd, caress'd like some first peer of Spain?
Was it that I might fall most suddenly
From honour's summit to the sink of scandal!
'Tis done, 'tis done!—what madness is ambition!
What is there in that little breath of men,
Which they call Fame, that should induce the brave
To forfeit ease and that domestic bliss
Which is the lot of happy ignorance,
Less glorious aims, and dull humility? –
Whoe'er thou art that shalt aspire to honour,
And on the strength and vigour of the mind
Vainly depending, court a monarch's favour,
Pointing the way to vast extended empire;
First count your pay to be ingratitude,
Then chains and prisons, and disgrace like mine!
Each wretched pilot now shall spread his sails,
And treading in my footsteps, hail new worlds,
Which, but for me, had still been empty visions.

PICTURE XVIII.

Columbus at Valladolid

1

How sweet is sleep, when gain'd by length of toil!
  No dreams disturb the slumbers of the dead—
To snatch existence from this scanty soil,
  Were these the hopes deceitful fancy bred;
And were her painted pageants nothing more
Than this life's phantoms by delusion led?

2

The winds blow high: one other world remains;
  Once more without a guide I find the way;
In the dark tomb to slumber with my chains—
  Prais'd by no poet on my funeral day,
Nor even allow'd one dearly purchas'd claim –
My new found world not honour'd with my name.

3

Yet, in this joyless gloom while I repose,
  Some comfort will attend my pensive shade,
When memory paints, and golden fancy shows
  My toils rewarded, and my woes repaid;
When empires rise where lonely forests grew,
Where Freedom shall her generous plans pursue.

4

To shadowy forms, and ghosts and sleepy things,
  Columbus, now with dauntless heart repair;
You liv'd to find new worlds for thankless kings,
  Write this upon my tomb – yes – tell it there –
Tell of those chains that sullied all my glory –
Not mine, but their's – ah, tell the shameful story.

The Pictures of Columbus (1788)

Joel Barlow (1754–1812)

Land of delights! ah dear delusive coast,
To these fond aged eyes for ever lost!
No more thy flowery vales I travel o'er,
For me thy mountains rear the head no more,
For me thy rocks no sparkling gems unfold,
Nor streams luxuriant wear their paths in gold;
From realms of promised peace for ever borne,
I hail mute anguish, and in secret mourn.
　　But dangers past, a world explored in vain,
And foes triumphant speak but half my pain.
Dissembling friends, each early joy who gave,
And fired my youth the storms of fate to brave,
Swarm'd in the sunshine of my happier days,
Pursued the fortune and partook the praise,
Now pass my cell with smiles of cold disdain,
Insult my woes and triumph in my pain.
　　One gentle guardian once could shield the brave;
But now that guardian slumbers in the grave.
Hear from above, thou dear departed shade!
As then my hopes, so now my sorrows aid,
Burst my full heart, afford that last relief,
Breathe back my sighs and reinspire my grief;
Still in my sight thy royal form appears,
Reproves my silence and demands my tears.
Even on that hour no more I joy to dwell,
When thy protection bade the canvas swell,
When kings and churchmen found their factions vain,
When superstition shrunk beneath her chain,
The sun's glad beam led on the circling way,
And isles rose beauteous in Atlantic day.
For on those silvery shores, that new domain,
What crowds of tyrants fix their murderous reign!
Her infant realm indignant Freedom flies,
Truth leaves the world and Isabella dies.
　　Ah lend thy friendly shroud to veil my sight,
That these pain'd eyes may dread no more the light;
These welcome shades shall close my instant doom,
And this drear mansion moulder to a tomb.

Thus mourn'd the hapless man: a thundering sound
Roll'd thro the shuddering walls and shook the ground;
O'er all the dungeon, where black arches bend,
The roofs unfold and streams of light descend;
The growing splendor fills the astonisht room,
And gales etherial breathe a glad perfume.
Robed in the radiance, moves a form serene,
Of human structure but of heavenly mien;
Near to the prisoner's couch he takes his stand
And waves, in sign of peace, his holy hand.
Tall rose his stature, youth's endearing grace
Adorn'd his limbs and brighten'd in his face;
Loose o'er his locks the star of evening hung,
And sounds melodious moved his cheerful tongue:
    Rise, trembling chief, to scenes of rapture rise,
This voice awaits thee from the western skies;
Indulge no longer that desponding strain,
Nor count thy toils nor deem thy virtues vain.
Thou seest in me the guardian Power who keeps
The new found world that skirts Atlantic deeps;
Hesper my name, my seat the brightest throne
In night's whole heaven, my sire the living sun.
My brother Atlas, from his birthright boast,
Claims the wild wave, but mine the solid coast.
This hand, which form'd, and in the tides of time
Laves and improves the meliorating clime,
Which taught thy prow to cleave the trackless way,
And hail'd thee first in occidental day,
To all thy worth shall vindicate thy claim,
And raise up nations to revere thy name.
    In this dark age tho blinded faction sways,
And wealth and conquest gain the palm of praise;
Awed into slaves while groveling millions groan,
And blood-stain'd steps lead upward to a throne;
Far other wreaths thy virtuous temples twine,
Far nobler triumphs crown a life like thine;
Thine be the joys that minds immortal grace,
As thine the deeds that bless a kindred race.
Now raise thy sorrow'd soul to views more bright,
The vision'd ages rushing on thy sight;

Worlds beyond worlds shall bring to light their stores,
Time, nature, science blend their utmost powers,
To show, concentred in one blaze of fame,
The ungather'd glories that await thy name.
  As that great seer, whose animating rod
Taught Jacob's sons their wonder-working God,
Led far thro dreary wastes the murmuring band,
And reacht the confines of their promised land,
Forbid to enter, but from Pisgah's height,
On fruitful Canaan feasted long his sight;
View'd unborn nations from his labors blest,
Forgot his toils and sooth'd his soul to rest;
Thus o'er thy subject wave shalt thou behold
Far happier realms their future charms unfold,
In nobler pomp another Pisgah rise,
Beneath whose foot thy new found Canaan lies;
There, rapt in vision, hail my favorite clime
And taste the blessings of remotest time.

The Columbiad (1807)

* * *

America did not have to wait for Richard Henry Lee's motion in Congress on 2 July, 1776, or for its proclamation two days later, to be pictured as an independent nation. When a young student of literature called John Trumbull took his master's degree at Yale in 1770, his valedictory oration included verses on the 'Prospect of the Future Glory of America'. A year later Philip Freneau said goodbye to the College of New Jersey (later Princeton) with a long dialogue in decasyllabic blank verse read out and partly composed by his classmate Hugh Brackenridge, later editor of the *United States Magazine* and author of the novel *Modern Chivalry*. 'The Rising Glory of America' outlines the discovery and settlement of the continent, engages in 'a philosophical enquiry' into the American Indians, and projects a millennial future in which 'independent power shall hold her sway' and 'Paradise anew / Shall flourish, by no second Adam lost'.

  It was not entirely by chance that the nation emerged in fiction before it did in fact. What prompted these productions was not so much a fanciful ideology as an ideology of the fancy. A year before he left Princeton Freneau had already written a poem of over 150 tetrameter lines in praise of 'The Power of Fancy' (the term meant the imagination before Coleridge later made the distinction). Trumbull had campaigned at Yale for a liberalization of the curriculum to include studies in modern poetry, and his 'Prospect of the Future Glory . . .' had been part of an oration on the 'Uses and Advantages of the Fine Arts'. The same ceremony that included Freneau's and Brackenridge's 'Rising Glory' also featured a debate, to which Freneau contributed as well, on whether 'ancient poetry excel[ls] the modern.'

Why should projects for a course of study and for a nation share the same occasion? Americans have always been great makers of curricula, and the most progressive spirits of the American Revolution were also the most forward in designing systems of higher education for the new citizenry. Franklin, Jefferson and Benjamin Rush, the surgeon-general of the Continental Army and member of the Continental Congress, all argued for educational reform in favour of practical and contemporary subjects ranging from the natural sciences to the fine arts. As Governor of Virginia and Visitor of the College of William and Mary, Jefferson had recommended changes in the subjects professed at his old alma mater: law, medicine and modern languages in place of ancient languages, Hebrew and theology. In planning the curriculum for the University of Virginia, the founding of which was one of three things he wished to be remembered for in his characteristically self-composed epitaph (the others were his authorship of the Statute of Virginia for Religious Freedom and the Declaration of Independence), Jefferson extended the list to include military and naval architecture, astronomy, mineralogy, geography and belles-lettres.

The momentum for these reforms, as for the shape of most American universities, the University of London (and hence the English redbrick universities and the 'daughter' colleges of the Empire), came from Scotland. The more progressive and democratic Americans were particularly attracted to the Scottish model of higher education because it had found a way of introducing a far higher proportion of the population to university training than had been (or still is) the case in England. The Scottish method depended not only on forms of instruction new to the English-speaking world, such as the vernacular lecture course professed by scholars who could be sacked by students whom they failed to instruct and entertain, but also on an opening into new, more practical studies in the natural and social sciences, law and medicine. In American university curricula, in American library lists both private and institutional, even in American commonplace books, the names that recur pre-eminently are of Scottish thinkers: Adam Ferguson, Lord Kames, Adam Smith, the historian William Robertson, and the moral philosophers of the common sensibility, Francis Hutcheson, Thomas Reid, James Beattie and Dugald Stewart (see, for example, May, 1976, 343 ff). 'America in general [writes Garry Wills, 176] had gone to school to the Scots in its last colonial period.' The College of William and Mary had been founded by a Scot educated in Aberdeen, James Blair. The Provost of the College of Philadelphia (later the University of Pennsylvania) in the crucial years from 1775 to 1779 was the Scottish-born educational theorist William Smith. Most famously, the President of Princeton from 1768 was the Scottish Presbyterian minister John Witherspoon, also a member of the Continental Congress and a signer of the Declaration, whose progressive curriculum and personal instruction in the common-sense philosophy shaped the early careers not only of James Madison but of his classmate, Philip Freneau.

The idea of a sensibility common to all mankind grounded moral criteria on a principle that could be applied readily to aesthetic judgement. If moral 'sense' were common to all, then so was taste as a benchmark for excellence in literature or the fine arts, as Kames argued in his *Elements of Criticism* (1762). The common-sense philosophy would come to be used conservatively in the American cultural debate, as a universal standard of decorum from which it became increasingly difficult to deviate, an unanswerable argument for the probable, as against the fanciful in art – or even as an attack on imaginative literature itself (see, for example, Martin, 1961, *passim*). But because the idea admitted all kinds of men – poor as well as rich, unlettered and educated, dull and clever – into the ranks of the 'sensible', it had its radical implications too. In the same year in which Kames published his *Elements of Criticism*, the first chair in what has come to be called English literature was established in Edinburgh. Hugh Blair's *Lectures on Rhetoric and Belles Lettres*, first published in 1783, widely reprinted in America and much studied there, begins its course of instruction with a confident connection between aesthetic judgement and an imaginative process not accessible to reason and common to all conditions:

For nothing can be more clear, than that taste is not resolvable into any such operation as reason. It is not merely through a discovery of the understanding, or a deduction of argument, that the mind receives pleasure from a beautiful prospect or a fine poem. Such objects often strike us intuitively, and make a strong impression, when we are unable to assign the reasons of our being pleased. They sometimes strike in the same manner the philosopher and the peasant; the boy and the man. (Lecture II)

Blair's categories of rhetoric (the sublime, structure of sentences, figurative language, hyperbole, comparison, and so forth) and his literary genres (public speaking, pastoral and epic poetry, tragedy and many more) cut across the old debate between ancient and modern. His examples and passages for close examination came as readily from Swift, Milton or an essay in the *Spectator* as from the classics of Greek and Roman writing. Given this context, one can see how his project might translate itself to an American university setting, why a young American might come to associate the revolution in letters with a revolution in politics, and finally why the liberation of the imagination might be thought a proper and necessary concomitant to the liberation of the common man in the nation yet to emerge in fact.

Yet the widely noticed feature of the poetry of the American Revolution is that it was anything but original. Deriving their diction and prosody almost slavishly from recent English verse, American poets kept the Augustan conventions on life-support systems until well into the nineteenth century. This irony was inherent even in those optimistic graduation ceremonies at Yale and Princeton. Trumbull's valedictory oration, to cite the *Dictionary of American Biography* (xix, 10), 'was distinguished by its early plea for the abandonment of neo-classical rules in poetry; but the verses which concluded the oration were an egregious example of the very practices its thesis had condemned'. Even Freneau, though confident in the luxury of the modern syllabus at Princeton which Trumbull had missed at Yale, came down on the side of the ancients in the debate on literary periods.

To a certain extent this persistence of stereotypes can be explained simply by distance from, and difficulty of access to, the place where new fashions were set. Think of the colonial poet Edward Taylor in the frontier town of Westfield, Massachusetts, writing his *Preparatory Meditations* in the style of Donne's *Holy Sonnets* almost until his death in 1729. But even when it is easier than it was for Taylor to keep up with trends, the provincial address to the metropolitan model has been characteristically ambiguous, a mood epitomized by the British title of Stephen Spender's book on the Anglo-American cultural debate, *Love–Hate Relations* (1974). The provincial writer may both resent the dominance of metropolitan culture and also, in the face of what he takes to be anarchic forces on the margins of empire, seek to uphold it even more rigidly and self-consciously than would his contemporary at home. (When he himself makes a visit 'home', of course, the provincial may get a lot of mileage out of acting the rough frontiersman, because in the metropolis, with actual barbarism well at bay, this kind of behaviour can be tolerated, or even taken as diverting.)

This anxiety of the provincial must have been heightened in the province evolving into a nation, and especially in one that was making itself out of a wilderness. The common complaint of early American authors was that poetry and fiction − or even non-fictional writing − was a hard profession to pursue in a country where building and business were the urgent concerns of the population. The novelist Charles Brockden Brown expressed this problem in a preface to the first bound volume of his literary review, the *American Review and Literary Journal* (1802):

> The people of the United States are, perhaps, more distinguished than those of Europe as a people of business; and by a universal attention to the active and lucrative pursuits of life. This habit has grown out of the necessities of their situation, while engaged in the settlement of a new country, in the means of self-preservation, in defending their possessions, in removing the obstacles and embarrassments arising from their colonial condition, and in forming and establishing independent systems of government.   (ed. Spiller, 1967, 32–3)

This may explain why, though he is often cited as the first professional author in the history of the United States, Brown had himself to go into business, including the business of journalism. Writing under the fictional name of 'Mr Robert Slender', Freneau too had complained that

> There are few writers of books in this new world, and amongst those very few that deal in works of the imagination. . . . In a country which two hundred years ago was peopled only by savages . . . it is really wonderful there should be any polite original authors at all in any line.
> (*The Miscellaneous Works of Mr Philip Freneau . . .*, 1788; see
> Spiller, 6–7)

Freneau's advice to aspiring writers was 'to graft your authorship upon some other calling, or support drooping genius by the assistance of some mechanical employment . . . in plain language . . . make something by weaving garters, or mending old sails, when an Epic poem would be your utter destruction' (ibid.). He took his own advice. During a life-long career as a writer, and despite the patronage of Jefferson in the form of a government appointment in Washington, Freneau also worked as the secretary to a planter in the West Indies, as a clerk in the Philadelphia Post Office, and (repeatedly, as the occasion demanded) as an editor and a ship's captain.

His predicament is neatly exemplified even in 'The Power of Fancy'. The poem is 'provincial' in its debt to a metropolitan model – in this case that kind of versified praise of the imagination by those authors sometimes cited as precursors of the Romantics, like Edward Young ('Night Thoughts', 1742–6) and Mark Akenside (*The Pleasures of Imagination*, 1744) (see, for example, Abrams, 1953, 57–69). Its immediate source is Joseph Wharton's ode 'To Fancy' (1746), which, like Freneau's imitation, pictures Fancy as a goddess freely circulating the whole world from Lapland (Wharton) to 'Norwegia' and Bermuda (Freneau). Each poet finds the goddess attendant on poets that matter to him, but in Wharton's case these are English (Spenser, Shakespeare), while Freneau is forced to cast his net of reference wider in both time and place, from Sappho and Homer to Virgil and Ossian. But the most revealing difference lies in the two endings. Wharton is able to turn his invocation into a celebration of national talent:

> With native beauties win applause,
> Beyond cold critics' studied laws;
> O let each Muse's fame increase,
> O bid Britannia rival Greece!

While in Freneau's version, Fancy goes into a period of decline from which, if she is to be revived, she will become, not the muse of a whole community (let alone a country) but the companion of the alienated poet: 'Come, O come – perceiv'd by none, / You and I will walk alone.'

So despite the bold proclamations of the graduation ceremonies, the American poets could not feel quite so confident about founding the nation on works of the imagination. Much as they championed fancy as the medium of the bold new Republic, they had first to authenticate it by grounding the imaginative construct on something verifiable. Just as the various accounts of American exploration were ballasted by catalogues of things to be found in the New World – lists of actual, three-dimensional objects that could be handled, described or even sent back home – so speculative projects, whether intellectual, political or literary, exploring figurative space had to be buttressed by something reassuringly 'known' to the audience they sought to persuade. In these cases the commonest authenticator was a reference to what might loosely be called 'history' – that is, something that was widely accepted as having happened already, a public repository of verifiable facts. These 'facts' might seem at other times and in other places to be little more than legends or even rumours, but the point is that they were accepted as actual at the time they were uttered. Thus, the risky project of the Reformation was justified as a return to the moral and institutional candour of the primitive church, and revolutionary programmes in seventeenth-century England and eighteenth-century America called for a return to the happy days when Anglo-Saxons were supposed to have lived as free and equal citizens, before the Normans imposed their 'yoke' of king and landlord (see, for example, Hill, 1958, 50–122).

The case of a new nation, anxious to assert a characteristic culture to suit its newly established political independence, might be thought the most desperate project of all. From the time of Virgil, poets have managed the difficult task of authenticating the vision of the emergent nation by means of a special kind of reference to the community's sense of its shared past that might be termed proleptic (or anticipatory) history. When Virgil wanted to celebrate the new Roman Empire under Caesar Augustus, he turned to one of the oldest motifs in European literature, the visit of the epic hero to the Underworld to secure important knowledge forbidden ordinary men. Aeneas, guided by the Cumean Sybil, travels to Hades to consult the shade of his father, Anchises, who shows him a vision of his illustrious progeny and prophesies the hero's expedition to Italy, the war in Latium and the triumphant completion of Roman history in the establishment of the Empire. The same device is used in Ariosto's *Orlando Furioso* (1516), where the spirit of Merlin foretells the role of Bradamante in founding the Italian city states. Spenser takes the idea over in support of the Tudor myth of history when, in Book III of *The Faerie Queene* (1590), he has Merlin show Britomart how her offspring will revive and perfect the Brithonic line in Henry VII and VIII and the 'royal virgin' Elizabeth. Even Shakespeare uses the device, when in the last act of *Henry VIII* (1612–13) Cranmer enters the king's presence carrying the infant Elizabeth in his arms and proceeds to prophesy 'Upon this land a thousand thousand blessings, / Which time shall bring to ripeness'.

The crucial tactic in all these cases is a sense of two 'times' – that of the fictional characters (or, to be more exact, the 'historical' figures who have been made into fictional characters), and that of the audience. What appears to the characters to be a wonderful future – too good to be believed – is taken by readers or listeners as past history. Yet before they read or saw the fiction in question, they may well have come to think of their past as a humdrum affair. It is their recognition that the past was once exciting and hopeful to their founding hero (or heroine) that renews their sense of its importance. This sense is produced not only by the double 'time' in the fictional episode, but also by a dual tone reflecting the conflation of verifiable history and fanciful prophecy. While the hero recoils in wonder, the prophet continues in a matter-of-fact manner that does not even pause to register the effect on the hero: 'Sic pater Anchises, atque haec mirantibus addit: / "adspice, ut insignis spoiliis Marcellus opimus / ingreditur . . ."' ('So [speaks his] father Anchises; while [Aeneas and the Sybil] marvel still, he adds, "Lo, how Marcellus advances, glorious in his splendid spoils . . ."') (*Aeneid*, VI, 854–6). And:

CRAN.   In her days every man shall eat in safety,
        Under his own vine what he plants; and sing
        The merry songs of peace to all his neighbours. . . .
KING   Thou speakest wonders.
CRAN.   She shall be, to the happiness of England,
        An aged princess. . . .

                                            (*Henry VIII*, v, v)

The great American foundation narrative in this tradition is Joel Barlow's *The Vision of Columbus* (1787), revised and expanded as *The Columbiad* (1807). Like Freneau's 'Rising Glory', *The Columbiad* is a prospect of the past and future of America, but it is much longer (ten books of around 700 lines each) and its elaborate narrative is substantiated by the device of the proleptic history. Indeed, it consists of little else, since most of its bulk is taken up with the prophetic vision granted to the dying Columbus by Hesper, 'the guardian genius of the western continent'. Immediately following this extract from the first Book of the poem, Hesper takes Columbus up to the 'Mount of Vision' to see the present state and future development of the continent he has discovered: its rich natural resources and colourful native inhabitants, its rapidly increasing population, the startling progress of its cultivation, its struggle for independence from Europe, and its example to the world. Thus far, through Book VII, the poem had the authenticity of history to its contemporary readers, and what was more, the flattering comfort of a history all their own – an American epic founded on verifiable fact. It then branches out into subjects restricted neither to American concerns nor to the past; untraditionally, considering the Virgilian example, but following the precedent of Milton's *Paradise Lost*, Book IX of *The Columbiad* moves into the mode of general instruction – in this case a history of the development of ideas, political institutions, the arts and the sciences – to illustrate the inevitability of progress in all human pursuits, and then in the final book – abandoning even the Miltonic model – into a prophecy of future harmony (that is, the future for Barlow and his readers that even they might have taken as a trifle optimistic) involving a universal language and the union of all mankind in a single world government.

Compared to *The Columbiad*, Freneau's *The Pictures of Columbus* is both more modest and more malleable. Written in 1774 and published in 1788, the poem is a sequence of eighteen 'pictures' (of which the extract comprises the last two) showing the stages of Columbus's discovery of America: his attempts to convince Ferdinand and Isabella of the feasibility of the venture, his troubles with a fearful crew, his discovery of San Salvador, his doubts as to what the European incursion will do to the paradisal New World, his disgrace, imprisonment and death. The element of proleptic history, which may have given Barlow the idea for *The Columbiad*, is here a mere sketch – a vision imparted not by a seraph but by the poet's own 'golden fancy', giving a mysterious, understated lift to the end of the sequence.

The Pictures feels more supple than *The Columbiad* partly because its rhythms vary to suit the speaker and his mood. Columbus's anger in Picture XVII ('Columbus in Chains') is reinforced by clever substitutions, like the trochee at the beginning of line 2 which places the indignant stress on 'Chains' and in 'Authors of wrong, and slaves to fortune merely!', where the attention is arrested by another trochee at the beginning, and the feminine ending casts the 'Authors' away in contempt. The possibilities of the blank verse are exploited to dramatize the turmoil. Short periods alternate with long, and the long are enlivened by enjambement. The run-on of 'brave / To forfeit', for example, speeds the tempo of the sentence running from lines 11 to 14, and the highly relevant stress on 'Vain . . .' in line 18 is made possible by 'mind / Vainly depending'.

By contrast, the unvaried iambics of the following Picture XVIII ('Columbus at Valladolid') strike the reader not as the leaden decasyllabics of *The Columbiad*, but as expressing the relative calm achieved by the protagonist as he nears his death. Now the rhythm is quiet, the stresses few, and only two enjambements, significantly at the points where fancy stirs his repose, quicken the beat. And the samples provided by the extract by no means exhaust the variety of verse forms employed in the poem as a whole. As the pictures change from descriptive passage, to dialogue and dramatic monologue, so the metre moves from octosyllabic couplets, decasyllabic couplets and blank verse, and even (in a sort of anti-masque in which a sailor argues with his wife about whether he should sign on with Columbus), anapests of varying line lengths.

The variety and responsiveness of the verse has something to do, of course, with the models Freneau chose for his poem. Unlike *The Columbiad*, bound by the unified tone of the secondary epic, *The Pictures* is derived from more dramatic forms, in which the poetry is customarily altered to suit both speaker and occasion. One classical precedent almost certainly known to Freneau, as suggested by the title of his even earlier poem on the Columbus theme, 'Columbus to Ferdinand', is Ovid's *Heroides*, a sequence of verse letters like 'Dido to Aeneas' and 'Ariadne to Theseus', in which the legendary heroines reproach their men for abandoning them. The *Heroides* format still had to do with 'history', but with the woman's view of it – the less glorious, more pathetic implications of the heroes' great deeds. Michael Drayton used the idea in his *England's Heroical Epistles* (1619) to add the dimension of love between the sexes to the sterner affairs of Edward the Black Prince, Richard II, Owen Tudor and others (and he fleshed out the scheme by adding the men's answers), and – most famously and perhaps best known to Freneau – Alexander Pope reworked the concept in 'Eloisa to Abelard' (1717).

The unfortunate women of history were given fuller dramatic voice in the early eighteenth century in the 'she-tragedies' of Nicholas Rowe (*The Tragedy of Jane Shore*, 1714, and *The Tragedy of Lady Jane Gray*, 1715), and James Thomson (*The Tragedy of Sophonisba*, 1730). But these were the same Whig dramatists who turned history and legend to the cause of the Glorious Revolution. Rowe's *Tamerlane* (1701–2) converted the tyrant into 'a monarch of almost priggish rectitude . . . intended by Rowe to represent William III' (Sutherland, 1929), and the play was regularly revived on the anniversary of the landing of William of Orange. Thomson celebrated liberty in a long poem of that name (1735) in which a goddess shows the poet a vision comparing the glory of Republican Rome with the present state of Italy, depraved by superstition (that is, Catholicism), 'slavery, vice and unambitious want'; then traces the history of the idea of freedom, from Egypt through Greece and Rome to the Saxons, the Cantons of Switzerland and the House of Orange. William Bond's play, *The Tuscan Treaty: or, Tarquin's Overthrow* (1733) and Addison's enormously popular *Cato* (1713) used crucial moments in Roman history (the beginning and tragic end of the Republic) to glorify liberty of conscience against the encroachments of absolutist government. The tradition of Whig drama goes right back to *Lucius Junius Brutus* by Nathaniel Lee, performed in 1680, two years after the Popish plot in the midst of the controversy over the Exclusion Bill. 'Lee's subject, Brutus's expulsion of Tarquin and the establishment of the Roman Republic [writes the modern editor of the play], was a precedent often cited in the seventeenth century by the theorists who advocated a form of government with powers divided among a chief of state, an aristocracy, and the people' (Loftis, 1968, xiv). Charles II had his Lord Chamberlain shut it down after it had run only a few days. It is the plays in this tradition that Freneau's work most resembles, not only in attitude but also in details of diction and versification.

So a symmetrical pattern begins to emerge of two opposed traditions in the American political poetry of the early Republic: the one (represented by *The Columbiad*) imperial, heroic, masculine and doggedly declamatory, and the other (*The Pictures of Columbus*) republican, subversive, feminine and dialectical. If one gives way to the temptation to extend the enquiry into the lives of the poets themselves, however, the picture becomes less distinct. Both Barlow and Freneau were warm supporters of the revolution; both held various government jobs; both were friends of Jefferson (though Freneau was the more closely associated with the Anti-federalist party); Barlow had even spent time in France, where, like his friend Paine, he was made a citizen out of respect for his defence of the Jacobin cause, and his long essay, *Advice to the Privileged Orders* (1792), was suppressed by the Pitt government in England. Surely Barlow also deserves the sobriquet assigned to Freneau as 'the poet of the American revolution'?

The difference lies in their works. Whenever he wrote on public themes, Barlow tended towards a premature, unearned synthesis of contradictions he himself had perceived and expressed. *The Columbiad* ends with a vision of universal government and a common world language; it is not that no one believes such things could or should come about, just that there is nothing in the logic of the earlier Books of *The Columbiad* to convince the reader that it will. While Barlow reworked *The Vision of Columbus* so as to extend and elaborate this vision of harmony, the real world in America was moving in the opposite direction. The arguments over the nature of the Constitution, culminating in the great Federal Constitutional Convention of 1787, had resulted in the inevitable polarization into political parties: the Federalists, who stood for mercantile interests and advocated a strong central government and a national bank to finance native industry; and the Antifederalists, or Democratic Republicans, who represented labourers and small farmers, and argued for a government devolved into the state legislatures.

These events overtook even Barlow's non-fiction. His *Advice to the Privileged Orders* is often cited alongside Paine's *Rights of Man*, from which it took some of its ideas, but the difference between the two books is that Barlow argues that the state must represent the whole society, not just one class, while Paine recognized the inescapable consequence of democracy that sovereignty resides in the majority. Both books attacked the contemporary English system, where power was held by the land-owning class, but the one replaced that condition with an ideal and the other (given that the majority can change, that one party can replace another in power) with a fact that was already emerging in the United States.

This is why Freneau, with his life-time of partisan politics, his editing of the Jeffersonian *National Gazette* and (to set alongside his poems of the sea, about the beauties of the Bermudas, or 'The Indian Burial Ground') a long list of satirical and patriotic verses (sharpened by the actual adversity of having been captured at sea and incarcerated in a British prison hulk), looks more like the true 'poet of the American Revolution'.

And the question of what genre the American poets chose will not serve, either, as the overriding variable. After all, think of what Milton did to Virgil's epic (while still retaining the masculine 'voice', to be sure): he overturned its conventional ideals of heroism and empire, and made even the fallen world delectable. Freneau's achievement in *The Pictures of Columbus* is in the way he contains the extremes of promise and disappointment, vision and fact, in the same fiction. He was perfectly aware, for example, of the dark side of the European development of the New World, as his poem 'Discovery' (written in 1772) makes clear:

> What charm is seen through Europe's realms of strife
> That adds new blessings to the savage life? –
> On them warm suns with equal splendour shine,
> Their each domestic pleasure equals thine . . .
> And the gay soul, in fancy's vision blest,
> Leaves to the care of chance her heaven of rest. –

> What are the arts that rise on Europe's plan
> But arts destructive to the bliss of man?
> What are all wars, where'er the marks you trace,
> But the sad records of our world's disgrace?
> Reason degraded from her tottering throne,
> And precepts, called divine, observed by none.
>   Blest in their distance from that bloody scene,
> Why spread the sail to pass the gulphs between? –

Columbus in *The Pictures* marvels at the natural innocence of the new land he has discovered, then comes upon the body of a native killed by one of his own men for a pair of golden earrings. His ecstasy is shattered:

> Is this the fruit of my discovery!
> If the first scene is murder, what shall follow
> But havoc, slaughter, chains and devastation
> In every dress and form of cruelty!
> O injur'd Nature, whelm me in the deep,
> And let not Europe hope for my return. . . .
>
> > (Picture XIV)

Nature does almost whelm him in the deep; the following 'picture' finds him in a storm on his return to Spain, and the rest of the poem is taken up with his disillusionment, imprisonment and death.

Yet the sombre mood is recuperated by the poem's strategy of proleptic history. Columbus may have been disappointed, but 'we', at least, know what came of his discovery. And even if the threat to nature extends beyond the Spanish explorers to the English settlers, at least the contemporary reader might be forewarned and make a better job with his piece of the dispensation. What Freneau questions is the inevitable beneficence of progress (here again, he differs from Barlow), but at least the potential for a harmonious relation between art and nature remains.

And the same might be said for reason and fancy. Again and again Freneau expresses Columbus's vision of a new world still to be discovered in terms of a fanciful projection distrusted by the Spanish court. 'His head at last grows dizzy with this folly,' says Ferdinand's prime minister, 'And fancied isles are turned to real lands.' 'The clergy have no relish for your scheme, / And deem it madness,' writes Isabella's page of honour in a reply to Columbus's application. A man of reason, a mathematician called Orosio, says: 'This simple man would sail he knows not where; / Building on fables, schemes for certainty'. Even

Columbus himself begins to doubt his project: 'Shadows and visions for realities! – / It is a bold attempt! – Yet I must go. . . .'

To some extent the issue of the fancy is resolved within the fictional time of Columbus and his contemporaries. Ferdinand, following Shakespeare's Hippolyta, reasons that 'a plan pursued with so much obstinacy / Looks not like madness' and sees in Columbus a 'soul of so much constancy / As to bear up against the hard rebuffs, / Sneers of great men'. But as in the old story of Theseus and Hippolyta, it is the woman who is moved by his 'something of great constancy', and acts on it. 'One weak woman only hears my story! – ,' says Columbus ruefully; but Isabella it is who finances the venture.

Yet for the modern reader what authenticates the fancy is the comic irony of the proleptic history. Orosio may prophesy:

> Let him advance beyond a certain point
> In his fantastic voyage, and I foretell
> He never can return: ay, let him go! –

But we know better, and we also know that Orosio's 'reason' served him badly in this case. It is by thus emphasizing the theme of fancy and fact – or different kinds of 'fact' – that Freneau authenticates not only the American project, but also the role of the imagination in its production. The trick is to make the fanciful side of the debate seem almost impossible – to intensify its unlikeliness – and simultaneously ground it in what the reader knows to be true. And here again the comparison with Barlow is instructive. For not only did *The Columbiad* outrun that which could be verified by its contemporary readers (or modern readers, for that matter); it also failed to account for all that had already happened in history. In the whole of his long account of the American Revolutionary War in Books v–vii, and despite finding room for the names of generals, statesmen, philosophers both great and small (whole catalogues of them in Book v), Barlow makes not one mention of his old friend Tom Paine. The history of the American Revolution without Tom Paine is strikingly incomplete.

Perhaps this too-rapid leap from the quotidian to the monumental is what doomed *The Columbiad* to obscurity; like the statue of General Du Puy in Wallace Stevens's *Notes toward a Supreme Fiction*, it was rubbish in the end, unread and ridiculed even in America, before Barlow's death, while from Freneau lines and whole stanzas began to be stolen by British poets (see Tyler, i, 177–80) and continued to be imitated by American ones – Whitman and Hart Crane, to name just two. Two contemporary poets addressed a classical model; the one made it new, and the other turned it into a fossil. And Whitman would follow, more closely than any other American poet, the lead first given in Freneau's 'The Power of Fancy', by making Columbus the type of the alienated, romantic artist. In his 'Prayer of Columbus', written in 1874 toward the end of his productive life and after suffering a stroke, he had Columbus utter yet another prophecy – though this one was undercut by doubt – from the depression of his imprisonment:

> Is it the prophet's thought I speak, or am I raving?
> What do I know of life? what of myself?
> I know not even my own work past or present,
> Dim ever-shifting guesses of it spread before me,
> Of newer better worlds, their mighty parturition,
> Mocking, perplexing me.

References

Abrams, M. H. (1953), *The Mirror and the Lamp: Romantic Theory and the Critical Tradition*, New York: Oxford University Press.

Hill, Christopher (1958), *Puritanism and Revolution: Studies in Interpretation of the English Revolution of the Seventeenth Century*, London: Secker & Warburg.

Loftis, John (1968) (ed.), *Lucius Junius Brutus*, London: Edward Arnold (Regents Restoration Drama Series).

Martin, Terence (1961), *The Instructed Vision; Scottish Common Sense Philosophy and the Origins of American Fiction*, Bloomington, Ind.: Indiana University Press.

May, Henry F. (1976), *The Enlightenment in America*, New York: Oxford University Press.

Spiller, R. E. (1967) (ed.), *The American Literary Revolution*, New York: New York University Press.

Sutherland, J. R. (1929) (ed.), *Three Plays by Nicholas Rowe*, London: Scholaritis Press.

Tyler, Moses Coit (1897), *The Literary History of the American Revolution, 1763–1783*, 2 vols, New York: Barnes & Noble (Facsimile Library, 1941).

Wills, Garry (1978), *Inventing America: Jefferson's Declaration of Independence*, New York: Random House.

Further reading

TEXTS

William K. Bottorff and Arthur L. Ford (eds), *The Works of Joel Barlow*, 2 vols, Gainesville, Flo.: Scholars' Facsimiles and Reprints, 1970.

Louis Leary (ed.), *The Miscellaneous Works of Mr. Philip Freneau*, Delmar, New York: Scholars' Facsimiles and Reprints, 1975 (reprint of the 1788 edition).

Fred Lewis Pattee (ed.), *The Poems of Philip Freneau, Poet of the American Revolution*, 3 vols, Princeton: University Library (Oxford: Oxford University Press), 1902.

CONTEXTS

Walter Jackson Bate, *From Classic to Romantic*, Cambridge, Mass.: Harvard University Press, 1946.

Benjamin T. Spencer, *The Quest for Nationality: an American Literary Campaign*, Syracuse, N.Y.: Syracuse University Press, 1957.

Robert E. Spiller (ed.), *The American Literary Revolution, 1783–1837*, New York: Anchor Books, 1967; reprinted New York University Press, 1969.

Moses Coit Tyler, *The Literary History of the American Revolution, 1763–1783*, 2 vols, New York: Barnes & Noble (Facsimile Library), 1941.

CRITICAL AND BIOGRAPHICAL

May Bowden, *Philip Freneau*, Boston, Mass.: Twayne (United States Authors Series, 260), 1976.

Arthur L. Ford, *Joel Barlow*, New York: Twayne (United States Authors Series, 193), 1971.

Lewis Leary, *That Rascal Freneau: a Study in Literary Failure*, [n.p.]: Rutgers University Press, 1941.

Richard C. Vitzhum, *Land and Sea; the Lyric Poetry of Philip Freneau*, Minneapolis, Minn.: University of Minnesota Press, 1978.

9

Washington Irving
(1783-1859)

Poor Rip was at last reduced almost to despair; and his only alternative to escape from the labour of the farm and the clamour of his wife, was to take gun in hand and stroll away into the woods. Here he would some-times seat himself at the foot of a tree and share the contents of his wallet with Wolf, with whom he sympathised as a fellow sufferer in per-secution. 'Poor Wolf,' he would say, 'thy mistress leads thee a dog's life of it, but never mind my lad, whilst I live thou shalt never want a friend to stand by thee!' Wolf would wag his tail, look wistfully in his master's face, and if dogs can feel pity I verily believe he reciprocated the sentiment with all his heart.

In a long ramble of the kind on a fine autumnal day, Rip had uncon-sciously scrambled to one of the highest parts of the Kaatskill mountains. He was after his favourite sport of squirrel shooting and the still solitudes had echoed and re-echoed with the reports of his gun. Panting and fatigued he threw himself, late in the afternoon, on a green knoll, covered with mountain herbage, that crowned the brow of a precipice. From an opening between the trees he could overlook all the lower country for many a mile of rich woodland. He saw at a distance the lordly Hudson, far, far below him, moving on its silent but majestic course, with the reflection of a purple cloud, or the sail of a lagging bark here and there sleeping on its glassy bosom, and at last losing itself in the blue highlands.

On the other side he looked down into a deep mountain glen, wild, lonely and shagged, the bottom filled with fragments from the impend-ing cliffs and scarcely lighted by the reflected rays of the setting sun. For some time Rip lay musing on this scene, evening was gradually advanc-ing, the mountains began to throw their long blue shadows over the valleys, he saw that it would be dark, long before he could reach the village, and he heaved a heavy sigh when he thought of encountering the terrors of Dame Van Winkle.

As he was about to descend he heard a voice from a distance hallooing 'Rip Van Winkle! Rip Van Winkle!' He looked around, but could see nothing but a crow winging its solitary flight across the mountain. He thought his fancy must have deceived him and turned again to descend, when he heard the same cry ring through the still evening air: 'Rip Van Winkle! Rip Van Winkle!' – at the same time Wolf bristled up his back and giving a low growl, skulked to his master's side, looking fearfully down into the glen. Rip now felt a vague apprehension stealing over him; he looked anxiously in the same direction and perceived a strange figure slowly toiling up the rocks and bending under the weight of something he carried on his back. He was surprised to see any human being in this lonely and unfrequented place, but supposing it to be some one of the neighbourhood in need of his assistance he hastened down to yield it.

On nearer approach he was still more surprised at the singularity of the stranger's appearance. He was a short, square built old fellow, with thick bushy hair and a grizzled beard. His dress was of the antique Dutch fashion, a cloth jerkin strapped round the waist, several pair of breeches, the outer one of ample volume decorated with rows of buttons down the sides and bunches at the knees. He bore on his shoulder a stout keg that seemed full of liquor, and made signs for Rip to approach and assist him with the load. Though rather shy and distrustful of this new acquaintance Rip complied with his usual alacrity, and mutually relieving each other they clambered up a narrow gully apparently the dry bed of a mountain torrent. As they ascended Rip every now and then heard long rolling peals like distant thunder, that seemed to issue out of a deep ravine or rather cleft between lofty rocks, toward which their rugged path conducted. He paused for an instant, but supposing it to be the muttering of one of those transient thunder showers which often take place in mountain heights, he proceeded. Passing through the ravine they came to a hollow like a small amphitheatre, surrounded by perpendicular precipices, over the brinks of which impending trees shot their branches, so that you only caught glimpses of the azure sky and the bright evening cloud. During the whole time Rip and his companion had laboured on in silence, for though the former marvelled greatly what could be the object of carrying a keg of liquor up this wild mountain, yet there was something strange and incomprehensible about the unknown, that inspired awe and checked familiarity.

'Rip Van Winkle' (1820)

*   *   *

There can be scarcely a reader of English who does not know how this story proceeds: how Rip Van Winkle finds the spirits of the Dutch explorer Hendrick Hudson and his crew playing at ninepins in the mountains, how a drink from their flagon of gin sends him into a twenty-year sleep, from which he awakes to find his scolding wife dead, his village transformed and his country changed from a British colony into an independent republic. The story was enormously popular both in and since its time. When the collection in which it appeared first began to be serialized in New York, it rapidly became the American best-seller for 1819 (see Morris, 1976, 851), and the English edition of 1820 (the very year in which the Rev. Sydney Smith asked, 'In the four quarters of the globe, who reads an American book?') made Irving the first American author to attain an international reputation.

So popular was *The Sketch Book of Geoffrey Crayon, Gent.* that it might be said to have inaugurated the American version of a genre developed by Walter Scott and others, of which Hawthorne's *Twice-Told Tales* (1837) and *Mosses from an Old Manse* (1846) were later developments: the collection of sketches – fictional, factual, fanciful, realistic, bitter and sweet – in which the author disguises himself under a whimsical pseudonymn or pretends to have got the story from a manuscript or an old legend. In Irving's instance the narrative mask was chosen to embrace the English contents of the book ('gents' being in short supply in the new republic); by the time he published *The Sketch Book* Irving had been for four years in England on his brothers' business, and was to remain in Europe for another fifteen; so many of the sketches are the essays of an American traveller. But there is also a slashing attack on 'English Writers on America', two sensitive and intelligent appreciations of American Indian manners and customs, and two short stories, 'Rip Van Winkle' and 'The Legend of Sleepy Hollow', both apparently authenticated by footnotes tracing them to actual events in their native American setting.

The role of the skittish narrator was hardly new of course. Various versions of the device were put to different uses in Henry Fielding's *Tom Jones* (1749), Laurence Sterne's *Tristram Shandy* (1759–67) and in gothic novels like Horace Walpole's *The Castle of Otranto* (1765). American literary journalism, especially of the superciliously conservative variety, had sprouted the odd whimsical pseudonym, such as Messrs Spondee and Colon of the *Port Folio* (1801–27), but this was a speciality for which Irving had become particularly well known. His first extended work, a series of nine essays on the drama, manners, dress and other contemporary fashions published in the New York *Morning Chronicle* in 1802–3, was signed 'Jonathan Oldstyle, Gent.' When he collaborated with his brother William and brother-in-law J. K. Paulding to produce the periodical series of satirical miscellanies called *Salmagundi* (1807–8), the authors were given out (among others) as Launcelot Langstaff, Esq., Anthony Evergreen and Will Wizard. His serio-comic *A History of New York* (1809) appeared under the name of Diedrich Knickerbocker. Probably 'this cavalier air, together with the mystery, and . . . the secrecy was a mere matter of sport', wrote R. H. Dana, reviewing *The Sketch Book* in *The North American Review* for September, 1819 (IX, 322). 'It is now well understood who the gentlemen were.'

Later on an American narrator's mystifications, as to who he was, where he got his stories, what he thought about them – even whether he could vouch for them – might be taken not so much as sport as profound scepticism (this, at least, is what Melville thought of Hawthorne's *Mosses*, in his now famous essay on the subject, published in 1850). Even later these authorial obliquities would be taken as daring experiments with the nature of fictional narrative itself (see, for example, Kermode, 1975, 83–114), for even when a narrator authenticates his fiction by tracing it to a documentary source, he also deconstructs it by introducing the possibility of faulty transmission. Both Hawthorne and Melville played this game with the pseudo-documentary several times.

Compared to later stories told by even trickier narrators, therefore, 'Rip Van Winkle' is really quite a simple affair. Or so it appears at first. At the literal level, it is a diverting tale of the supernatural. As an allegory in which family relationships stand for international alliances, it works as a parable of the emerging American republic. Rip's sleep projects him into an unfamiliar, even uncongenial world, but at least it frees him from the wife who was always nagging him about his idleness. Thus the story is a kind of daydream of independence, both personal and national, a celebration of that yearning – though not unconnected with the sense of loss accompanying the desire – for western flight from female domestic entanglements felt by so many Americans, and to which Irving himself would return in his 'A Tour on the Prairies' (1835). Hawthorne would write another version of the parable, though one more acutely angled towards the violent disorientations of the adolescent nation's initiation rites, in 'My Kinsman, Major Molyneaux' (1832). A young man from the country arrives in colonial Boston seeking his influential kinsman, who has promised to advance his fortunes. After his numerous enquiries meet with mysterious, almost Kafkaesque, hostility on the part of those he asks, he finally sees the major led out of town by a mob, tarred and feathered and riding a rail. Deciding to leave town himself after this horrific scene, he is prevented by a friendly stranger who tells him he may yet 'rise in the world without the help of your kinsman, Major Molyneux'.

Yet there are details of 'Rip Van Winkle' that hardly seem to be working towards a development of this theme. In this passage alone, at the important point in the story when Rip first sees the odd little man carrying the keg, two paragraphs interrupt the action to describe what Rip sees from the top of the mountains. Perhaps they work mainly as a pacing device, providing a moment of pause before the climax, but why are they so specific about two different landscapes, and what are they saying about the scenes? They seem to be portents of a crucial choice; but if so they provide a false lead in the plot, for Rip never makes the decision, or even considers it.

Then there seem to be difficulties quite out of proportion to a short story. Take, for example, the confusion between old and young, new and ancient. Rip's 'new acquaintance' is an 'old fellow' (very old, as it turns out) dressed in the 'antique Dutch fashion'. Rip himself (his first name suggests both a 'tearaway' and the gravestone letters for 'Rest in Peace') enters into the youth of his country as an old man, a 'patriarch' who finally has to be looked after like a child by his own daughter. (It is a joke something like that in Act II of *As You Like It*, when, shortly after Duke Senior praises the paradisal Forest of Arden because 'Here feel we not the penalty of Adam', the old Adam himself enters, tended by Orlando.) Again, are these paradoxes simply there to serve the tale – to accentuate the supernatural disruption of time – or do they communicate something else beside?

The answer, for once, is not far to seek. It comes in the preface to the collection, a short essay called 'The Author's Account of Himself', in which Irving crowds a surprising number of diverse topics: his love of travel, the reasons why he felt European travel answered his interests better than American, even an apology for having studied 'the shifting scenes of life', not 'with the eye of a philosopher, but rather with the sauntering gaze with which humble lovers of the picturesque stroll from the window of one print-shop to another'. 'The Author's Account' even finds room for a brief counterblast to the critical books written by British travellers in America:

I had, beside all this, an earnest desire to see . . . the great men of

Europe; for I had read in the works of various philosophers, that all animals degenerated in America, and men among the number. A great man of Europe, thought I, must therefore be as superior to a great man of America, as a peak of the Alps to a highland of the Hudson; and in this idea I was confirmed by observing the comparative importance and swelling magnitude of many English travellers among us; who, I was assured, were very little people in their own country.

Like Franklin, at his Paris dinner party, Irving turns the old hypothesis of Buffon and Raynal into a good joke. But clearly the issue still rankled, or at least still needed some sort of answer, even in a preface of less than three pages. And the same question might be asked of 'Rip Van Winkle', a mere sketch of a tale, apparently too short for more than one theme, which is nevertheless shot through with references to degeneration. For example, Rip is a 'sauntering' idler, and not much of a farmer. 'His patrimonial estate had dwindled away under his management, acre by acre, until there was little more left than a mere patch of Indian corn and potatoes.' This is an interesting detail for a writer who rebuts Buffon so robustly in his preface, especially since the only two species of vegetables said to remain *at all*, are both native to the new world. But there is no mistaking the emphasis. The words 'patrimonial' and 'estate', both more appropriate to an old country than to a new, accentuate the narrative point that Rip himself has fallen off since his family's transplanting: 'He was a descendant of the Van Winkles who figured so gallantly in the chivalrous days of Peter Stuyvesant, and accompanied him to the siege of Fort Christina. He inherited, however, but little of the martial character of his ancestors.'

The process of degeneration is not confined to Rip or to the plot of ground which he fails to cultivate energetically. Nor is it, as it might have been in a more patriotic tale, arrested and reversed with American independence. The sharpest paradox of youth and age in the story comes when Rip returns twenty years later to the village inn where he used to sit and discuss the affairs of the day with 'the sages, philosophers, and other idle personages of the village'. Now, as befits the new country, there is a new inn in its place, with the portrait on its sign metamorphosed from that of George III to George Washington, and before it a spanking new flagpole 'with something on the top that looked like a red night-cap'. But the new building is already decrepit: 'large, rickety, wooden . . . with great gaping windows, some of them broken and mended with old hats and petticoats, and over the door was painted, "the Union Hotel, by Jonathan Doolittle".'

The 'Author's Account' also provides a clue to the strange inclusion of the two landscape descriptions just before Rip meets the first of the ancient Dutchmen. 'Had I been merely a lover of fine scenery', Irving writes, 'I should have felt little desire to seek elsewhere' than America:

> for on no country have the charms of nature been more prodigally lavished. Her mighty lakes, like oceans of liquid silver; her mountains, with their bright aerial tints; her valleys, teeming with wild fertility; her tremendous cataracts, thundering in their solitudes; her boundless plains, waving with spontaneous verdure; her broad, deep rivers, rolling in solemn silence to the ocean; her trackless forests, where vegetation puts forth all its magnificence; her skies, kindling with the magic of summer clouds and glorious sunshine – no, never need an American look beyond his own country for the sublime and beautiful of natural scenery.

'Sublime' and 'beautiful' were technical words that would have been understood by any aesthetician (whether professional philosopher or lay describer of landscape on the grand tour) among Irving's contemporary readers. Edmund Burke had discriminated between the terms in his seminal *A Philosophical Enquiry into the Origin of Our Ideas of the Sublime and Beautiful* (1757). Roughly speaking, sublime feelings were sensations aroused by the harsh extremities of nature – steep crags, waterfalls, thunder and lightning, storms at sea, and so on – while the beautiful had to do with nature in a softer and more rounded aspect, as with grassy hills and placid lakes on a sunny day. What Irving is saying is that nature in America provides the full range of landscapes. Indeed Rip seems to have the whole panoply at his feet, as he stands on the summit of the Catskills. To the east lies a typically 'beautiful' scene: lush woodland, a sailing barge on the 'glassy bosom' of the river, all set against the backdrop of the 'blue highlands'. To the west the scene is sublime – not only uncultivated but even uneroded except by catastrophe: 'wild, lonely and shagged, the bottom filled with fragments from the impending cliffs.' Rip stands on the cusp between the west and east, between the unexplored and the settled, the youth and middle age of the continent. He has also arrived at the crucial moment in his life and, through a trick of the event about to happen to him, the turning point in the life of his country as well.

If Rip and his country stand, each in a different sense, between two possibilities represented by the attractions of the opposing landscapes, why, when Rip awakes, is the actual scene so shabby – so without either sublimity or beauty? Again, an answer is suggested by the 'Author's Account'. Immediately following the paragraph about American scenery Irving explains why he preferred to live and write in Europe:

> But Europe held forth the charms of storied and poetical association. There were to be seen the masterpieces of art, the refinements of highly cultivated society, the quaint peculiarities of ancient and local custom. My native country was full of youthful promise; Europe was rich in the accumulated treasures of age . . . I longed . . . to tread, as it were, in the footsteps of antiquity – to loiter about the ruined castle – to meditate on the falling tower – to escape, in short, from the commonplace realities of the present, and lose myself among the shadowy grandeurs of the past.

'Association' was another term of contemporary philosophy. For the English philosopher David Hartley the association of ideas was the basic principle of psychology. Irving and his readers probably best understood the aesthetic applications of the idea as promulgated by Archibald Alison's *The Nature and Principles of Taste* (1790), which argued that sublimity and beauty in natural scenery does not exist in its own right but only in so far as it arouses associations in the mind of the beholder. If the observer is one of those 'more disposed to the employment of attention than of imagination' or a sensitive soul whose mind happens to be 'in such a state as to prevent this freedom of imagination, the emotion, whether of sublimity or beauty, is unperceived' (Essay i, Section ii). The best perceivers are the 'vacant and the unemployed' whose imaginations are free to 'extend themselves to analogies with the life of man and bring before us all those images of hope and fear which, according to our peculiar situations, have the dominion of our hearts' (ibid.). Indeed:

> This is very obviously the effect of all associations. There is no man who has not some interesting associations with particular scenes, or airs, or books, and who does not feel their beauty or sublimity enhanced to him by such connexions.
>
> (Essay i, Section iii)

Associations are drawn from history – whether personal ('the view of the house where one was born, of the school where one was educated') or national ('There are scenes undoubtedly more beautiful than Runny-mead, yet to those who recollect the great event which passed there, there is no scene perhaps which so strongly seizes upon the imagination'); there are associations to add to the power of everything from 'the beauty of a theory' to 'a relic of antiquity' (ibid.).

It is because of this rather particular context of the word 'association' that it would be unfair to characterize Irving's paragraph about Europe merely as the gushings of a snobbish tourist. What his sense of the European past provides is not just the glamour attaching to an ordinary object in the present, and not only (as T. S. Eliot would say later) a sense of scale by which to proportion contemporary events, but also and above all the incitement to imaginative effort. Whereas the tremendous volume of the American landscape overwhelmed and ultimately left dull his passive senses, the varied scenery of Europe – in its social as well as its physical sense – left space for invention. To use the disjunction popularized by Roland Barthes (1970), America was *lisible* (can only be read), Europe *scriptible* (susceptible to being written).

Since the assignment of these values runs directly contrary to the usual one (America having been conventionally thought of as under-plotted, and Europe overplotted), Irving risks being misunderstood on this point. But that he felt it this way round is unmistakable; it is even in his syntax. The paragraph on nature in America is really an elaboration of the old positive catalogue, used at least since the time of Captain John Smith to describe the American landscape. Stripped of modifiers, it is a simple series of which nothing is predicated. But unlike Captain Smith, or Whitman after him, Irving could not allow the bare catalogue to stand alone; he felt the need – as though in desperation at a stream of plenitude which could go on for ever and of which nothing could be said except that it was there – to fill every white space in the verbal matrix, to load each substantive with adjectival words and phrases. The paragraph is saturated, like a molecule with all its valences filled, and ordinary things like grass and waterfalls have become elaborated into 'verdure' and 'cataracts'. By contrast the paragraph on the attractions of the European scene is much more supple and varied rhetorically, with short and long sentences, verbal sequences, antitheses, appositives. The syntax is subordinated as well as paratactic; everything is focused, pointed, framed.

So, to return to 'Rip Van Winkle', there are two ways of reading the tale – one for its story line and another attending to the odd bumps, knobs and narrative *culs de sac*, like the references to degeneration and the landscape scenes, which seem to have little to do with the story. Rip possesses all the advantages of the observer of the sublime and beautiful – save one. He has the scenery, representing the full potential of the American continent; he has the leisure, or takes it; but he lacks the 'association'. Cut off from his European parent stock, he has degenerated not only physically but psychologically. His break with European history is, in a sense, a break with all history. Unable to connect, he cannot perceive. His response to the magnificent panorama is dullness, then oblivion. While he sleeps, 'history' in another sense overtakes him.

Thus described, 'Rip Van Winkle' sounds a much more pessimistic story than the one admired for so long since its first appearance in *The Sketch Book*. 'Amiableness is so strongly marked in all Mr Irving's writings as never to let you forget the man,' wrote Richard Henry Dana in his review in the *North American* (336). Dana liked 'Rip Van Winkle' best of all the sketches in the collection. 'Rip's idle good nature, which made him the favorite of the boys – his . . . "thinking it no use to work upon his own farm because everything about it went wrong" . . . yet always ready to help his neighbours . . . these show a thorough understanding of the apparent contradictions in character, and are set forth in excellent humour' (354–5). More recent criticism has interpreted these amiable contradictions as a myth of the American character in general:

> As Irving gave local habitation to a myth, perhaps as old as any which has beguiled the mind of man – that of Epimenides, Endymion, Sleeping Beauty, and the seven sleepers of Ephesus – he added such other familiar elements of popular lore as the thunder of the gods, birds of ill-omen, a magic potion . . . and dwarfs who are spectral spirits, transporting Valhalla and the Brocken to the Catskills, where Rip still triumphantly postures as the man-boy American (Huck Finn and Anse Bundren) who never grows up, the New World innocent who yearns to return to prelapsarian freedom from work and responsibility, to retire like Franklin at forty and fly a kite.
>
> (Leary, 1963, 26)

The comparison with Huck Finn is interesting, especially because his popularity with generations of readers owes as much to the sense of unfamiliarity and even danger he arouses, as to his amiability. How old is Huck? What are his origins? How can he live in a hogshead in a tanyard? What happens to him at the end of the story? In a sense Huck can be incorporated within the accepted ideals of civilized society (never better than when he comforted Mark Twain's post-bellum readers by turning instinctively, before his time and out of his place, into an abolitionist), but the threat of his anarchic life-style remains as salt to the story. (Indeed it is his antipathy to southern society that makes his conversion to northern values credible.) At a deeper level than contemporary satire Huck lives on as an American myth because he lives on the border between civilization and barbarism, generation and degeneration, history and oblivion. The 'blood lines' of aristrocracy (including his own) interested Mark Twain at least as much as they did Irving, and both authors were ambivalent about them. Rip and Huck are free because they have cut themselves off from the generations of Europe, but because unlike their authors they have made the break authentic – have taken it to its logical conclusion – they are alienated also from their American communities, perhaps even from history itself, in so far as 'history' provides a sense of the past and a conventional memorial to one's own life. Both forget, and both disappear.

This is not how Irving's American contemporaries saw the setting of 'Rip Van Winkle'. They were delighted that at last an American author not manifestly absurd, as they judged poor Joel Barlow to be, had found the present and the past of the American scene sufficiently rich to serve as a fictional background. Edward Everett, editor of the *North American Review* from 1819 to 1826, kept a particularly close watch on the nationality of Irving's settings. Reviewing *Bracebridge Hall* (1822), a second collection of tales and sketches by 'Geoffrey Crayon, Gent.', Everett preferred the story called 'Dolph Heyliger', about an American boy who encounters a ghost and recovers a buried treasure, because it 'is of the true Knickerbocker and Rip Van Winkle school', 'where his fort lies' (xv, 215). Eight years later, in the course of a long piece defending the *North American* against accusations in the *Scotsman* and the *Edinburgh Reivew* that the Boston journal lacked the confidence to foster truly native growths in American literature and political ideology, Everett made his judgement more explicit: 'The best of Mr Irving's works are those in which he has drawn his inspiration wholly from American sources, and those of which the scene is laid abroad, though often beautiful, are uniformly feebler than the former' (xxxi, 44). By this time Irving had been living in Europe for fifteen years, and his search for the picturesque had taken him as far afield as Andalucia, which provided historical and folkloristic material for a sort of Spanish *Sketch Book* called *The Alhambra* (1832). It was not until

Irving's triumphant return to the United States that he began to consider the possibility of an American legendary past. Perhaps inspired by his patron Scott's treatment of the Highlanders, he turned his mind to the American Indians, and in particular the tribes then being moved forcibly westward as a result of Andrew Jackson's Indian Removal Bill of 1832. He accompanied one of the marches, and the result, 'A Tour of the Prairies', was published as part of *The Crayon Miscellany* (1835). Everett was delighted with it. 'We are proud of Mr Irving's sketches of English life,' he wrote in his review in the *North American* for July 1835, 'proud of the gorgeous canvas upon which he has gathered in so much of the glowing imagery of Moorish times . . . but we glow with rapture as we see him coming back from the Prairies, laden with the poetical treasures of the primitive desert. . . . We thank him for turning these poor, barbarous *steppes* into classical land' (LXXXVIII, 14).

My own opinion* is that Irving's 'Tour' does indeed answer to something like Everett's description of it. But in 'Rip Van Winkle' the American past — in fact, the American setting both past and present — is treated with much less certainty. In 'Rip' the American break with history is total. This catastrophe is dramatized in two quite different ways: first, in the chronological dislocations and the paradoxes of youth and age; second, in the insubstantiality or decrepitude of whatever 'historical' characters and references remain in the text. Rip's ancestors '*figured gallantly* in the *chivalrous* days of Peter Stuyvesant'. The Dutch crew are literally ghostly, 'dressed in quaint, outlandish fashion', reminding Rip 'of the figures in old Flemish painting'. The effect everywhere is to associate the 'antique' with the figurative, the theatrical and the melodramatic. Irving invents the American picturesque only to erase it: 'and there were some of the houses of the original settlers . . . built of small yellow bricks brought from Holland, having latticed windows and gable fronts, surmounted with weathercocks . . . and in one of these very houses (which, to tell the truth, was sadly time-worn and weather-beaten), there lived . . . a simple, good-natured fellow of the name of Rip Van Winkle.' In this landscape without frames, 'lovers of the picturesque' cannot 'stroll from the window of one print shop to another'. The dislocation of the setting extends even to the bedrock of geology. The Catskill Mountains, or so the reader is told in the second sentence of 'Rip Van Winkle', 'are a dismembered branch of the great Appalachian family'.

---

* Developed at some length in Fender (1981), 20–5, 167–71.

This last detail, the first in the story, might alert the attentive reader to the possibility that the narrator is playing games with him. And maybe that is what is happening. Perhaps Irving was countering his doubts about association in America (a special, aesthetic kind of 'degeneration') just as he countered Buffon in his 'Author's Account' – with a joke. Only, as befits a fiction told by an intermediary with an ironically 'picturesque' name, this joke is subtly extended into narrative evasions, half-truths, even lies. And the best part of the joke, considering how anxious his well-wishing American contemporaries were that he stick to native materials, is that 'Rip Van Winkle' is not native to the American scene at all. Neither is 'The Legend of Sleepy Hollow' or 'Dolph Heyliger', for that matter. Despite the mock-scholarly protestations of the narrator to the contrary, they come from German fiction and folklore: 'Rip' from the old tale 'Peter Klaus', 'The Legend' virtually translated from Bürger's *Der wilde Jäger*, and the second part of 'Dolph' an adaptation of the Flying Dutchman story. It would seem that even before Hawthorne the American narrator became obscurely frolicksome.

References

Barthes, Roland (1970), *S/Z*, Paris: Editions du Seuil.

Fender, Stephen (1981), *Plotting the Golden West; American literature and the Rhetoric of the California Trail*, Cambridge: Cambridge University Press.

Kermode, Frank (1975), *The Classic*, London: Faber & Faber.

Leary, Lewis (1961), *Washington Irving*, Minneapolis, Minn.: University of Minnesota Press (Pamphlets on American Writers, 25).

Melville, Herman (1850), 'Hawthorne and his mosses', *Literary World*, 17 and 24 August 1850; reprinted in Edmund Wilson (ed.), *The Shock of Recognition*, 2nd edn, 2 vols, New York: Grosset & Dunlap, 1955, I, 187–204.

Morris, Richard (1976) (ed.), *Encyclopedia of American History*, Bicentennial edition, New York: Harper & Row.

Further reading

TEXT

Henry Pochmann, Herbert Kleinfield, Richard Rust (eds.), *The Complete Works of Washington Irving*, Madison, Wisc.: University of Wisconsin Press (Boston: Twayne), 1970– ; vol. VIII, *The Sketch Book of Geoffrey Crayon, Gent.*, ed. Haskell Springer, 1978.

CONTEXTS

Van Wyck Brooks, *The World of Washington Irving*, New York: Doubleday, 1944.
Christopher Hussey, *The Picturesque: Studies in a Point of View*, London: Putnam, 1927.

CRITICAL AND BIOGRAPHICAL

William Hedges, *Washington Irving: an American Study*, Baltimore: Johns Hopkins Press, 1965.
Lewis Leary, *Washington Irving*, Minneapolis, Minn.: University of Minnesota Press (Pamphlets on American Writers, 25), 1963.
Philip McFarland, *Sojourners*, New York: Atheneum, 1979.
Stanley T. Williams, *The Life of Washington Irving*, 2 vols, New York: Oxford University Press, 1935.

10

James Fenimore Cooper
(1789–1851)

'Listen, Hawkeye, and your ear shall drink no lie. 'Tis what my fathers have said, and what the Mohicans have done.' He hesitated a single instant, and bending a cautious glance toward his companion, he continued, in a manner that was divided between interrogation and assertion, 'Does not this stream at our feet run towards the summer, until its waters grow salt, and the current flows upward?'

'It can't be denied that your traditions tell you true in both these matters,' said the white man; 'for I have been there, and have seen them; though, why water, which is so sweet in the shade, should become bitter in the sun, is an alteration for which I have never been able to account.'

'And the current!' demanded the Indian, who expected his reply with that sort of interest that a man feels in the confirmation of testimony, at which he marvels even while he respects it; 'the fathers of Chingachgook have not lied!'

'The Holy Bible is not more true, and that is the truest thing in nature. They call this up-stream current the tide, which is a thing soon explained, and clear enough. Six hours the waters run in, and six hours they run out, and the reason is this: when there is higher water in the sea than in the river, they run in, until the river gets to be highest, and then it runs out again.'

'The waters in the woods, and on the great lakes, run downward until they lie like my hand,' said the Indian, stretching the limb horizontally before him, 'and then they run no more.'

'No honest man will deny it,' said the scout, a little nettled at the implied distrust of his explanation of the mystery of the tides; 'and I grant that it is true on the small scale, and where the land is level. But everything depends on what scale you look at things. Now, on the small scale, the 'arth is level; but on the large scale it is round. In this manner, pools and ponds, and even the great fresh-water lake, may be stagnant, as you and I both know they are, having seen them; but when you come to spread water over a great tract, like the sea, where the earth is round, how in reason can the water be quiet? You might as well expect the river to lie still on the brink of those rocks a mile above us, though your own ears tell you that it is tumbling over them at this very moment!'

If unsatisfied by the philosophy of his companion, the Indian was far too dignified to betray his unbelief. He listened like one who was convinced, and resumed his narrative in his former solemn manner.

'We came from the place where the sun is hid at night, over great plains where the buffaloes live, until we reached the big river. There we fought the Alligewi, till the ground was red with their blood. From the banks of the big river to the shores of the salt lake, there was none to meet us. The Maquas followed at a distance. We said the country should be ours from the place where the water runs up no longer on this stream, to a river twenty suns' journey toward the summer. The land we had taken like warriors, we kept like men. We drove the Maquas into the woods with the bears. They only tasted salt at the licks; they drew no fish from the great lake; we threw them the bones.'

'All this I have heard and believe,' said the white man, observing that the Indian paused: 'but it was long before the English came into the country.'

'A pine grew then where this chestnut now stands. The first pale-faces who came among us spoke no English. They came in a large canoe, when my fathers had buried the tomahawk with the redmen around them. Then, Hawkeye,' he continued, betraying his deep emotion only by permitting his voice to fall to those low, guttural tones, which rendered his language, as spoken at times, so very musical; 'then, Hawkeye, we were one people, and we were happy. The salt lake gave us its fish, the wood its deer, and the air its birds. We took wives who bore us children; we worshipped the Great Spirit; and we kept the Maquas beyond the sound of our songs of triumph!'

'Know you anything of your own family at that time?' demanded the white. 'But you are a just man, for an Indian! and, as I suppose you hold their gifts, your fathers must have been brave warriors, and wise men at the council fire.'

'My tribe is the grandfather of nations, but I am an unmixed man. The blood of chiefs is in my veins, where it must stay forever. The Dutch landed, and gave my people the fire-water; they drank until the heavens and the earth seemed to meet, and they foolishly thought they had found the Great Spirit. Then they parted with their land. Foot by foot, they were driven back from the shores, until I, that am a chief and a sagamore, have never seen the sun shine but through the trees, and have never visited the graves of my fathers!'

'Graves bring solemn feelings over the mind,' returned the scout, a good deal touched at the calm suffering of his companion; 'and they often aid a man in his good intentions; though, for myself, I expect to leave my own bones unburied, to bleach in the woods, or to be torn asunder by the wolves. But where are to be found those of your race who came to their kin in the Delaware country, so many summers since?'

'Where are the blossoms of those summers! — fallen, one by one: so all of my family departed, each in his turn, to the land of spirits. I am on the hill-top, and must go down into the valley; and when Uncas follows in my footsteps, there will no longer be any of the blood of the saga-mores, for my boy is the last of the Mohicans.'

The Last of the Mohicans (1826)

* * *

Two men sit talking. They have done so since the beginning of the chapter and will continue almost until the end. A novel with so much physical action — of chases, skirmishes and Indian captivities — seems an odd context for an extended debate. Is the subject of their discussion relevant to the action? Does it hint at what is about to happen and recapitulate what already has? No. Does it comment on the action, drawing subtle meaning from it? Not apparently, or at least, not immediately. So what do these two men represent in *The Last of the Mohicans*, and what is the significance of their discussion?

In the first place, they 'represent' their respective races, both in what they are and in what they say. One is Chingachgook, the old chief of the Mohicans and father of the novel's Indian hero, Uncas, the 'last of the Mohicans' himself. The other is an American of English extraction named Nathaniel (Natty) Bumppo, the transcendent figure of Cooper's Leather-Stocking Tales, who appears in the various books of the series under different sobriquets — 'Deerslayer', 'Pathfinder', 'Leather-Stocking' and 'the trapper' — according to his age and *métier* at the time of the story's setting. Here, at his prime, he is called 'Hawkeye'.

In addition to representing, however, they are also, in a sense, meeting to negotiate; so both are described as different kinds of blend of savage and civilized qualities. The Indian's body 'presented a terrific emblem of death, drawn in intermingled colors of white and black', but sports a 'chivalrous scalping tuft' on the top of his head. That is, though savage, he is prepared to give his enemies a chance, like a medieval knight. Moreover, certain implements of his savagery are manufactured and supplied by the 'civilized' whites: 'A tomahawk and scalping-knife, of English manufacture, were in his girdle; while a short military rifle, of the sort with which the policy of the whites armed their savage allies, lay carelessly across his bare and sinewy knee.' As for his age, he has 'reached the vigor of his days, though no symptoms of decay appeared . . . to have yet weakened his manhood'.

The American 'exhibited, through the mask of his rude and nearly savage equipments, the brighter, though sunburnt and long-faded complexion of one who might claim descent from a European parentage'. The narrator's tentative tone on the matter of Hawkeye's race contrasts sharply with the hero's own insistence, repeated occasionally and sometimes in oddly inappropriate circumstances, that he is all white, without the 'cross' of Indian or Negro blood. Perhaps his wild environment and his role as interpreter, in both language and customs, between white and Indian requires him to be quite definite about his heredity. In any case his clothing declares his intermediate status: 'a hunting shirt of forest green, fringed with faded yellow, and a summer cap of skins . . . a knife in his girdle of wampum' and moccasins 'ornamented after the gay fashion of the natives'. His principal weapon is the long rifle, 'which the theory of the more ingenious whites had taught them was the most dangerous of all firearms' (24–5). It is not just that Hawkeye combines Indian and white accoutrements – his 'natural' colours setting him off sharply from the red, black and pipeclay white of the English army – but also that the 'savage' side of his clothing is itself an exotic blend of 'gay fashion' and feral utility suggesting the noble savage of the French Romantics – of Baudelaire's Indian dandy, for example. John Cawelti (1971, 45) has shown how this picturesque dress has been duplicated in the hero's costume in the western movies.

The conversation, like the disputants' clothing, seems to exhibit the relative merits of white and red culture – which is closer to nature, and which more savage? Hawkeye thinks they come out about equal in the latter respect: 'Your fathers came from the setting sun, crossed the big river [a footnote glosses this as the Mississippi], fought the people of the country, and took the land; and mine came from the red sky of the morning, over the salt lake, and did their work much after the fashion that had been set them by yours; then let God judge the matter between us, and friends spare their words!' But Chingachgook thinks that the white man's method of population resettlement, 'the leaden bullet with which you kill', was much more effective than 'the stone-headed arrow of the warrior'. Hawkeye doubts that the blunderbusses of the early settlers were any more deadly than 'a hickory bow and a good flint-head' (25–6).

And so on. It soon develops that they are also comparing the premises and processes of white and Indian knowledge. Hawkeye admits he cannot know the whole truth even about his own culture, because white men 'write in books what they have done and seen, instead of telling them in villages, where the lie can be given to the face of a cowardly boaster'. This observation is followed by the passage excerpted here, in which Chingachgook relates the 'authentic' history of his tribe, as handed down by his fathers.

The discussion is rendered portentous partly by its subject and partly by the sonority of the special 'Indian' English in which it is held. Subsequent imitations in popular fiction and western films have by now dulled something of its strangeness, but the original literary effect, prompting contemporary readers to reconstitute references to the 'salt lake', and 'place where the sun is hid at night' and 'twenty suns' into the common 'white' parlance of 'Atlantic Ocean', 'west', and 'twenty days', must have accentuated the apparent distance – both chronological and cultural – between the events in the book and the time of its publication. It might also have afforded a new perspective of the history they learned at school. Cooper thought he was representing Indian speech as it was. As he puts it in the introduction to the book, the Indian 'draws his metaphors from the clouds, the seasons, the birds, the beasts, and the vegetable world. . . . His language has the richness of and sententious fullness of the Chinese.'

Other people have not been so sure. Leslie Fiedler (1960, 198) says Cooper made his 'Indians talk like mythic Celts out of Ossian', and contemporary critics were only slightly less severe. W. H. Gardiner and General Lewis Cass, in different articles in the *North American* in 1826 and 1828, both took Cooper to task for relying too credulously on the *Account of the History, Manners, and Customs of the Indian Nations Who Once Inhabited Pennsylvania* (1819), by the Moravian missionary to the Indians on the Susquehanna, John Gottlieb Heckwelder. 'He has relied exclusively [wrote Gardiner] upon the narrations of the enthusiastic and visionary Heckwelder, whose work is a mere eulogism upon the virtues of his favorite tribe, and contains, mixed with many interesting facts, a world of pure imagination' (XXIII, 166). Gardiner wondered whether 'such a civilized warrior as Uncas ever flourished' in a real Indian tribe:

> Uncas is represented as falling in love with Cora at first sight. This we do not object to, as we suppose an Indian is about as likely to fall in love at first sight as a white man. But then, we apprehend, he has his own aboriginal mode of expressing the tender passion. We remember once to have had the honor of meeting a deputation of Pawnee chieftains in a fashionable drawing room. One of the Sagamores, intoxicated partly with beauty and partly with rum, approached a young belle, and raising his hands, explained, 'Oh!' (or it might have been Hugh!) 'pretty!' This we took, at the time, to be the beginning of an Indian courtship; though great doubts were entertained whether the admiration of the savage had been thus excited by the beauty of the lady, or the brilliancy of her necklace.   (167)

General Cass, Governor of Michigan from 1813 to 1831, had commanded American Army detachments against the Indians and knew a good deal of frontier conditions. If only Cooper too, he wrote, could have collected 'his materials from nature, instead of the shadowy representations he has studied [in Heckwelder] . . . he would find that an Indian does not always speak in figures and parables'. He added a good pastiche, drawn from phrases in *The Last of the Mohicans* and *The Prairie*, to show all that he thought false in Cooper's Indian speech:

> A gull fans a thousand miles of air to find the sea; the women and children of a pale face cannot live without the meat of a bison; a head is white, but there is a forked tongue; the leaves cover the trees in the season of fruits. . . . If any of his words fall to the ground, they will pick them up and hold them to their ears. He gave them tongues like the false call of the cat-bird; hearts like rabbits; the cunning of the hog (but none of the fox), and arms longer than the legs of the moose.'   (XXVI, 48–9)

There is clearly more at stake here than the virtues and vices of a novelist's dialogue. Cass's opinion of Cooper comes from his doubts about the thought and behaviour of the Indians themselves. Reviewing two recent books on the Indians in a long, learned article in the *North American* for January 1826, he declared:

> The range of thought of our Indian neighbors is extremely limited. Of abstract ideas they are almost wholly destitute. They have no sciences, and their religious notions are confused and circumscribed. They have but little property, less law, and no public offences. They soon forget the past, improvidently disregard the future, and waste their thoughts, when they do think, upon the present.   (XXII, 79)

He also suggested that what had been taken as complex words in Indian languages were really simple monosyllables run together (77) and that the so-called 'richness of . . . grammatical forms' of Delaware (i.e. Mohican) verbs were 'useless appendages, adding no precision to the language, condensing its phraseology but little, and perplexing it with an almost infinite variety of combinations' (80).

Cass's view of the Indian languages is not wholly inconsistent with Cooper's, since the corollary of his opinion that they have little abstract vocabulary and that their words are mainly monosyllables denoting material objects to hand, is that they might well use figures drawn from everyday things to express ideas beyond the immediate scene. The real dispute underlying the issue is between those who believed the American Indians represented a sane ecology and rich culture that was fast disappearing, and those who thought they had no culture at all. Cass was clearly in the latter camp, but the former had many adherents apart from Cooper and Heckwelder. Indeed, the idea that Indian speech is picturesquely figurative is surprisingly strong in American thinking. The *American Museum* for January 1789 began a series by Jonathan Edwards (son of the revivalist preacher) on the language of the Mohicans, flanking the first instalment of Edwards's treatise with an old letter from the late British superintendent of Indian Affairs in North America, Sir William Johnson, to the effect that 'though not very wordy, [the language of the Mohicans] . . . is extremely emphatical; and . . . adorned with noble images, strong metaphors, and equal in allegory to any of the eastern nations' (v, 21). *Niles' Register* (II, 81–2) printed verbatim the speech of a Tonnawonta Indian called John Sky at a council of principal chiefs in Gennessee County, New York, on 2 March 1812, under the (apparently unironic) title 'Indian Eloquence'. Indeed respect for the poetic possibilities of Indian speech goes back to Roger Williams's classic *Key into the Language of America* (1643), a description, dictionary and primitive grammar of the Narragansett

Indians (like Cooper's Mohicans, a branch of the Algonquin tribe) in Rhode Island and Long Island. Cadwallader Colden, later Governor of New York State from 1761 to 1776, made the first carefully documented study of the Iroquois Confederacy (Cooper's treacherous Mingoes) in his *The History of the Five Indian Nations* ... (1727), which included numerous verbatim reports of transactions between the whites and Indians, such as this speech by the Mohawk Cadianne to Francis, Lord Howard of Effingham, Governor-General of Virginia:

> Assarigoa, you are a man of knowledge and understanding, thus to keep the covenant-chain bright as silver; and now again to renew it, and make it stronger. (Then pointing to the three other nations, said,) But they are chain-breakers. I lay down this as a token, that we Mowhawks have preserved the chain entire on our parts. Gives two beavers and a racoon.
>
> The covenant must be kept; for the fire of love of Virginia and Maryland burns in this place, as well as ours, and this house of peace must be kept clean. Gives two beavers.
>
> We now plant a tree, whose top will reach the sun, and its branches spread far abroad, so that it shall be seen afar off; and we shall shelter ourselves under it, and live in peace without molestation. Here he gave two beavers.   (I, 41–2)

Colden glosses the reference to the tree with the note: 'The five nations always express peace by the metaphor of a tree.' His preface (I xxxiv–xxxv) praises their 'fluency of words' and 'elegancy in varying and compounding their words', which he says exceeds that 'any man could expect, among a people entirely ignorant of all the liberal arts and sciences'.

Of course, Colden's report cannot be taken as a document of what was actually spoken; the late-seventeenth-century reverberations of 'covenant' and 'chain' (like a governor's badge of office) suggest that the speech was as much a matter of what the white negotiators heard as what the Indian orator said. In other words, Europeans and Americans saw in the Indians what they needed to see. For General Cass, who first suggested the Indian Removal Bill to President Jackson and who believed it was the destiny of Americans of British origin to occupy the continent coast to coast, the claim of a distinct Indian culture had to be denied in order to justify the displacement and ultimately (though he would surely and sincerely have disowned the motive) the near-genocide of the American natives. But it was equally necessary for other Americans to re-invent the Indian as an exotic noble savage, as part of the process by which the surrounding wildnerness was recuperated as what Edward Everett would call 'classical land'.

Another version of the same argument centred on the quality of the language spoken by American whites. The British reviews had included in their charges against the culture of the new republic the allegation that Americans were allowing the English language to deteriorate, especially by their tolerance of neologisms. 'To the charges of ignorance and dullness', wrote Everett in his riposte to the *Scotsman* and the *Edinbugh Review*, 'we of course, plead guilty with great cheerfulness.' No doubt their condition results 'from the well-known degeneracy of the race on this side of the water' (*North American Review*, XXXI, 59). In another salvo nine years earlier he had rounded on the *New London Monthly Magazine* for February 1821, with the neat debating point, 'Whence should we learn our bad English', when 'we are derided and taunted with our dependence on the English press, when we are said to have no literature of our own, and when most of our books, from children's readers to college text books, are English in origin'? As for American coinages, 'language is a fluctuating thing' and Americans may need new words for new ideas and institutions, such as 'congressional' for 'a body of representatives equally chosen by the people, a sort of body, we believe, unknown in England' or 'presidential' for 'a chief magistrate ruling by the consent of the people, an idea also not familiar to the old world' (XIII, 30–1).

But it was not just the British who expressed anxieties about where American English was heading. Indeed if Everett seems to be answering any specific argument, it is that of Sidney Willard, Professor of Hebrew and Oriental Languages at Harvard, reviewing John Pickering's *Vocabulary, or Collection of Words and Phrases which have been supposed to be peculiar to the United States . . .* (1816) – in the *North American*, of all places – in which 'presidential' and 'congressional' are instanced as particularly 'barbarous' innovations, and the linguistic version of Buffon's law by no means brushed aside so lightly:

> Violations of the genuine idiom, in a country separated from the parent stock, but professing to speak and write the same language, often escape with impunity. They are commonly the result of negligence; sometimes, however, of pardonable ignorance. Even where the language is most cultivated, all the vigilance of criticism is requisite to preserve its idiom pure. (III, 359–60)

It was Walter Channing (1786–1876), Professor of Obstetrics at Harvard and brother of the Unitarian minister, who grasped the literary implications of the American-language issue. He too deplored American coinages (*North American Review*, II, 14) but in reviewing various causes commonly alleged for the 'literary delinquency of America' – too little leisure, no profession of authorship, no clear copyright, lack of antiquity, and so on (ibid., 37–41) – he himself came down strongest for the disadvantage that the emerging country shared a language with the metropolitan culture. 'If then we are now asked, why is this country deficient in literature?' he wrote in the *North American* for September 1815, 'I would answer, in the first place, because it possesses the same language with a nation, totally unlike it in almost every relation' (I, 307–8). A national literature must have a national language; but Americans were for too long colonials who had to 'wait for all improvements from abroad [and] acquire a literary tone from the mother country' (312).

But if only they knew where to look, Channing continued, Americans would find a native literature expressed in its own language, already flourishing on the continent. 'I now refer to the oral literature of [the] aborigines' whose 'words of description' are 'the very language for poetry'. The Indians' language 'is now as rich as the soil on which he was nurtured, and ornamented with every blossom that blows in his path. It is now elevated and soaring . . . now precipitous and hoarse. . . . In the oral literature of the Indian, even when rendered in a language enfeebled by excessive cultivation, every one has found genuine originality' (313–14).

This was to turn the metaphor of cultivation back in the faces of the Buffonists; it was also to attribute to the Indian languages the merits ascribed by Kames and Blair to good, imaginative English, and finally to claim for the Indian 'nations' the power of 'association'.

So the status of American Indian culture, and particularly of their languages, was a counter not only in debates about American policy relating to the frontier, but also in the disputes of transatlantic literary politics. And it is this latter context, particularly, that is most useful to an understanding of Cooper's Indians. Like Irving (at leisure) and 'Crèvecoeur (by force of circumstance), Cooper had his doubts about the American scene as a setting for imaginative literature, but he was able to meet the issue more positively than either of them. Crèvecoeur, frightened off his farm in the violent, faction-ridden neutral ground above and to the west of New York City, simply lacked the peace to continue writing in the vein of *Letters from an American Farmer*. So he returned to his metropolitan centre and reinvented America after the contemporary French fashion for the exotic. Irving found his native materials too raw and commonplace to excite the associations necessary for the perception of imaginative literature, so he too retreated to the metropolis to write about – and to exemplify through a subtle narrative joke – his failure to write about America. Cooper too was worried about 'association'. As he wrote in his third preface to *The Spy*, native materials were so accessible to American readers, and democratic manners had so restricted the range of social references, that there was too little beyond the ordinary that an author of fiction could present so as both to convince his readers and still evoke a sense of the mysterious and unexpected. While in Europe he expanded on this theme in a work of non-fiction he called *Notions of the Americans* (1828). In a vigorous refutation of some of the grosser European prejudices against American politics and society, Cooper nevertheless had to admit, in one of those negative catalogues characteristic of nineteenth-century American literary people resident in, or newly returned from, Europe, that America had:

> no annals for the historian; no follies (beyond the most vulgar and commonplace) for the satirist; no manners for the dramatist; no obscure fictions for the writer of romance . . . nor any of the rich artificial auxiliaries of poetry. . . . There is no costume for the peasant, (there is scarcely a peasant at all) no wig for the judge, no baton for the general, no diadem for the chief magistrate. . . . However useful and respectable all this may be in actual life, it indicates but one direction to the man of genius. (II, Letter 23)

But Cooper had already been more fortunate and resourceful than this gloomy generalization would suggest. Unlike Crèvecoeur, he was born too late for first-hand experience of the Revolutionary War, the events of which were already acquiring the focus and depth of field bestowed by the reversed telescope of history. So he could make fiction even out of that troubled and ill-defined guerrilla battleground of lower New York State – the very country Crèvecoeur had to flee – in his historical novel *The Spy* (1821), whose subtitle is 'A Tale of the Neutral Ground'. In other words, Cooper was perceptive enough to realize that the United States was already acquiring a history, that there were, after all, 'annals for the historian', or at least for the historical novelist. So Cooper headed for his true, native metropolis – New York City – and began to write historical novels set in the Revolutionary War on land (*The Spy*, *Lionel Lincoln*, 1825) and on the sea (*The Pilot*, 1824). In this period came also the first two, and most of the third of the Leather-Stocking Tales (he finished *The Prairie* in Paris in 1826). And this simple fact of chronology and context, together with the evidence of Cooper's letter to his publishers that he first intended *The Pioneers* (1823), *The Last of the Mohicans* (1826) and *The Prairie* (1827) as a trilogy (ed. Beard, 1960, I, 168), are timely reminders that whatever else the first three Leather-Stocking Tales are (romances? fantasies? extended allegories of the human condition?), they are also historical fictions set, respectively, in a frontier community of the early 1790s, the French and Indian War at the time of Montcalm's assault on Fort William Henry on Lake George (1757), and the year of the Louisiana Purchase of 1803. American history, not European antiquity, was Cooper's first route to 'association', and that may be why his most popular books in his own country (all those mentioned above, save *Lionel Lincoln*, were best-sellers in America) – and one might say his best – were written before he left, with his wife and family, for his first trip to Europe.

Cooper also realized that America had a history of literature. Though he was certainly aware of European precedents, he had an equally good eye for native literary growths. The Leather-Stocking Tales exploited the popular cult of Daniel Boone (1734–1820), the explorer and scout, agent for the Transylvania Company and local official in many border communities, who kept 'lighting out' for settlements ever more remote from civilization. Boone had been glamourized as an explorer, discoverer and the greatest of frontiersmen by John Filson's widely read account, supposedly based on dictation taken from the man himself, *Discovery, Settlement and Present State of Kentucke* (1784). More particularly, *The Last of the Mohicans* exploits the perennial popularity in America of tales about captivity (whether the captives were women or men, and the captors Indians, Jesuits or – in Mrs Stowe's ingenious modification of the genre – southern whites), which were best-sellers from the time of Mary Rowlandson's *Captivity and Restauration* (1682, fifteen editions by 1800) down to that of Lew Wallace's *Ben-Hur* (1880, two million copies sold, many foreign translations).

So America also had, after all, some 'obscure fictions for the writer of romance'. And the darkest and most pervasive of them all, enhanced as it was by the additional 'associative' resonance (Scott's discovery, really) of the disappearing tribe, was the exotic recuperation of the American Indian. Yet historical novels and native fictional forms though they were, the Leather-Stocking Tales are not just conflations of the factual and imaginative materials their author found to hand.

Cooper obviously felt he had to add some 'framing' to his native resources, over and above that which an English novelist of manners had to add to his – or more often, hers. He needed to find an American equivalent of the social gradations he felt conferred such an advantage upon the European novelist, to synthesize hierarchies of appearance, modes of dress and levels of speech to replace the abandoned 'costume', wig, baton and diadem. Being American, however, these tokens had to be earned, not inherited – that is, they had to represent professional, temperamental and moral hierarchies a democratic reader would consider appropriate to their bearers. Thus Cora and Alice Monro in *The Last of the Mohicans* are distinguished by complexion and hair colour in order to indicate their capacities for feeling and to hint at their degree of sexual responsiveness. Thus too the clothing of Hawkeye and Chingachgook is carefully described in order to indicate their marginal status between the worlds of red man and white.

Once again, it is in the realm of spoken style that Cooper devoted most attention to these gradations. In a famous attack on Cooper, Mark Twain later complained that all his characters speak as though their mouths were rolling-mills busying themselves 'all day long in turning four-foot pigs of thought into thirty-foot bars of conversational railroad iron by attenuation' ('Fenimore Cooper's Literary Offenses', 1895). This is certainly true of the personnel in *The Last of the Mohicans*; everyone seems to take longer than necessary to say what he means. At times this periphrasis seems intended to achieve a particular rhetorical or comic effect, as in the case of Chingachgook's history of his tribe or the verbal perambulations of the singer David Gamut:

> 'This beast, [of a horse] I rather conclude, friend, is not of home raising, but is from foreign lands, or perhaps from the little island itself over the blue water? . . . I may speak of these things, and be no braggart; for I have been down at both havens; that which is situate at the mouth of Thames, and is named after the capital of Old England, and that which is called "Haven," with the addition of the word "New".' (9)

Mark Twain, of course, was very proud of his 'ear' for the spoken American word. *Huckleberry Finn* is prefaced by the author's explanatory note claiming to have caught no fewer than seven 'dialects' and accents heard on the Missouri and Mississippi rivers. But the distance between Cooper and Mark Twain is not so much one of ability as of purpose. Whereas Mark Twain was trying to convey local colour,

Cooper was attempting to generate meaning out of stylistic shadings between speeches the reader is extremely unlikely to have heard, had he been there in 'real life'. Take, for example, Chingachgook's history of his tribe in the passage selected for close examination. There are other ways of telling the same story. One is Hawkeye's, also in the passage. Another comes from the narrator's introduction to the book:

> The Mohicans were the possessors of the country first occupied by the Europeans in this portion of the continent. They were, consequently, the first dispossessed; and the seemingly inevitable fate of all these people, who disappear before the advances, or it might be termed the inroads of civilization, as the verdure of their native forests falls before the nipping frost, is represented as having already befallen them.   (v)

This is a neutral voice, earmarked as 'unfictional' (in terms of this novel, anyway) by its lack of periphrasis. Compared to Chingachgook's account, it is both direct and abstract. The Indian's narrative is more beautiful and less efficient. His sense of his displacement from his homeland is communicated through figures like 'I, that am a chief and a sagamore, have never seen the sun shine but through the trees' and the powerful summary of the Mohicans' life on the coast, touching only on the essentials of sustenance, reproduction and defence – the natural balance of the native culture. The white narrator can get something of the same meaning, though nothing of its nostalgic resonance, through the ironic revision of 'advances' into 'inroads'.

Yet in this book the contrast between white and Indian speech is not just one of abstractions versus concrete figures. The narrator has his simile of the frost, and Hawkeye (who, as we shall see, talks like a white though in the requisite Indian language) uses an analogy as acutely appropriate as an aphorism out of Francis Bacon, to explain the tides. The real difference is that the Indians' figures (in Cooper, anyway) are mainly metonymic, and the whites' metaphorical; and this distinction covers an even deeper one: that the whites are capable of irony, can make comparisons, can doubt the whole truth of what they proclaim, whereas the Indians can perceive one truth only, which they express in greater or lessser portions of the whole. Magua, the Indian villain of the book, says later that the whites 'have two words for each thing, while a redskin will make the sound of his voice speak for him'. This is meant as an insult, but it also epitomizes the 'pale-faces'' ability to see everything relatively – to compare and qualify. Even Hawkeye's version of Mohican history, though tricked out like his clothing in Indian references ('setting sun', 'big river'), is 'white' in that it poses one 'scale' (whether narrative or topographical) against another. It is he, not Chingachgook, who is aware of plural interpretations of nature and history – oral traditions, books – who believes in an objective truth of which these are only partial accounts, who knows what he does not know and would like to know it: 'though why the water, which is so sweet in the shade, should become bitter in the sun, is an alteration for which I have never been able to account.' As he finishes this sentence, as 'white' a passage of detached scientific speculation as one could imagine, his diction and tone become as scholarly as the narrator's 'Evidence of their Asiatic origin is deduced from the circumstances, though great uncertainty hangs over the whole history of the Indians.' As for what Hawkeye does know, some of it at least comes from books, not from what he can sense for himself, for how else would he know that the earth is round? Chingachgook, on the other hand, knows what he knows, which is what he has seen and heard and does not doubt.

So Cooper exploits a particular tradition (we have called it exotic) by which some Americans thought of the Indians and their language in order to meditate on the differences between white and Indian culture. The comparison, of course, is not quite on all fours. The Indians were already vanishing – had all but disappeared from that part of New York State in which *The Last of the Mohicans* is set – by the time the novel was written and read. Perhaps that is what made them accessible to the romanticizing imagination of both writer and reader. Certainly Cooper does his best to magnify the nostalgia generated by their disappearance. Chapter 3, from which the passage is taken, opens with an epitaph from the American nature poet William Cullen Bryant (1794–1878):

> Before these fields were shorn and tilled,
>   Full to the brim our rivers flowed;
> The melody of waters filled
>   The fresh and boundless wood;
> And torrents dashed, and rivulets played,
>   And fountains spouted in the shade.

Even to the reader unable to trace their source to Bryant's 'An Indian at the Burial-Place of his Fathers', these lines would announce a case of loss, of a primeval natural plenty (whether innocent or otherwise it does not say) gone for ever.

The American wilderness had vanished with them. Cooper prepares the scene of this chapter very carefully, so as to suggest a moment frozen, like the frame of a movie momentarily held by a jammed projector, in the midst of a process. Like Chingachgook's age, both the season and the landscape have just passed high summer. Already 'the rays of the sun were beginning to grow less fierce', but as yet no clearing has been made for cultivation, and 'the vast canopy of woods spread itself to the margin of the river overhanging the water' (23). Even the woods have a history; even in the vegetable world one species supplants another. As the sharp-eyed Indian observer of nature points out, a chestnut tree has taken the place of a pine. And by the time of the book's appearance, as the narrator's introduction and subsequent footnotes make clear, the wilderness has long passed its zenith. Though the country has undergone little apparent change, the Indians have since vanished – which is to say that everything is different: the wilderness has become a vacationers' park. 'There are fashionable and well-attended watering-places at and near the spring where Hawkeye halted to drink,' says the introduction, 'and roads traverse the forests where he and his friends were compelled to journey without even a path' (5–6). From primeval wood to spa in less than a lifetime!

Yet it would be a serious mistake – especially given its position in the first three of the Leather-Stocking Tales that Cooper wrote and which he originally intended as a trilogy – to read *The Last of the Mohicans* as an elegy for a lost Eden. Before the Dutch and the English, the Mohicans too came and supplanted the indigenous peoples. We are told so no fewer than three times. The ominous corollary, that one day may yet see the last of the Americans, is made explicit (or as explicit as a Cooper Indian can make it) by the old Indian sage Tamenund towards the end of *The Last of the Mohicans*: 'I know that the pale-faces are a proud and hungry race. I know that they claim not only to have the earth, but that the meanest of their color is better than the sachems of the redman. . . . But let them not boast before the face of the Manitou too loud. They entered the land at the rising, and yet may go off at the setting sun' (368).

And Cooper's famous antinomies – the good and bad Indian, the good and bad outlaw, the 'dark' and 'light' woman, the 'natural' and rapacious use of the environment – are not allegories for timeless verities of the human spirit, as in a pastoral romance (much as the book resembles and refers to the pastoral at times) to be resolved at the end in fictional harmony, but dialectical oppositions of particular moments in history. The word 'dialectical' is a reminder that the Marxist critic Georg Lukács once praised Cooper for catching that moment in history when 'the colonizing capitalism of France and England destroy[ed] physically and morally the gentile society* of the Indians which had flourished almost unchanged for thousands of years' (1962, 64). This is nearly right, though if anything it underestimates the rate of flux of the historical situation Cooper dramatizes. For one thing, the Indians had not remained 'unchanged for thousands of years', and for another, after the last of the Mohicans disappears, Cooper's whites sweep on westwards to make a different kind of wilderness of the landscape – and possibly of themselves. The famous irony underlying *The Prairie* is that though set on the Great Plains, when this enormous expanse of the continent had just been opened to American exploration and settlement, the story takes place in an atmosphere of death and degeneration:

> The harvest of the first year of our possession had long been passed, and the fading foliage of a few scattered trees was already beginning to exhibit the hues and tints of autumn. . . .

and:

> Amid the monotonous rolling of the prairie, a single naked and ragged rock arose on the margin of a little watercourse. . . . A swale of lowland lay near the base of the eminence, and as it was still fringed with a thicket of alders and sumac, it bore the signs of having once nurtured a feeble growth of wood.

Now the American landscape has gone from summer to late autumn; the hunters of bear and deer have become hunters of bees. Even Natty Bumppo (who will die at the end of this book) has become a beaver trapper. This time the Indians are defeated not by brave men with blunderbusses, but sold by foreign governments six thousand miles away. '"And where were the chiefs of the Pawnee Loups when this bargain was made?" suddenly demanded the youthful warrior. . . . "Is a nation to be sold like a skin of beaver?" "Right enough – right enough [answers Natty helplessly], and where were truth and honesty

---

* Not a misprint for 'gentle [much less genteel] society' but the translators' attempt to find an English equivalent for the German *Gentilgesellschaft*. This is apparently a coinage made up (as I guess, anyway, given that Lukács discusses Cooper alongside Scott) from the word for 'society' and *Gentil*, a loan word from the Latin *gens*, a race or clan supposedly descended from a common ancestor and sharing a name and certain religious rites; so 'tribal society' would probably serve as a suitable English equivalent.

also? But might is right according to the fashions of the 'arth; and what the strong choose to do, the weak must call justice." '

By now, though, the real struggle is not between white and Indian, but between Americans who are willing to live at peace in their environment, to tolerate what they cannot understand completely, accommodate diversity of landscape and peoples (even Spanish-speaking Roman Catholics, perhaps even what is left of the Indians), and other Americans who continue to look for virgin land to exploit in a hurry for quick profits, who kill what they cannot understand and therefore fear. ' "What the world of America is coming to and where the machinations and inventions of its people are to have an end, the Lord only knows," ' says Natty to Paul Hover and Captain Duncan Middleton. ' "How much has the beauty of the wilderness been deformed in two short lives! . . . and I, miserable and worn out as I seem, have lived to see it all!" "That you must have seen many a chopper skimming the cream from the face of the earth, and many a settler getting the very honey of nature, old trapper," said Paul, "no reasonable man can, or for that matter shall, doubt." '

In *The Prairie* the old ways of the explorer and settler are dead, or going through the hectic thrashings of a beheaded chicken. The independent spirit, the courageous, innovative, ingenious pioneer has become the restless, irritable emigrant Ishmael Bush, wandering pointlessly around the trackless prairie, having kidnapped a 'female' whose ransom his meanderings prevent his collecting, going nowhere. It is as though the novelist himself had joined the dance of death, miming the dissolution with a kind of crazy rush to the head of superfluous plots. Although criticized by contemporary reviewers for making too much happen too quickly in *The Last of the Mohicans* (see Dekker and McWilliams, 1973. 97–118), Cooper nevertheless multiplied the confusion in *The Prairie*, raising the total of captivities to three and producing a mystifying swirl of marches, attacks, prairie fires, counter-marches, counter-attacks and back-fires, single and general conflict, torture, an amateur trial and execution, a buffalo stampede and even a recognition scene. It is as though in killing off Natty Bumppo he was also trying to expel from his system the flotsam of the Daniel Boone fiction, the romance of the wandering, unattached American explorer. And so he was – for a while – until nearly fifteen years of assorted non-fiction and unsuccessful attempts at novels of manners drew him back to the Leather-Stocking series in the shape of *The Pathfinder* (1840) and *The Deerslayer* (1841).

For the deepest meaning of that discussion in the woods is not the relative merits of Indian and white wisdom. The Indian there, as elsewhere in the American imagination, is a projection of American pre-occupations – of the fears or hopes of an immigrant people on the margin of traditional experience, and of a novelist trying to pioneer an American fiction. Chingachgook's fatalistic vision is used to set off something more relativistic: intellectual curiosity, the ability to compare, the uneasy awareness that the past can be 'read' in more than one way and that the future holds several possibilities, not all of them pleasant. This is Natty Bumppo's mentality and it is also Cooper's – the ironic perspective of the American caught between the old world and the wilderness. At its worst it hates what it sees in the dark mirror of its other self, shuts it out and kills it (Natty's insistence on the purity of his race and the confections of Cooper's more crystalline romance structures are alike in their paranoia), but at its best it makes compromise possible, allows alternative systems to exist side by side, lets 'God judge the matter between, and friends spare their words'. In either case, its greatest strength, the tragic dimension which makes Cooper's Leather-Stocking Tales such magnets to the imagination, is that it knows its own limitations.

References

Beard, James Franklin (ed.) (1960–8), *The Letters and Journals of James Fenimore Cooper*, 6 vols, Cambridge, Mass.: Harvard University Press.

Cawelti, John (1971), *The Six-Gun Mystique*, Bowling Green, Ohio: Bowling Green University Popular Press.

Dekker, George and McWilliams, John (1973), *Fenimore Cooper; the Critical Heritage*, London: Routledge.

Fiedler, Leslie (1960), *Love and Death in the American Novel*, New York: Criterion.

Lukács, Georg (1962), *The Historical Novel*, trans. Hannah and Stanley Mitchell, London: Merlin.

Twain, Mark (1895), 'Fenimore Cooper's literary offenses', *North American Review*, reprinted in e.g. Edmund Wilson (ed.), *The Shock of Recognition*, 2 vols, New York: Doubleday, 1955, I, 580–94.

Further reading

TEXTS

James Franklin Beard and James Elliott (eds), *The Writings of James Fenimore Cooper*, Albany, N.Y.: State University of New York Press, 1980 (four volumes to date).

The Last of the Mohicans, Mohawk Edition, New York: Putnam (n.d.).

CONTEXTS

William Charvat, *The Profession of Authorship in America, 1800–1870*, ed. Matthew Bruccoli, n.p.: Ohio State University Press, 1968.

Richard Chase, *The American Novel and its Tradition*, Garden City, N.Y.: Doubleday, 1957.

Leslie Fiedler, *Love and Death in the American Novel*, New York: Criterion Books, 1960.

Richard Slotkin, *Regeneration through Violence; the Mythology of the American Frontier, 1600–1860*, Middletown, Conn.: Wesleyan University Press, 1973.

Henry Nash Smith, *Virgin Land; the American West as Symbol and Myth*, Cambridge, Mass.: Harvard University Press, 1950.

CRITICAL AND BIOGRAPHICAL

George Dekker, *James Fenimore Cooper, the Novelist*, London: Routledge, 1967.

D. H. Lawrence, *Studies in Classic American Literature*, London: Secker, 1924, pp. 50–66.

H. Daniel Peck, *A World by Itself; the Pastoral Moment in Cooper's Fiction*, New Haven, Conn.: Yale University Press, 1977.

Joel Porte, *The Romance in America; Studies in Cooper, Poe, Hawthorne, Melville and James*, Middletown, Conn.: Wesleyan University Press, 1969, pp. 3–52.

Donald Ringe, *James Fenimore Cooper*, New York: Twayne (United States Authors Series, 11), 1962.

Index